PIT BOSS WOOD PELLET GRILL & SMOKER COOKBOOK

200 Tasty and Delicious Recipes to prepare Stunning Meals and become the Undisputed King of Neighborhood

Luke Gray

The information provided herein is stated to be true and consistent, in that any liability arising from the use or abuse of any policies, processes, or directions contained herein, whether due to inattention or otherwise, is solely and completely the responsibility of the recipient reader. Under no circumstances will the publisher be held liable for any reparation, damages, or monetary loss incurred as a result of the information contained herein, whether directly or indirectly.

All copyrights not held by the publisher belong to the authors.

The information provided here is solely for educational purposes and is therefore universal. The information is presented without any type of contract or guarantee assurance.

The trademarks are used without the trademark owner's permission or backing, and the trademark is published without the trademark owner's permission or backing. All trademarks and brands mentioned in this book are the property of their respective owners and are not affiliated with this document.

TABLE OF CONTENTS

SMOKING RECIPES...393

INTRODUCTION

Pellet grills are the hottest sensation in the BBQ and grilling world. People are enthusiastic about the many features and conveniences that pellet grills are bringing to the market because technology in the sector hasn't advanced much in the last 30 years or so. However, in order to fully appreciate everything, they have to offer, it is necessary to understand how they work. So, if you're new to pellet grilling or smoking and wondering, "How do pellet grills work?" you've come to the right place!

What is a pellet grill?

Pellet grills are outdoor cookers that combine aspects of smokers, charcoal and gas grills, and ovens into one unit. Pit Boss Pellet Grills employ 100 percent natural hardwood pellets as a fuel source, allowing them to generate direct or indirect heat.

How do pellet grills work?

The wood pellets are placed into a hopper that serves as a storage bin. After that, the pellets are fed into a cooking chamber by an electric auger. The wood pellets ignite by combustion, heating the cooking chamber. The air is then drawn in using intake fans. After that, the heat and smoke are disseminated throughout the cooking area.

Pellet grills, like ovens, let you set the temperature digitally or with a dial, often between 180°F and 500°F. As a result, you can choose between "low and slow" or "searing hot" cooking.

A meat probe that connects to the control board on most pellet grills can be used to monitor the internal temperature of the meat. On Pit Boss Grills, the revolutionary SearZone plate allows either indirect or direct heat, as well as eight different cooking options.

How are the pellets made?

Pellet grills are the only place to get wood pellets. Pit Boss hardwood pellets are comprised entirely of 100% natural hardwood that has been dried and ground into sawdust. The dust is then compressed at high temperatures to form compact pellets that are covered and kept together by the natural lignin in the wood. Wood pellets are also regarded for being the most user-friendly fuel. Because they emit less than 1% ash, a 40 pound bag of pellets will only produce 12 cup of ash, making cleanup a snap. They also provide a lot of flavor without having to worry about the air-to-fuel ratio like wood chips or chunks do.

How long do the pellets last in a pellet grill?

When checking for gas in the truck, as with every road trip, the first thing you should do is double-check that you have plenty of pellets in the hopper. A decent rule of thumb is to have 2 lbs. of pellets each hour of low and slow smoking or 4 lbs. per hour of high and fast grilling.

Why pellet grills?

Smoking on a Pit Boss is unlike any other grilling experience. Everything becomes infused with a real wood smokey flavor when hardwood pellets are burned. Because Pit Boss pellet grills include fan forced convection, they may be used with direct or indirect heat. Which means that no matter what happens, hot smoky air will continue to circulate inside the grill, generating an equal cloud of flavor.

You may smoke dishes low and slow for hours, in addition to providing smoky tastes. Some Pit Bosses even leave their grills unattended for hours at a time while at work or sleeping at night to get flawlessly smoked meats without having to babysit them. This makes smoking even the most difficult cuts, such as brisket, a breeze. When brisket is prepared, everyone likes it; now you can enjoy it while making it as well.

To do so, simply set up your grill as directed in the "Pellet Grill Setup" section, turn it on "smoke," and monitor the progress with a remote thermometer or a meat probe.

1. Starting Up Your Wood Pellet Grill - The Steps

Use this simple guide to ensure that you can safely and successfully use your Pit Boss Grill:

1. Have Fuel In The Hopper:

When checking for gas in the truck, as with every road trip, the first thing you should do is double-check that you have plenty of pellets in the hopper. A decent rule of thumb is to have 2 lbs. of pellets each hour of low and slow smoking or 4 lbs. per hour of high and fast grilling.

2. SET YOUR GRILL TO SMOKE AND OPEN THE LID:

Once you've fueled up, open the hood of your grill and set it on "smoke." Because the grill only feeds pellets for 3 to 4 minutes before stopping, this is crucial. Give the igniter a chance to spark before adding more fuel. If the grill is set to 400°F right away, it will continue to feed pellets until it reaches that temperature, and if there is too much fuel over the igniter, it may begin to muffle and never light. In that situation, the pellets would simply build up in the pot. You don't want it to leak all over the place, do you?

3. Go In and Prep Your Foods:

Pit Boss grills light up in a flash. It simply takes approximately 3 minutes from the time you switch it on to the time you have a fire. That is the ideal time to go in and prepare all of your food.

4. Watch for Thick Smoky Clouds:

When you see heavy clouds of smoke rising from your grill, you know it's on the correct track. That signifies your pellets are on fire and your pot has caught fire. We've heard some amusing stories about neighbors being frightened by the amount of smoke and not realizing it's coming from the grill. Pit Bosses, on the other hand, recognize that this is a positive thing. For 3 to 4 minutes, it will billow out of the grill. It will eventually fade away.

5. Crank It Up and Start Grillin':

You'll hear the boom of a fire after the pot catches. That's the fan-assisted convection blowing on your grill's flame. After that, you may turn up the heat and be ready to start grilling. Within 5 to 6 minutes, the heat will reach the appropriate temperature.

PIT BOSS MAIN BENEFITS

2.Heating Prowess & Adjustments

Pellet grills used to be programmed to reach a predetermined temperature using a specific amount of pellets. The rudimental options such as low, mid, high, and shutdown were present in those repeated cycles, but there was no further fine-tuning process. As if it weren't awful enough, the temperature wasn't as precise as it is now.

Traeger pellet grills with the Advanced Grilling Logic technology can maintain a temperature range of 180°F to 450°F with a 25°F increment. Pit Boss, meanwhile, employs a dial-in digital control board with an LED-lit LCD to provide a temperature range of 200°F to 500°F in 50°F increments.

The convection method, just like in an oven, is the key to evenly dispersed heating in a pellet grill. The air is dispersed and circulated by a built-in fan, resulting in the same temperature throughout the cooking chamber. Furthermore, both manufacturers offer low-heat smoking alternatives, which are ideal for pork shoulder and briskets, at roughly 160°F.

When you have to constantly monitor the grill while missing out on the enjoyment, it's easy to lose patience. As a result, the set-and-forget feature will keep the fire under control while you take care of other matters. Whether you're slow-roasting for a few hours or a whole day, the heat will remain constant.

3. Craftsmanship & Quality

The brands do an excellent job of weatherproofing their grills against everyday wear and tear as well as intense heat. While not as durable as stainless steel, the powder-coated steel exterior should be able to withstand the elements. The paint job may take years to begin cracking or flaking.

Porcelain-enameled cast iron cooking grates, on the other hand, have nearly the same heating efficiency and retention capabilities as stainless steel cooking grates. When it comes to cleaning, there will be certain standards to follow, but grillers find the headaches worthwhile.

We have little to no complaints about both manufacturers' general quality and craftsmanship. Although using stainless steel for all of the components would be ideal, it would be more expensive. Besides, most people don't mind if the grills' integrity isn't damaged (at least for a few years).

The double-walled design produces an excellent layer of insulation to prevent heat loss to the surrounding environment. As a result, even if you reside in a cooler part of the country, your food will always be hot. This design will come in handy even more during late-night smoking sessions or in the winter when it snows.

4. Cooking & Smoking Area

The size of the cooking varies greatly depending on the menu and the number of people you plan to serve. However, when comparing the catalogs of both brands, Traeger has a little advantage over Pit Boss. Traeger always has something for everyone, so whatever you're looking for, you'll be able to find it here.

Because pellet grills are meant for large gatherings, double- or triple-decked grates are typical. It just goes to show that even a mid-range pellet barbecue can feed up to 15 people at once. Certain versions can hold an incredible amount of food while still leaving enough for side dishes.

5. Exterior Dimensions & Portability

Going small is a good option if you frequently go camping or throw tailgate parties. Both brands, thankfully, have travel-size units that can make a great meal on the go. You'll be fine if you have access to a stable power source from a portable generator, your RV, or the campsite.

6. Mobile App & User Experience

Moving on to the software side of things, Pit Boss has developed their own mobile apps to control these grills. You can also expect a smooth user interface and a diverse menu with adjustable options thanks to frequent firmware updates.

Connection issues, on the other hand, may include lagging and time-out sessions as a result of distance and other obstructions such as walls. While both brands use Wi-Fi, Pit Boss grills also have Bluetooth pairing capabilities.

Pellet grills don't require a seasoned pitmaster with years of experience. Anyone who enjoys barbecuing should be able to pick it up quickly after a few tries. All you have to do now is set the temperature, and the grill will do the rest. In the meantime, you can prepare other side dishes or take a quick break without having to worry about the food getting cold.

7. Warranty Terms & Customer Service

When it comes to after-sales service, few things speak louder than a generous warranty policy. The longer and more specific the warranty, the better the overall quality is almost always. It demonstrates that businesses have great faith in their products and are willing to vouch for their validity.

When it comes to warranty length, Pit Boss wins hands down with its generous five-year warranty. In addition, the company has a strong social media presence and uses a variety of platforms to communicate with customers.

8. Value

A propane grill is available in a variety of price ranges. Whether you are looking for a small, inexpensive grill to barbecue hot dogs and burgers on or a massive stainless-steel contraption to look good on your patio (which will run you close to 5 figures) there is a propane grill for everyone.

The price range for Pit Boss Wood Pellet Grills, on the other hand, is more focused. Our grills range in price from $296 to $700, depending on whether you want a small Tailgater Grill or a large Pro Series 1100.

By far the best value on the pellet grill market, but how do we stack up against gas grills?

When it comes to determining value, price isn't the only factor to consider. This section would otherwise be referred to as "Cheapest." And Pit Boss Grills aren't cheap (in the sense that they aren't well-made).

The following questions should be considered when discussing value.

On the grill, how many different types of cooking can you do?

Is it constructed to last?

Is the manufacturer's customer service exceptional?

A Pit Boss Grill is an 8-in-1 grill, which means it can be used for grilling, smoking, baking, roasting, searing, charring, braising, and, of course, grilling.

The grills have a 5-year warranty and are built to last. In the unlikely event that an issue arises, our outstanding customer service team will assist you in troubleshooting, repairing, and/or replacing whatever is causing the problem.

Since there are hundreds of gas grill companies out there, it's difficult to honestly assess their build quality and customer service.

For this reason, we will call this one a wash, even though there isn't a gas grill out there that can offer 8 in 1 cooking...not even the fancy expensive ones.

9. Temperature control

Temperature control on a gas barbecue is a completely manual procedure. Adjust up your dial, wait for the temperature gauge to reach your preferred temperature, then turn it down or up again, depending on how much the temperature fluctuates.

A computerized control board, along with meat probes and an auger that feeds pellets into the burn plate, are used in a Pit Boss Grill. This entire procedure works together to ensure that your grill reaches and maintains the proper temperature. Your grill should maintain its temperature as long as your hopper doesn't run out of pellets.

Gas grills are notorious for being manufactured in such a way that they do not allow for true convection heating. Most gas grills have a blocky, angular form, which contributes to this. On the other hand, Pit Boss Grills have a spherical, dome-shaped lid that circulates air and heat. This heat and air circulation helps to limit heat loss, lowering fuel costs and reducing extreme temperature changes.

10.   Cooking Options

A Pit Boss Grill, as previously said, provides you with eight various cooking alternatives. Thanks to the hardwood pellets used as fuel, you may grill, bake, char, sear, smoke, roast, BBQ, and braise your way to excellent and naturally flavored meals.

You can grill, sear, char, bake, and roast using a gas grill. However, depending on the grill, even the latter two may be difficult. On gas grills, slow and low cooking is not suggested because they are not meant to do so.

KIND OF PELLETS

11.   Hardwood Smoker Pellets

The top smoker pellet manufacturers utilize high-quality wood in a range of natural flavors to satisfy even the pickiest griller. These pellets will provide a woodsy, smoky taste to your meat.

To help you select the right smoker pellet taste for your next barbeque, take a look at the pellet/food combinations listed below.

- Oak. Oak smoke pellets have a gentle and familiar flavor. When grilling fish or beef, use oak smoke pellets for the best results.
- Alder. This pellet pairs well with a variety of meats, including chicken, lamb, hog, turkey, fish, and beef. Alder imparts a great, earthy flavor to your meat that isn't overpowering.
- Maple. The maple smoker pellets are the finest choice if you want meat with a tang of sweetness, such as pig, beef, or turkey.
- Pecan. Pecan smoker pellets offer a flavor that will blow your taste senses away. Pecan is very good with pork and beef.
- Hickory. Do you want something you can use on a regular basis? Then hickory is a great option. Hickory may be used to cook any form of meat. It does not, however, go well with fish, so keep that in mind!
- Mesquite. If you want to barbecue fish on your BBQ day, mesquite is the way to go. Mesquite pellets will enhance the fish's natural flavor and add a hint of spice. It's also good for chicken and beef.

The hardwood smoker pellets are made from actual trees that have been processed into the finished product. It isn't made from recycled content, which can be difficult or impossible to trace back to their source. The chemical makeup of the hardwood smoker pellets, as well as the specified ash weight and heat value, are all tested in a laboratory. This is done to make sure they're made entirely of wood fiber. It has a tiny diameter to allow for a hotter burn and more smoke due to the increased surface area. It comes in a variety of flavors, including pure and blended mixes.

Let's move on to the fruity-flavored wood pellets!

12. Fruitwood Smoker Pellets

You might want to try some fruit-flavored smoker pellets when looking for the best smoker pellets. You will not be sorry! Fruity pellets will elevate your smoking experience to new heights.

- Apple. Apple is excellent for poultry and pig because it provides a tangy flavor to the meat.
- Cherry. Use cherry-flavored smoker pellets on pork, beef, or poultry for a gourmet flavor.

Fruitwood smoker pellets are best used for pork or veal. It's also good for poultry and game birds. Fruitwood smoker pellets are combined with hickory wood pellets for a little stronger smoke flavor with a distinct flavor. There are no fillers, binders, or additions in them. For easy handling and storage, they are packaged in a heavy-duty plastic bag.

13.   BBQrs Delight Wood Smoking Pellets

BBQrs is the sixth most popular wood smoking pellet on the market. These food-grade wood pellets are the fastest and most natural way to add smoky flavor to your meal on any electric outdoor cooker, as well as any charcoal or gas grill. Any impurities found in BBQrs wood smoking pellets are eradicated since pellets are produced from sawdust by pressure, which causes heat.

HOW TO COOK WITH THE PIT BOSS

So you got a Pit Boss and followed the instructions for the initial burn off (wow!). then you're all set to start cooking, right? Not so quickly! To prevent food from adhering to your grates and rust from forming on your grates and Flame Broiler Plate, season your grill today. We'll walk you through the process of seasoning your barbecue.

Seasoning a Pit Boss Pellet Grill

1. Make sure you have a high temperature oil or bacon grease

It's critical to use a high-temperature-resistant oil, such as canola, peanut, or coconut oil. We all love olive oil, but when heated at high temperatures, it has a strong flavor that doesn't go well with most BBQ. Some argue that consuming olive oil that has reached its smoke point of 375°F is unhealthy (but the science is still out on that one).

If you don't mind the flavor of bacon in anything you cook on your grill, bacon grease can be an acceptable substitute for cooking oil. It everything boils down to personal taste.

Note: It's easiest to use a spray oil, but if you don't have any or don't want to use bacon fat, a basting brush will suffice.

2. Apply a liberal amount of oil or grease to the grates and Flame Broiler Plate

If you're using a spray, distribute the oil evenly between the grates and the Flame Broiler Plate with a dry paper towel. Slide the plate back and forth on the plate to get the oil into the crevices between the plates. Apply to other steel sections inside the grill, such as the probes, if desired.

3. Put the plate and grates back on the grill and turn it on

Follow the startup methods described in your manual and raise the temperature to 375°F once the initial startup is complete. Allow about 15 minutes for your Pit Boss to run.

4. Smoke on!

You're now ready to fire up your Pit Boss and start cooking!

GRILL BEEF RECIPES

1. GARLIC LOVERS ROAST BEEF

Prep Time: 5 Minutes

Cook Time: 1hrs 15min

Rest Time: 1hr

Total Time: 2hours 20 Min

Serving :10

Ingredients

- All fat should be removed from a 2-3-pound roast or eye round.
- 3-4 garlic cloves, sliced into thin slivers
- I used my misto to spray olive oil.
- to taste kosher salt
- to taste with freshly cracked pepper
- 2 tsp rosemary, chopped (dry)
- thermometer for meat

Instructions

1. 1 hour before cooking, take the roast out of the refrigerator to bring it to room temperature. Remove all of the fat from the meat. Using a sharp knife, puncture the meat about 1/2-inch deep and put slivers of garlic all the way into each hole. Season the meat generously with salt, pepper, and rosemary after lightly spraying it with olive oil. Insert the thermometer all the way into the meat's core.

2. Preheat the oven to 350 degrees Fahrenheit. Place the roast in a roasting pan and place it in the oven when the temperature reaches 350 degrees Fahrenheit.

3. Roast until the internal temperature reaches 130 degrees for rare, 140 degrees for medium rare, 150 degrees for medium, and 155-160 degrees for well done. Remove the roast from the oven and set it aside for 10-20 minutes before slicing it to ensure that the juices are equally distributed. When my roast beef reaches 135°F for medium rare, I take it out of the oven. As it sits, the temperature will rise another 5 degrees.

4. Serve thinly sliced.

Nutrition:
Calories: 142
Fat: 4.07g
Carbs: 0.5g
Protein: 24.1g

2. GRILL-ROASTED BEEF

Prep Time: 15 Minutes

Cook Time: 1hrs 15min

Total Time: 1hours 30 Min

Serving: 5

Ingredients

- 6 minced garlic cloves
- 2 tbsp fresh rosemary, minced
- 4 teaspoons kosher salt
- 1 teaspoon pepper
- 3 pound prime sirloin roast with all visible fat removed
- 1 disposable aluminum roasting pan (13 x 9 inches).

Instructions

1. In a mixing dish, combine the garlic, rosemary, salt, and pepper.
2. Using paper towels, pat the roast dry and evenly sprinkle with the salt mixture.
3. Refrigerate the roast for 18 to 24 hours after wrapping it in plastic wrap.
4. Set aside fifteen 1/4-inch holes in the roasting pan's middle, which should be about the size of the roast.

For a charcoal grill:

1. Completely open the bottom grill vents.
2. Fill a huge chimney starter halfway with charcoal briquettes and light it (50 briquettes; 3 quarts).
3. When the coals are hot, spread them out over one-third of the grill in a uniform layer.
4. Place the cooking grate on top, cover, and partially open the lid vents. Heat the grill for about 5 minutes, or until it is very hot.

For a gas grill:

- Turn all of the burgers to high, cover, and cook for about 15 minutes.
- Reduce the heat on the primary burner to medium and turn off the others. (If necessary, adjust the primary burner to keep the grill temperature about 325 degrees F.)

Once Your Grill is Ready

1. The cooking grate should be cleaned and oiled.
2. Place the roast on the hotter area of the grill and cook (covered if using gas) for about 10 minutes, flipping as needed, until nicely browned on both sides.
3. Transfer the pan to the cooler area of the grill and place the roast in it over the holes.
4. Cook, covered (with the lid vents over the meat if using charcoal), for 40 to 60 minutes, or until the roast registers 125 degrees F on an instant-read thermometer (for medium-rare), rotating the pan halfway through.
5. Allow the roast to rest for 20 minutes on a wire rack put over a rimmed baking sheet, covered loosely with foil. Transfer the roast to a carving board and cut thin slices across the grain.

Nutrition:
Calories: 324
Fat: 2.07g
Carbs: 27.4g
Protein: 4.1g
Fiber: 5.1g

3.STEAKHOUSE-STYLE RIB EYES

Prep Time: 40 Minutes

Cook Time: 1hrs 15min

Total Time: 1 hours 55 Min

Serving: 5

Ingredients

- 1 tablespoon kosher salt Diamond Crystal
- 2 pound (1 1/2 pound) Bone-in 1 1/2-inch thick rib eye steaks
- grapeseed oil, 2 tblsp.
- a quarter teaspoon of black pepper
- 1 tablespoon unsalted butter, sliced into cubes
- 2 cloves garlic

Directions

1. Salt both sides of steaks evenly in a steady stream, holding salt approximately 1 foot above steaks and pressing gently to adhere. Steaks should be placed on

a wire rack within a rimmed baking pan. Chill for 72 hours, uncovered, turning twice a day.

2. Take the steaks out of the fridge. Allow 1 hour for cooling. Preheat the oven to 400 degrees Fahrenheit. In a 12-inch cast-iron skillet, heat the oil on high. Sprinkle pepper on both sides of the steaks. When a wisp of smoke rises from the skillet, put the steaks in a single layer and cook, undisturbed, for about 4 minutes, or until a light brown crust forms. Cook for another 4 minutes after flipping the steaks. Turn steaks on fatty edges with tongs, leaning steaks against skillet sides to keep them steady if needed. Cook, rolling occasionally to render fat on the edges, for 4 to 5 minutes, or until caramelized all over. Place steaks flat in skillet and cover with butter and garlic.

3. Preheat the oven to 350°F. Place the skillet in the oven. 5 minutes of roasting steaks Place the skillet on the stovetop over medium heat. Slightly tilt skillet toward you to allow butter to pool in the bottom; spread brown butter over steaks. Flip the steaks carefully and baste them again. Return skillet to oven and roast for 4 to 6 minutes, or until a thermometer inserted in thickest area registers 120°F.

4. Place the steaks on a cutting board and let aside for 10 minutes to rest. Remove the bones from each steak and separate the fatty strip. Reassemble steaks on a dish by slicing thinly against the grain and fanning

pieces out slightly. Place bones on plates and sel gris on the steaks.

5. Use any well-marbled piece of red meat for this approach, such as prime rib (increase the cook time), T-bone steaks, or pork shoulder steaks.

Nutrition:
Calories: 186
Fat: 107g
Carbs: 7.4g
Protein: 14.1g
Fiber: 5.1g

4.BUTTER-BASTED RIB EYE STEAKS

Prep Time: 25Minutes

Cook Time: 1hrs 10min

Total Time: 1hours 35 Min

Serving: 4

Ingredients

- Two Bone-in rib eye steaks weighing 1 1/4 pound
- Salt that has been koshered.
- pepper, freshly ground
- 2 tblsp. oil from canola
- 4 tblsp. butter (unsalted)
- 4 sprigs of thyme
- 3 cloves of garlic
- 1 sprig rosemary

Instructions

1. Season both sides of the rib eye steaks with salt and freshly ground pepper. Allow 30 minutes for the meat to come to room temperature.

2. Heat the canola oil in a large cast-iron skillet until it shimmers. Cook the steaks over high heat for 5 minutes, or until crispy on the bottom. Toss the steaks in the skillet with the butter, thyme, garlic, and rosemary. Cook 5 to 7 minutes longer over high heat, basting the steaks with the melted butter, garlic, and herbs until medium-rare. Place the steaks on a cutting board and let aside for 10 minutes to rest. Remove the bone from the steaks before slicing the meat across the grain and serving.

Nutrition:
Calories: 175.26
Fat: 13.07g
Carbs: 17.4g
Protein: 8.1g
Fiber: 5.1g

5. BALSAMIC MARINATED FLANK STEAK

Prep Time: 5 Minutes

Cook Time: 25min

Total Time: 30 Min

Serving: 8

Ingredients

- 2 chopped garlic cloves
- 1 tablespoon leaves of rosemary
- 1 tablespoon oregano, dry
- 2 tblsp mustard (whole grain)
- a half-cup of balsamic vinegar
- 1 cup extra-virgin olive oil plus a little extra for grilling
- Salt that has been koshered.
- pepper, freshly ground
- 1 flank steak, 3 lbs.

Instructions

1. Puree the garlic, rosemary, oregano, mustard, and vinegar together in a blender until the garlic is minced. While the machine is running, slowly drizzle in the oil and combine until smooth. Season with salt and pepper to taste.

2. Pour all but 1/4 cup of the vinaigrette over the meat in a glass or ceramic baking dish, turning to coat. Refrigerate for at least 4 hours and up to 24 hours after wrapping in plastic wrap.

3. Grates should be oiled and a grill should be lit. Remove the steak from the marinade and drain any excess. Salt & pepper to taste. Grill the steak over medium heat, rotating periodically, for 10 to 12 minutes, or until moderately browned and an instant-read thermometer inserted in the thickest section registers 125°. Allow the steak to rest for 5 minutes on a carving board. Serve the meat thinly sliced against the grain, with the remaining vinaigrette passed around the table.

Serve With

Grill half cherry tomatoes and sliced leeks while the grill is hot. Serve everything on toasted bread with the remaining 1/4 cup vinaigrette drizzled over the grilled vegetables and meat. Here are some more amazing grilled veggie recipes.

Nutrition:
Calories: 215
Fat: 24.07g
Carbs: 17.4g
Protein: 2.1g
Fiber: 5.1g

6. GRILLED HANGER STEAK WITH KIMCHI-APPLE SLAW

Prep Time: 15 Minutes

Cook Time: 30 min

Total Time: 45 Minutes

Serving: 4

Ingredients

- 2 tblsp. oil (canola) (plus more for grilling).
- 3 teaspoons of sugar (plus 1 teaspoon).
- a third of a cup of soy sauce
- 2 tablespoons sesame oil, roasted
- 1 teaspoon of ginger (finely grated).
- 3 garlic cloves (minced).
- 1 shallot 1 shallot (minced).
- Salt that has been koshered.
- Pepper.
- Hanger steak, 2 lbs.
- a third of a cup of mayonnaise
- apple cider vinegar, 2 tblsp.

- 1 apple, Granny Smith (small peeled and julienned).
- 1 slice of cucumber (small julienned).
- 1 cup kimchi with juices from cabbage (chopped)
- Seeds of sesame (for garnish)
- scallion slices (for garnish)

Instructions

1. Combine the canola oil, 3 tablespoons sugar, soy sauce, sesame oil, ginger, garlic, and shallot in a large mixing bowl; season with salt and pepper. Allow for 15 minutes of resting time after adding the meat.
2. Meanwhile, whisk together the mayonnaise, vinegar, and remaining 1 teaspoon of sugar in a medium mixing bowl. Season with salt and chill the apple, cucumber, and kimchi.
3. Light a grill and brush the grate with oil. 4 to 5 minutes per side, grill the steak over moderate heat until browned and medium-rare inside. Allow to rest for 5 minutes on a chopping board.
4. Thinly slice the steak and serve with the slaw, topped with sesame seeds and scallion.

Nutrition:
Calories: 112
Fat: 11.07g
Carbs: 10.4g
Protein: 5.1g
Fiber: 6.1g

7. THROWBACK PORTERHOUSE STEAKS

Prep Time: 25 Minutes

Cook Time: 30min

Total Time: 55 Min

Serving: 4

Ingredients

- 1 1/4-pound porterhouse steaks (1 1/4-inch thick cut).
- Salt.
- Pepper.
- 12 cup barbecue sauce, bottled
- 14 cup of beer (preferably American lager).
- Oil made from vegetables (for brushing).

Instructions

1. Turn on the gas grill. Season the steaks well with salt and pepper and let aside for 30 minutes at room temperature. Whisk the barbecue sauce and beer together in a small basin.

2. The grill grate should be oiled. Grill the steaks over high heat for 6 minutes total, flipping once, until lightly browned on both sides. Grill, turning and basting regularly, until the steaks are glazed and an instant-read thermometer inserted in the thickest portion registers 120° for medium-rare meat, about 3 to 5 minutes more. Before serving, transfer the steaks to a carving board and let aside for 10 minutes to rest.

Nutrition:
Calories: 143
Fat: 11.07g
Carbs: 17.4g
Protein: 101g
Fiber: 5.1g

8. MINUTE STEAK STACKS WITH HERBED ANCHOVY BUTTER

Prep Time: 10 Minutes

Cook Time: 20min

Total Time: 30 Min

Serving: 1

Ingredients

- 2 tablespoons anchovy fillets, diced and drained in oil
- 1 minced shallot
- 2 tbsp. of red wine vinegar
- 1 pound unsalted unsalted butter, room temperature
- 1/4 cup chopped parsley, tarragon, and chives in equal portions
- 1/2 teaspoon pepper, finely ground
- 2 tblsp. oil from canola
- 12 to 16 ounces top round—each slice split crosswise into four slices.
- hammered to a thickness of 1/4 inch

Instructions

1. Combine the anchovies, shallot, and vinegar in a skillet. Cook, stirring constantly, for about 5 minutes, or until the anchovies have broken down and the vinegar has evaporated. With a wooden spoon, mash the anchovies. Allow the mixture to cool to room temperature in a small basin. Mix in the butter, herbs, and pepper thoroughly. Scrape the butter onto parchment paper and roll it into a log or store it in an airtight container.

2. Heat the canola oil in a large cast-iron skillet until it begins to smoke. Season both sides of the steaks with Montreal steak spice. Sear the steaks in two batches over high heat for 30 to 40 seconds per side, or until nicely browned on the exterior but still rare. Place the steaks on a rack in front of a baking sheet.

3. Stack the steak slices on a serving platter, with a generous pat of anchovy butter between each slice. Serve immediately with a large pat of butter on top, separating the stack at the table.

Nutrition:
Calories: 251
Fat: 18.07g
Carbs: 27.4g
Protein: 4.1g
Fiber: 5.1g

9. SPICE-RUBBED T-BONE STEAKS

Prep Time: 10 Minutes

Cook Time: 10 min

Total Time: 20 Min

Serving: 5

Ingredients

- 2 tablespoons powdered ancho chile
- 1 1/2 tablespoons cumin powder
- 1 tsp. paprika (hot)
- 1 teaspoon powdered garlic
- freshly ground pepper and kosher salt
- 2 T-bone steaks, 1 inch thick, at room temperature (3 1/4 pounds total).

Instructions

Preheat the grill. Combine the ancho chile powder, cumin, paprika, and garlic powder in a small bowl with 1 tablespoon salt and 1 teaspoon pepper. Use the spice rub to season the steaks. For medium-rare, grill for 8 minutes on each side over moderate heat; move to a work surface and rest for 5 minutes before serving.

Nutrition:
Calories: 215
Fat: 24.07g
Carbs: 17.4g
Protein: 2.1g
Fiber: 5.1g

10.   Grilled Texas Rib Eye

Prep Time: 25 Minutes

Cook Time: 35min

Total Time: 1 hours

Serving: 10

Ingredients

- At room temperature, three 1 1/2 pound bone-in rib eye steaks, about 1 inch thick.
- Brush with canola oil.
- Kosher salt and black pepper, roughly ground

Instructions

1. Light a grill and heat it until it's very hot, covered. Season the steaks with salt and pepper after brushing them with oil. Grill the steaks for 1 1/2 minutes on each side over high heat. Place the steaks on a cutting board and set them to rest for 10 to 30 minutes.
2. Return the steaks to the hot grill, cover, and cook for 4 to 6 minutes, rotating once, until an instant-read

thermometer inserted in the center of the meat reads 130° for rare or 135° for medium-rare. Allow 10 minutes for the steaks to rest on the carving board. Serve the steaks thinly sliced across the grain.

Nutrition:
Calories: 227
Fat: 0.07g
Carbs: 17.4g
Protein: 4.1g
Fiber: 5.1g

11.   Balsamic and Rosemary-Marinated Florentine Steak

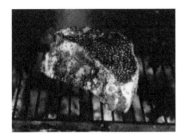

Prep Time: 20 Minutes

Cook Time: 40 Min

Total Time: 1 Hour

Serving: 4-6

Ingredients

- 1 c. balsamic vinaigrette
- 2 tablespoons extra-virgin olive oil plus 1/2 cup extra-virgin olive oil
- 1/4 cup rosemary, finely chopped
- 1 porterhouse steak, 3 pounds, 4 inches thick
- kosher salt, 2 tblsp.
- 2 tablespoons pepper, finely ground

Instructions

1. Combine the vinegar, 1/2 cup olive oil, and rosemary in a sturdy resealable plastic bag. Place the steak in

the bag, lock it, and refrigerate it overnight, flipping it several times.

2. Preheat the oven to 425°F and allow the steak to come to room temperature before cooking. A grill pan should be preheated. Season the steak with salt and pepper after removing it from the marinade. Rub the remaining 2 tablespoons of olive oil on the side. Grill until beautifully browned on top and bottom, about 5 minutes per side, over fairly high heat. Place the steak on a rimmed baking sheet and roast for 30 minutes, or until an instant-read thermometer inserted into the tenderloin (the smallest piece) registers 125 degrees. Alternatively, light a charcoal barbecue on one side or a gas grill on the other. Grill the steak for 5 minutes on each side over medium heat. Close the cover and cook the steak for another 30 minutes on the cool side of the grill. Allow the steak to rest for 10 minutes on a carving board. Serve the steak immediately after slicing it across the grain.

Nutrition:
Calories: 119
Fat: 5.07g
Carbs: 23.4g
Protein: 4.1g
Fiber: 5.1g

12. Grilled Steaks with Onion Sauce and Onion Relish

40 minutes of active time.

Total time: 3 hours.

The yield is 6.

Prep Time: 40 Minutes

Cook Time: 2 hrs 20 min

Total Time: 3 hours

Serving: 6

Ingredients

- 2 tblsp. black pepper, cracked
- 2 crushed dry bay leaves
- 1 tablespoon fish sauce from Asia
- 1 tablespoon extra-virgin olive oil
- 6 rib eye steaks, about 3/4 inch thick, 12 to 14 ounces
- 4 tblsp. butter (unsalted)
- 1 pound finely sliced red onions
- 2 seeded pickled jalapeos
- 1 tablespoon red wine, dry
- 2 tbsp. of red wine vinegar

- Season with salt and freshly ground black pepper.
- 1/2 cup roughly chopped drained cocktail onions
- 1/4 cup pitted and chopped Moroccan oil-cured olives
- a quarter cup of torn mint leaves

Instructions

1. Combine the cracked pepper, bay leaves, fish sauce, and 2 tablespoons olive oil in a large, shallow dish. Add the steaks to the dish and massage the mixture all over them. Allow for 2 hours at room temperature or 4 hours in the refrigerator.

2. Meanwhile, heat the butter in a saucepan. Cook the onions and jalapeos for 5 minutes over medium heat, or until the onions are just softened. Season with salt and pepper after adding the wine and 1 tablespoon of vinegar. Bring 2 cups of water to a boil, then reduce to a low heat. Cook, covered, over low heat for 40 minutes, or until the onions are very soft.

3. Uncover the onions and simmer over moderate heat, turning regularly, for about 10 minutes, or until the liquid has evaporated. Place the onions in a blender and blend until smooth. Puree in the remaining 1 tablespoon of vinegar until completely smooth. Season to taste with salt and pepper.

4. Toss the cocktail onions, olives, and mint leaves with the remaining 2 tablespoons of olive oil in a medium bowl.

5. Light a grill or preheat a grill pan. Grill the steaks until lightly browned, about 7 minutes for medium-rare meat, over moderate heat, rotating once or twice. Allow 5 minutes for the steaks to rest before serving with the onion sauce and pickled onion relish.

Nutrition:
Calories: 146
Fat: 0.07g
Carbs: 167.4g
Protein: 4.1g
Fiber: 5.1g

13.   Skirt Steak with Paprika Butter

Prep Time:35 Minutes

Cook Time: 1hrsmin

Total Time: 2hours 20 Min

Serving: 10

Ingredients

- 6 tblsp. butter (unsalted)
- 6 finely sliced garlic cloves
- smoky spicy paprika, 1 1/2 tablespoons
- 2 tblsp. freshly squeezed lemon juice
- Salt.
- Skirt steaks weighing 5 pounds
- Rub with vegetable oil.
- pepper, freshly ground
- Farro with Sunchoke-Kale Hash

Instructions

1. Prepare a grill or a grill pan by lighting it or heating it. Melt the butter in a small pot. Cook, stirring constantly, until the garlic is brown, about 3 minutes. Cook, stirring constantly, until the paprika is aromatic, about 30 seconds. Remove from the fire, mix in the lemon juice, and season with salt and pepper to taste; keep warm.

2. Season the skirt steaks with salt and pepper after rubbing them with oil. Grill for 3 minutes per side over high heat until well browned and medium-rare. Place the steaks on a cutting board and let them for 5 minutes to rest. Across the grain, thinly slice the steaks. Place the steak on top of the Sunchoke-Kale Hash with Farro on a big dish. Serve the steak immediately with the paprika butter.

Nutrition:
Calories: 90
Fat: 8.07g
Carbs: 17.4g
Protein: 20.1g
Fiber: 5.1g

14. Grilled Skirt Steak with Green Sriracha

Prep Time: 20 Minutes

Cook Time: 40 min

Total Time: 1 hours

Serving: 4

Ingredients

- 3 poblano peppers, big
- 2 stemmed serrano chiles
- 3 big peeled and smashed garlic cloves
- 1/2 cup fresh ginger, finely sliced
- 1/2 teaspoon ground turmeric or one 1/2-inch piece fresh turmeric, sliced
- 1 cup unsweetened shredded coconut
- 2 c. basil leaves, loose
- 2 c. mint leaves, loose
- 1 1/2 cups chives, clipped
- 1/2 cup cilantro, chopped
- 4 shredded kaffir lime leaves

- 1 lemongrass stalk—tender inner bulb, removed and thinly sliced bottom 4 inches
- 1 cup canola oil plus a little extra for grilling
- 2 tablespoons fresh lime juice plus 1/4 cup
- salt kosher
- 5 lb. skirt steak, cut into 4-inch chunks

Instructions

1. Turn the poblanos over a gas flame until they are roasted and soft. Place in a bowl and cover with plastic wrap to chill. Transfer the poblanos to a blender after peeling, coring, and seeding them. Pulse to chop the serranos, garlic, ginger, turmeric, coconut, basil, mint, chives, cilantro, lime leaves, and lemongrass Puree 1 cup of oil in the machine while it is running. Season the green Sriracha with salt and lime juice.

2. Preheat the grill. Season the steaks with salt and pepper after brushing them with oil. Oil the grill grates and cook the steaks in batches over high heat for 5 to 6 minutes, flipping once or twice, until lightly browned and medium-rare. Place the steaks on a cutting board and set aside for 5 minutes before slicing them across the grain. Serve the steak with a dollop of green Sriracha sauce on top.

Nutrition:
Calories: 565
Fat: 19.07g
Carbs: 17.4g
Protein: 30.1g
Fiber: 5.1g

15. Rib Eye Steaks with Pete's Barbecue Sauce

Prep Time: 15 Minutes

Cook Time: 30 min

Total Time: 45 Min

Serving: 2

Ingredients

- 1 cup vinegar made from red wine
- 1/2 teaspoon mustard powder
- a quarter teaspoon of ground cloves
- 2 tbsp. vegetable oil, plus additional for grilling
- 1/4 cup onion, finely chopped
- 2 minced garlic cloves
- 1 tblsp cumin powder
- 2 tbsp brown sugar, light
- 2 roughly chopped plum tomatoes
- 1 cup barbecue sauce with a smokey flavor
- 1 teaspoon sambal oelek (chili paste).
- Season with salt and freshly ground black pepper.

- 4 bone-in rib eye steaks, sliced 3/4 inch thick (about 1 pound each).
- Garnish with rosemary sprigs.

Instructions

1. Combine the vinegar, dry mustard, and cloves in a medium saucepan and reduce by half over medium heat, about 10 minutes. Fill a heatproof basin halfway with vinegar. Wipe the saucepan clean.

2. Toss the onion, garlic, and cumin into the saucepan with the 2 tablespoons of oil. Cook for 5 minutes over low heat, until the onion is mellow and aromatic. Cook, stirring occasionally, until the brown sugar has dissolved and the tomatoes have softened, about 5 minutes. Cook, stirring occasionally, until the vinegar has reduced to 2 cups, about 5 minutes. Puree the sauce in a blender until it is completely smooth. Season with salt and pepper after adding the sambal oelek.

3. Preheat the grill or a grill pan. Season the steaks generously with salt and pepper after rubbing them with oil. Grill the steaks over moderately high heat, rotating once, for about 6 minutes total, or until faintly browned and medium-rare. Allow 5 minutes for the steaks to rest before garnishing with rosemary and serving with the barbecue sauce.

Nutrition:
Calories: 172
Fat: 10.07g
Carbs: 17.4g
Protein: 9.1g
Fiber: 5.1g

16.   Ethiopian Spiced Steak

Prep Time: 20 Minutes

Cook Time: 1hrs 10min

Total Time: 1hours 30 Min

Serving: 5

Ingredients

- 1 1/2 pound steak of sirloin
- 1 1/2 tblsp. berbere seasoning
- 1 pint halved red cherry tomatoes
- 1 pint halved yellow cherry tomatoes
- 2 tbsp extra-virgin extra-virgin olive oil
- Black pepper, salt, and freshly ground black pepper
- 2 tblsp. freshly squeezed lemon juice
- 3 finely sliced celery ribs, plus 1/2 cup leaves
- 2 tablespoons parsley, chopped
- 2 tablespoons drained and chopped capers
- 2 tblsp. balsamic vinegar

- 1/2 finely sliced red onion
- 4 tblsp. butter (unsalted)
- 3 quarts of vegetable oil
- 1 big baked potato, peeled, cut into 3-by- 1/4-inch sticks, washed, and fully dried
- 1 head lettuce (Boston or green leaf), cut into leaves

Instructions

1. Allow 1 hour for the steak to come to room temperature after being seasoned with 1 tablespoon of berbere spice.
2. Preheat the oven at 350 degrees in the meantime. Toss the tomatoes with the olive oil on a wide rimmed baking sheet. Season with salt and pepper and bake for 45 minutes, or until the tomatoes begin to sizzle and color.
3. Combine the lemon juice and the remaining 1/2 tablespoon of berbere spice in a medium mixing bowl. Toss in the celery and leaves, as well as the parsley, capers, vinegar, and onion. Salt & pepper to taste.
4. Melt the butter in a big skillet. Season the steak with salt and pepper and cook for 5 minutes over moderately high heat, or until well browned. Cook for another 6 minutes over moderate heat until the steak is medium-rare. Allow the steak to rest for 10 minutes on a carving board.

Nutrition:

Calories: 119
Fat: 12.07g
Carbs: 17.4g
Protein: 7.1g
Fiber: 5.1g

17.   Mark Bittman's Grilled Skirt Steak with Chimichurri Sauce

Prep Time: 5 Minutes

Cook Time: 20min

Total Time: 25 Min

Serving: 8

Ingredients

- 2 cups parsley, chopped
- a third of a cup of extra-virgin olive oil
- 6 tbsp. freshly squeezed lemon juice
- 2 tablespoons garlic, minced
- 2 teaspoons red pepper, crushed
- Season with salt and freshly ground black pepper.
- Skirt steak, 4 pounds

Instructions

1. Preheat the grill. Combine the parsley, olive oil, lemon juice, garlic, and crushed red pepper in a mixing bowl; season to taste with salt and pepper.

2. Season the skirt steak with salt and pepper and grill over a high heat for 2 minutes each side, or until charred on the surface and rare on the inside. Allow to rest for 5 minutes on a carving board. Across the grain, thinly slice the meat. Serve immediately, with the chimichurri sauce passed around the table.

Nutrition:

Calories: 89
Fat: 16.07g
Carbs: 17.4g
Protein: 10.1g
Fiber: 5.1g

18.   Grilled Steak with Cucumber-and-Daikon Salad

Prep Time:10 Minutes

Cook Time: 30min

Total Time: 40 Min

Serving: 5

Ingredients

- 2 teaspoons soy sauce
- 1 tbsp. fresh lemon juice
- 1 tbsp rice vinegar, unseasoned
- 1 minced garlic clove
- 1/4 cup canola oil, plus additional for rubbing
- Season with salt and freshly ground pepper.
- 1/2 cucumber, seedless, thinly sliced
- 8 ounces peeled and thinly sliced daikon
- 4 x 8 to 10 oz. strip steaks (3/4 inch thick).
- 1 tablespoon lemon zest, minced
- 1 tsp fresh chile, minced
- 4 oz. baby arugula

- 1 cup daikon or radish sprouts (optional).
- 2 tbsp roasted sesame seeds

Instructions

In a small mixing bowl, combine the soy sauce, lemon juice, vinegar, and garlic. Whisk in 1/4 cup oil until emulsified. Season with salt and pepper to taste. Toss the cucumber and daikon with half of the dressing in a medium mixing dish. Allow for 30 minutes at room temperature. Any surplus liquid should be drained and squeezed out. Put the cucumber and daikon back in the bowl.

Preheat a grill or a grill pan. Season the steaks with salt and pepper after rubbing them with oil. Grill the steaks over medium heat, rotating once, for 7 minutes, or until lightly browned on both sides and medium-rare. Place the steaks on a work surface and let aside for 5 minutes to rest.

Combine the lemon zest and chile in a small bowl and season with salt and pepper; move the steaks to plates and pour the gremolata on top. Toss the cucumber and daikon with the arugula, sprouts, and remaining dressing. Serve the salad beside the steaks, topped with sesame seeds.

Nutrition:
Calories: 606
Fat: 31.07g
Carbs: 17.4g
Protein: 16.1g
Fiber: 5.1g

19. Grilled Rib-Eye Steaks with Roasted Rosemary Potatoes

Prep Time: 20 Minutes

Cook Time: 1hrs 10min

Total Time: 2hours 20 Min

Serving: 5

Ingredients

- 3 lbs Yukon Gold potatoes, peeled and sliced into 1-inch chunks
- Salt.
- 10 rosemary sprigs, 1 inch
- a third of a cup extra-virgin olive oil
- black pepper, freshly ground
- 2 lbs boneless rib-eye steaks

Instructions

1. Preheat the oven to 400 degrees Fahrenheit. Cover the potatoes with cold water in a big saucepan. Bring to a boil with a big pinch of salt. Simmer for 12 minutes over medium-high heat, or until the vegetables are soft. Drain.

2. Return the potatoes to the saucepan and shake over moderately high heat for 10 seconds, or until the potatoes are dry. On a rimmed baking sheet, arrange the potatoes and rosemary sprigs. Toss with the olive oil and season with salt and black pepper to coat. Cook for 45 minutes, stirring occasionally, until the potatoes are bubbling and beginning to brown. Pour out any excess oil by tilting the baking sheet. Cook for another 15 minutes, or until the potatoes are golden and crisp.

3. Meanwhile, preheat a grill or a grill pan. Season the steaks with salt and black pepper and grill over high heat, rotating once, for 8 minutes, or until well-browned and medium-rare. Place the steaks on a cutting board and let them for 5 minutes to rest. Serve the steaks in thick slices with the potatoes.

Nutrition:
Calories: 321
Fat: 23.07g
Carbs: 17.4g
Protein: 12.1g

20.   Grilled Flank Steak with Sichuan Peppercorns

Prep Time: 10 Minutes

Cook Time: 25min

Total Time: 35 Min

Serving: 5

Ingredients

- 1 1/2 tbsp Sichuan peppercorns
- 3 tbsp of dry white wine
- 2 1/2 tbsp Chinese black bean and garlic sauce
- 2 tablespoons sugar
- Three 14-pound flank steaks
- Salt.

Instructions

1. Toast the peppercorns in a small pan over moderately high heat for 30 seconds, or until aromatic. Allow it cool fully before transferring to a spice grinder. Transfer to a small bowl after grinding to a powder.

Combine the wine, black bean–garlic sauce, and sugar in a mixing bowl.

2. Start a grill. Place the steaks on a baking sheet and brush with the sauce all over. Allow for a 10-minute resting period.

3. Season the flank steaks gently with salt and pepper. Grill the steaks over moderately high heat, rotating once, until medium-rare, about 8 minutes. Place the steaks on a work surface and let aside for 5 minutes to rest. Serve the meat thinly sliced across the grain.

Nutrition:
Calories: 606
Fat: 313.07g
Carbs: 22.4g
Protein: 4.1g
Fiber: 5.1g

21.   Peppered Beef Tenderloin with Roasted Garlic-Herb Butter

Prep Time: 30 Minutes

Cook Time: 1hrs 10min

Total Time: 1hrs 40 Min

Serving: 6

Ingredients

- 2 tbsp black pepper, coarsely ground
- 1 tsp of kosher salt
- 1 tsp. dark brown sugar
- 1 tbsp. soy sauce
- 1/2 tsp apple cider vinegar
- 1 tbsp. + 1 tsp. extra-virgin olive oil
- 6 tenderloin steaks, approximately 1 1/2 inches thick
- 4 unpeeled garlic cloves
- a quarter teaspoon fresh thyme
- 1/4 teaspoon rosemary, fresh
- 1/4 teaspoon oregano, fresh
- 4 tablespoons softened unsalted butter.

Instructions

1. Preheat the oven to 275 degrees Centigrade. Combine the pepper, salt, brown sugar, soy sauce, vinegar, and 1 teaspoon olive oil in a mixing bowl. 2 teaspoons of the paste should be applied to each steak. Wrap each steak in plastic wrap and set aside at room temperature for 1 hour.

2. Meanwhile, mix the garlic with the herbs on a double-layer square of aluminum foil; sprinkle with the remaining 1 tablespoon of oil on top. Fold the foil around the garlic and place it on a baking sheet. Cook for 45 minutes, or until the garlic is tender.

3. When the garlic has cooled, remove the cloves from their skins and place them in a dish with the herbs. Mash the garlic, herbs, and butter together with a fork. Spoon the garlic butter onto a sheet of plastic wrap, form into a log, and chill for 30 minutes, or until hard.

4. Light a very hot fire on one side of a charcoal barbecue or turn on a gas grill. Unwrap each steak and cook for about 7 minutes over high heat, flipping once, for rare meat. To cook the steaks medium-rare, move them to the cold side of the grill, cover the lid, and cook for 4 minutes more, rotating once halfway through. Garnish the steaks with the garlic-herb butter and let aside for 5 minutes before serving.

Nutrition:
Calories: 152
Fat: 2.07g

Carbs: 17.4g
Protein: 14.1g
Fiber: 5.1g

22. Kalbi Beef Short Ribs

Prep Time: 40 Minutes

Cook Time: 15min

Total Time: 55 Min

Serving: 5

Ingredients

- 2 and 1/2 pounds Thinly cut beef short ribs
- 1 tbsp soy sauce
- 1 pound brown sugar
- 1/8 c. Mirin (rice wine).
- 2 tablespoons minced garlic
- 1 tablespoon sesame oil
- 1/8 cup onion, finely grated

Instructions

1. Combine soy sauce, brown sugar, Mirin, garlic, sesame oil, and shredded onion in a medium-sized mixing bowl.

2. Add the beef short ribs to the bowl with the marinade, coating well.
3. Refrigerate the bowl for 1-6 hours, covered with plastic wrap.
4. Start your Traeger grill and set the temperature to high. Ascertain that the grill has been adequately preheated.
5. Remove the marinated meat from the fridge and set it straight on the grill. Close the grill as quickly as possible to ensure that you lose as little heat as possible.
6. Cook for four minutes on one side, then turn and cook for another four minutes on the other. Remove the meat from the grill and serve with your favorite grilled veggies on a bed of rice.

Nutrition:
Calories: 355
Fat: 8.07g
Carbs: 17.4g
Protein: 4.1g
Fiber: 5.1g

23. Beef Short Rib Lollipop

Prep Time: 15 Minutes

Cook Time: 3 hours

Rest Time : 15 minutes

Total Time: 3hours 30 Min

Serving: 5

Ingredients

- 4 beef short rib lollipops
- Liberal amounts of BBQ Rub
- Barbecue Sauce

Instructions

- Preheat your pellet grill to 275°F according to the manufacturer's recommendations.
- 2. Rub the rub all over the lollipop before placing it on the grill.
- Cook for 3–4 hours, stirring occasionally, until the meat is cooked.

- If preferred, baste with barbecue sauce in the last 30 minutes of cooking.

Nutrition:
Calories: 265
Fat: 12.07g
Carbs: 17.4g
Protein: 19.1g
Fiber: 5.1g

24. BEEF ROAST

Prep Time: 10 Minutes

Smoke Time: 5 hrs

Braise Time: 4 hours

Total Time: 9hours 100 Min

Serving: 5

Ingredients

1. 1 3-4 pound beef sirloin tip roast
2. 1/2 cup bbq rub
3. 2 bottles/cans amber beer
4. 1 bottle barbecue sauce

Instructions:

- Select the "smoke" setting on your pellet grill.
- Remove any extra fat from the roast and thoroughly cover it with the barbecue dry rub.
- Place on the grill for an hour to smoke.

- Flip the roast every hour or so for the following 3-4 hours.
- Remove from the grill and combine with the two beers in your braising saucepan. If your braising container is very large, you may need three. It should come up approximately halfway up the roast.
- Cook until the meat is fork tender and shreddable. This will vary based on the roast and braising Instructions: you use.
- Braising on the stove takes 3-4 hours on average.
- Braising in an Instant Pot normally takes 60 minutes plus a 25-30 minute natural pressure release period.
- Remove the braising liquid from the pan after the roast is fork tender, reserving 1-2 cups.
- Return the remaining braising liquid to the pan after shredding the meat, discarding any extra fat or connective tissue. Stir with your preferred barbecue sauce and keep heated until ready to serve. This keeps and maintains quality for several hours and reheats well.

Nutrition:
Calories: 180
Fat: 10.07g
Carbs: 17.4g

Protein: 23.1g
Fiber: 5.1g

25. CHILI PEPPER RUBBED BRISKET

Prep Time: 10 Minutes

Cook Time: 3hrs 30min

Total Time: 3hours 40 Min

Serving: 2

Ingredients:

1. 2 ancho peppers, dried
2. 1/2 cup apple cider vinegar
3. 9 arbol chilies, dried
4. 12 lbs beef brisket, packer cut
5. 2 tsp coriander
6. 1 tbsp cumin seed, whole
7. 2 tsp garlic, granulated
8. 1/4 cup kosher salt
9. 2 tsp oregano, dried
10.   2 tsp smoked paprika
11.   3 cups water

Instructions:

1. Just when you thought smoked brisket couldn't get much better, this chili pepper rubbed beef arrives to prove you wrong. Toasted arbol chilies, ancho chiles, coriander, and savory herbs and spices are used to make the smokey and spicy chili pepper rub. The brisket is liberally rubbed before being slow-smoked then crutched until juicy and tender. As a consequence, the bark is bold and well-seasoned, with tender slices of succulent meat.

2. Set your pit boss to smoke and keep the lid open for 10 minutes.

3. Close the lid and turn the heat up to 350°F. Allow it to come to room temperature before using. Whether you're using a gas or charcoal grill, set the temperature to medium.

4. Grill the dried peppers for 5 minutes, or until aromatic and hot to the touch, in a large cast iron pan. After removing from the skillet, let aside to cool.

5. In a heated skillet, toast the cumin and coriander for 1 minute. Remove the seeds from the pan and place them on a plate to cool.

6. Remove the stems from the ancho peppers and throw them all in a food processor. Pulse a few times to start things going, then process for 2 minutes on high, or until the mixture is coarsely ground.

7. In a mixing bowl, combine the garlic, oregano, smoked paprika, and salt. Pulse 10 times to mix before transferring to a cup.

8. Remove the brisket from the box and lay it on a cutting board, patting it dry with paper towels.
9. Using a sharp knife, trim the brisket. Begin trimming from the fat side downward. Trim the silver skin off the flat surface to remove the sides and corners. Remove any excess fat from the stage area. Turn the brisket over and remove any excess fat, leaving approximately 14 inches of fat thickness.
10. After seasoning the brisket with the chili pepper rub, set it aside.
11. Set your pit boss to the smoke mode. Set up a low, indirect fire on a gas or charcoal grill.
12. Place the brisket on the grill, then raise the temperature to 250°F and smoke until the internal temperature surpasses 165°F. After 2 hours, begin spraying the brisket every 30 minutes to help conserve moisture.
13. Wrap the brisket tightly in pit boss butcher paper, then place it on the grill and smoke it until the internal temperature reaches 200°F.
14. Before slicing, remove the brisket from the gill and set it in a covered refrigerator for 1 to 2 hours.

Nutrition:

Protein 23g

Fat 10g

Calories 180g

26. HOT AND SPICY RIBS

Preparation Time: 10 minutes

Cooking Time: 6 hr

Servings: 2

Ingredients:

- 2 finely minced chipotle in adobo
- 1 cup (any kind) barbecue sauce
- 1/2 cup brown sugar
- 1/4 cup honey
- 1/4 cup olive oil
- 1 rack st. Louis-style rib(s)
- 3 tablespoons sweet heat rub

Instructions:

1. These tasty spicy ribs will be a big success at your next backyard barbecue! These st. Louis style ribs are sure to satisfy every crowd! They're sweet, smoky, and

have just enough fire to keep you coming back for more!

2. Drain and pat dry the ribs after removing them from their wrapping. Grasp the skin on the back of the ribs with a paper towel and slip it off. Remove the membrane and the paper towel.

3. Combine the brown sugar, olive oil, butter, bbq sauce, and adobo chiles in a deep mixing cup. Clean the front and back of the ribs liberally with the bbq paste using a basting brush. Save the basting brush and part of the sauce for later.

4. Season the ribs liberally with sweet heat rub, paying particular attention to the front of the ribs.

5. Set your pit boss to 225°f and start cooking. Set the barbecue to low heat whether you're using a gas or charcoal grill. Place the ribs on the grill and smoke at 225°f for 4-6 hours, basting every 2 hours with the sauce.

6. Remove from the grill and top with more barbecue sauce.

Nutrition:

Protein 23g
Fat 10g
Calories 180g
Carbs 0g

BACON SMOKED BRISKET FLAT

Preparation Time: 10 minutes

Cooking Time: 1 hr

Servings: 2

Ingredients:

1. 1/2 lbs bacon
2. 4 lbs brisket flat, trimmed
3. Tt pit boss lonestar brisket rub

Instructions:

- Smoked brisket is no exception to the rule that anything tastes better with bacon.
- Start your pit boss in smoke mode and let it run for 10 minutes with the lid open.
- Double the temperature of your barbecue to 250°f. Set up a gas or charcoal grill for low, indirect fire.

- Place the brisket in an aluminum pan lined with foil. Season the fat side of the brisket with pit boss lonestar brisket rub before flipping and seasoning the meat side.
- Place the brisket on the grill for 1 hour to smoke.
- Toss the brisket with tongs such that the fat side is up, then drape half of the bacon slices over the brisket. After 2 hours, cut the browned bacon and set aside.
- Continue cooking until the fresh bacon strips are browned and the internal temperature of the brisket reads 202°f, which will usually take a further 3 to 4 hours.
- Remove the brisket from the grill and let it rest for 1 hour before slicing thinly. Serve hot.

Nutrition:

1. Protein 23g
2. Fat   10g
3. Calories   180g
4. Carbs 0g

27. SMOKED DR. PEPPER RIBS

Preparation Time: 10 minutes

Cooking Time: 1 hr

Servings: 2

Ingredients:

1. Aluminum foil
2. 2 racks baby back ribs
3. 1 cup bbq sauce
4. 1 stick butter, melted
5. 1/2 cup dark brown sugar
6. 12 oz dr. Pepper soda
7. 1/4 cup pit boss sweet rib rub
8. 1/4 cup yellow mustard

Instructions:

- These dr. Pepper ribs are sweet, smoky, and succulent, falling off the bone tender. Meaty baby back ribs are liberally seasoned with sweet rib rub before being smoked low and slow. They're then braised in a butter, brown sugar, and dr. Pepper bath until tender, before being slathered in a sticky sweet dr. Pepper bbq sauce. The sauce caramelizes on the grill until mildly burnt and gooey for a finger-lickin' good treat.
- Preheat your pit boss to 225°f and your grill. Set up a gas or charcoal grill for low, indirect fire.
- Place the ribs directly on the grill grates after the grill has reached temperature, close the door, and smoke for 2 hours.
- Whisk together the butter, brown sugar, and 8 ounces of dr. Pepper in a glass measuring cup.
- Half of the mixture should be put on a sheet tray lined with foil.
- Place the ribs on top of the mixture, meat-side down, and then dump the remaining mixture over the bone-side. Send the sheet tray to the grill for another 2 hours, tenting it with foil.
- Remove the ribs from the liquid and position them directly on the grill grate, meat side up.

- Combine the bbq sauce and 4 ounces of dr. Pepper in a mixing bowl, then rub half of the sauce over the ribs.
- Cook for a further 30 to 60 minutes, or until the ribs are tender and the beef pulls away from the bones, at 275°f.
- Place the ribs on a sheet tray and set aside for 10 minutes before slicing and serving with the remaining bbq sauce.

Nutrition:

Protein 23g

Fat 10g

Calories 180g

28.   BEEF SHORT RIBS

Preparation Time: 10 minutes

Cooking Time: 1 hr

Servings: 2

Ingredients:

- 1 cup apple cider vinegar
- 1 cup apple juice
- 4 tablespoon olive oil
- 4 tbsp pit boss beef and brisket rub
- 2 1/2 pounds (or 6 large) beef short rib(s

Instructions:

- For full flavor absorption, these smoked beef short ribs are first smoked on the pit boss for 2 hours, naked on the grill gates. Since reaching an internal temperature of 145°f, at which point the beef can no longer contain smoke, the ribs are braised in an apple juice and apple cider vinegar blend, which breaks down the fat and collagen, yielding out-of-this-world fall-off-the-bone ribs.

- Internal temperature of smoked beef short ribs
- Beef short ribs are normally finished when they attain an internal temperature of 200 to 205°f, but this can vary somewhat. If you pick up the rack and it twists before beginning to come apart slightly, they are able to take off the rack.
- Switch on the pit boss. Then, set the thermostat to 225°f.
- Combine the apple cider vinegar and apple juice in a food-safe spray container. Place aside.
- Remove the thick membrane from the beef short ribs by flipping them over, bone side up. Throw out. Flip the short ribs over and strip away any extra fat from the end. Clean the short ribs liberally with olive oil and beef and brisket rub.
- Place the beef ribs in the middle rack of the oven. Smoke the short ribs for around 2 hours, or until they have formed a crust and are a dark lacquered color.
- After 2 hours, cut the beef short ribs from the smoker, put them in a heat-resistant baking dish, and pour in the apple cider vinegar and apple juice. Cover securely with foil and continue to smoke for 1 12-2 hours, or until the ribs are fall-apart tender and register 200°f. Serve shortly after removing from the smoker.

Nutrition:

Protein 23g

Fat   10g

Calories 180g

Carbs 0g

29.   PEPPERED SPICY BEEF JERKY

Preparation Time: 10 minutes

Cooking Time: 1 hr 10 minutes

Servings: 2

Ingredients:

1. 1 12 oz bottle dark beer
2. 1/4 cup brown sugar
3. 2 tbsp coarse black pepper
4. 4 tbsp garlic salt
5. 2 tbsp hot sauce
6. 2 tablespoons, divided pit boss sweet heat rub
7. 1 tablespoon quick curing salt
8. 1 cup soy sauce
9. 2 pounds trimmed flank steak
10.   ¼ worcestershire sauce

Instructions:

1. This tasty, protein-packed peppered spicy beef jerky is ideal for workouts or social gatherings! This recipe calls for trimmed flank steak, which is deeply flavored and smoky.
2. When you're about to smoke the jerky, take the beef out of the marinade and dump it.
3. Set the temperature of your pit boss smoker to 200°f. If you're using a sawdust or charcoal smoker, set the temperature to medium-low.
4. Place the meat in a single layer on the smoker grate. Smoke the beef for 4-5 hours, or until it is crispy but still chewy and bends slightly.
5. With tongs, remove the jerky from the grill and place it in a resealable plastic bag while it is still warm. Enable the jerky to sit at room temperature for 1 hour.
6. Refrigerate the jerky after pressing any air out of the resealable plastic container. It can be stored for several weeks. Have fun!

Nutrition:

Protein 23g

Fat 10g

Calories 180g

30.   PIT BOSS BBQ BEEF BRISKET

Preparation Time: 10 minutes

Cooking Time: 5 hr 20 minutes

Servings: 2

Ingredients:

- 1 cup beef broth
- 1, 10-12 pound brisket
- 1 bottle pit boss sweet rib rub

Instructions:

- Many will believe that the brisket beef cut is the mount everest of BBQ, grilling, and smoking. Beef brisket is a rugged cut of meat that takes hours to prepare. However, until juicy, it is one of the most delicious cuts of beef you can ever eat. As a result, considering the lengthy cooking time, many daring backyard cooks are up for the challenge. Fortunately, a pit boss wood pellet grill can help alleviate this problem by providing continuous heat for hours on end. Using our grills in conjunction with this pit boss type recipe is the one-two punch you need for perfectly smoked brisket.

- Discard some silver skin or extra fat from the flat muscle. The flat of the meat would then have a big, crescent-shaped fat portion.

- Trim the fat until it is smooth against the meat and seems to be a flawless transition from point to flat. Trim the fat cap to 14 inch thick and flip the brisket over. Cut between the stage and the flat, reserving the flat for later.

- Season the trimmed brisket point on both sides liberally with the sweet rib rub. Allow the brisket to marinate for 30 minutes.

- Set aside the beef broth in the spray bottle.

- Get your pit boss smoker or wood pellet barbecue going. Set the temperature to 225°f until it's started. Place the brisket in the smoker, insert the attached temperature probe if you have one, and cook for 6-8 hours, or until the internal temperature exceeds 165°f. To keep the brisket juicy, spray it with beef broth after 2 hours.
- Remove the brisket from the smoker until it reaches 165°f, wrap in peach butcher paper, folding the edges over to create a leakproof cover, and return to the smoker seam-side down for another 3-4 hours, or until the brisket hits 200°f.
- Remove the brisket from the smoker and set aside for at least an hour before serving.

Nutrition:

Protein 23g

Fat   10g

Calories   180g

Carbs 0g

31. COMPETITION SMOKED BABY BACK RIBS

Preparation Time: 10 minutes

Cooking Time: 4 hr 40 minutes

Servings: 2

Ingredients:

1. 2 cups apple, juice
2. 2 racks baby back rib
3. Pit boss competition smoked rub
4. Southern style bbq sauce

Instructions:

1. The rivalry smoked baby back ribs are easy to prepare, but the tastes are well worth the effort. This recipe calls for starting the ribs with a dry rub before adding a wet rub incorporating apple juice and your favorite southern style barbecue sauce halfway through the cook. Because of the 2-2-1 procedure, the baby back rack of ribs will be fall-off-the-bone juicy, with a tangy and sweet punch from the sauce. You'll be in hog

paradise if you pair these championship pork ribs with a side of coleslaw, mac & cheese, or potato salad.

2. Preheat to 200°F or smoke mode on your.
3. Remove the skin off the rear side of the ribs using a knife and a paper towel. Using your own spice blend or the competition's smoke-infused smoked rub.
4. Using your own spice blend or the competition's smoke-infused smoked rub.
5. Smoke the aged baby back ribs on the grill grates for 2 hours, meat side up.
6. After 2 hours, remove off the grill and adjust the temperature to 250°F.
7. Make an aluminum boat for each pair of ribs and place the ribs inside. Cover the boat with aluminum foil and pour in a cup of apple juice.
8. Return the ribs on the grill for another 2 hours.
9. Sprinkle the ribs with barbecue sauce after taking them from the apple juice wash.
10. Raise the temperature of the grill to 350 degrees Fahrenheit. Return the ribs to the grill when it has warmed.
11. Simply leave the ribs on the grill for around 15 minutes to harden up the barbecue sauce. Keep an eye on the grill during this stage since the sugar in the apple juice and barbecue sauce can readily burn.
12. Allow the ribs to rest for about 15 minutes after they have been removed from the grill, then serve hot and enjoy!

Nutrition:

Protein 23g

Fat 10g

Calories 180g

32.   ASIAN STYLE GRILLED BEEF SHORT RIBS

Preparation Time: 10 minutes

Cooking Time: 3 hr 50 minutes

Servings: 2

Ingredients:

- 2–3 racks of ribs per person
- 6 tablespoons hoisin sauce
- 2 tablespoons sesame seed oil
- 4 tablespoons soy sauce (full sodium)
- 1 cup brown sugar
- 4 ounces mirin
- 4 tablespoons rice vinegar (seasoned)
- a single apple (granny smith, fuji, braeburn, or honeycrisp)
- 1 ginger knob
- three tangerines
- 3 garlic cloves
- 2 tablespoons maraschino cherry juice
- 1 tbsp red pepper flakes (or 1 tsp if you want it less hot)

Salad components

- 1/2 head of napa cabbage (finely shredded)
- 1 carrot (grated)
- 4-5 small sweet peppers
- Handful of sugar snap peas
- Juice of 2 tangerines
- 1 apple (granny smith, fuji, braeburn, or honeycrisp)
- Pinch of red pepper flakes (optional)

Salad dressing

1. 1 small piece of ginger
2. 1 small clove of garlic
3. Juice of 1 tangerine
4. 4 tbsp rice vinegar
5. 1 tbsp mirin
6. 1/2 tbsp sesame oil
7. Large pinch of white sugar
8. Pinch of salt

Instructions:

1. So you'll start with 2 to 3 ribs per guy, at the very least. And i'm making a crosscut beef short rib, which is also known as flanking cut, asian cut, or simply crosscut. I know all of you have cooked ribs before beef and pork, but i want to make sure you understand that the membrane on your rib should be stripped. When you cook these, they do not get tender. So i'm just going to grab a knife and cut it as thin as possible.

2. Let's marinate the cross-cut ribs now. I already have mine in a vacuum-sealed bag, so they only need to marinate for around an hour. I've got 16 ribs in here with the marinade, and i'm going to put them in the fridge for an hour. It's not a great deal if you don't vacuum seal or don't have a vacuum sealer. Place them in a casserole dish or on a sheet plate, cover with the marinade, and place in the refrigerator. I'd give them at least six hours. No trouble if you need to do that overnight when you have to go to work the next day.

3. So, let's go over the ingredients. I combined all of these ingredients in a mixer, mixed it, poured it over the ribs, and vacuum-sealed it. So it's pretty easy. Let's begin with the ingredients. This is my hoisin sauce. I'm going to use 6 teaspoons hoisin sauce. I'm going to use 2 tbsp. Sesame seed oil. I'll use 4 teaspoons of soy sauce. Since we're not going to apply salt to this marinade, i recommend using the entire sodium, and i like this particular brand. It adds a good richness to the beef, in my opinion. I'll even add a half-cup of brown sugar and red pepper flakes. I used a tablespoon because i like them spicy. If you don't find anything so spicy, use just a teaspoon. Then we'll add mirin to the mix. We're going to use four ounces of sweet rice wine. Again, i'm dumping everything into the blender. Then we'll add four teaspoons of rice vinegar. I made use of the experienced. They offer both unseasoned and seasoned options. Salt has been applied to the seasoning. Again, we don't add any extra salt to this dish, so please find it seasoned. The apples have now been sliced. We use a granny smith, a fuji, a braeburn, or a honey crisp apple. You sliced them, finely chopped them, and threw them in your blender. Then i used a finger knob of ginger

that was around the size of my finger and a few inches long, peeled it, diced it up, and tossed it in the blender. Then i've got three tangerines. I halved them, squeezed the juice in, and tossed in one of the tangerines. Garlic: i took three cloves, peeled them, and blended them.

4. Maraschino cherry juice is the secret ingredient. I know it sounds strange, but i used 2 teaspoons of maraschino cherry juice. It adds a little depth of flavor as well as colour to the ribs. Keep the remainder for shirley temples for the girls. So, once again, i threw it into a blender, pureed it, poured it over my steak, and vacuum-sealed it. Again, if you don't want to use a vacuum sealer or don't have one, spread your flank and ribs over a sheet pan, spill the marinade on, cover with saran wrap, and place in the fridge for 6 hours or when you get home from work.

5. Then we'll fire up the grill and show you how it's handled. The asian style cross-cut ribs are served with a handmade asian salad. While you can buy good quality in a bag in the produce department, i prefer to make my own. So for the sauce, i finely shredded half a head of napa cabbage. Standard cabbage would be much too good for this dish. I grated one carrot and added it to the dish, then i bought some of the tiny sweet peppers and sliced them into matchsticks (four or five). Put in some lovely color and sweetness. Then, instead of asian snow peas, i used sugar snap peas because i like the flavor and crunch. I even cut them into matchsticks and throw them in. I cut a granny smith or a fuji apple into small dice and tossing them in the juice of two tangerines to keep them from turning brown. It also enhances the taste.

6. The dressing is now ready. It does not seem to be much, but it is extremely strong. I put one little piece of fresh ginger, about the size of a nickel, in my trusty bullet blender. I'd chop this up into a couple bits. 1 garlic clove, crushed and peeled crush it first with your knife to let the flavors escape more easily. Another tangerine, four tablespoons rice vinegar, one tablespoon mirin, a half teaspoon sesame oil (this is potent content, so don't use too much), and a big pinch of white sugar and salt i blended it in my blender. Nobody makes a small amount, so this will season the whole cup.

7. So, along with my apples, i'll toss this into the slaw. I like a little heat, so i'm going to throw in some red pepper flakes. It's a coin toss. It looks good and has a nice comparison taste to the sweetness of the ribs.

8. So it looks like it's time for me to take the ribs off the grill, and then we'll feast. I've set the pit boss to 375 degrees fahrenheit and am using wood pellets because, as you know, i used apple in this marinade, so i'm just trying to infuse the flavors. You'll have to wait outside while these cook because they only take about 8 minutes. 375 degrees in one Instructions:. I like grill labels, so i'll flip them. I'll give them another two to three minutes before flipping them over and repeating the process. Allow three to five minutes for these to rest before serving. Okay, here's our finished plate. I sprinkled it with toasted sesame seeds. Have fun, everybody!

9. **Nutrition:**

Protein 23g

Fat 10g

Calories 180g

Carbs 0g

33. HANGING ST. LOUIS-STYLE RIBS

Preparation Time: 10 minutes

Cooking Time: 3 hr 20 minutes

Servings: 2

Ingredients:

- 1 1/3 cup apple juice
- 1 2/3 cup bbq sauce, divided
- Tt pit boss pulled pork rub
- 4 half racks spare ribs, st. Louis style

Instructions:

1. With these succulent hanging st. Louis-style ribs, you can channel your inner pitmaster. The fat and juices run down the length of the rack when hanging and smoked vertically in the pit boss, making it super juicy and soft.

2. Preheat the pit boss to 250 degrees fahrenheit. Set up a gas or charcoal grill for low, indirect fire.

3. Strip the back membrane from the rib racks with a sharp knife and pat dry with a paper towel. Cut rib racks in two, then generously season with pulled pork rub.

4. Insert a hanging hook under the top rib, then transfer the racks to the smoking drawer. Smoke for a total of 2 1/2 hours.

5. Take the ribs out of the smoking cabinet and place them on heavy duty foil. Brush thinned bbq sauce on both sides of ribs after combining 2/3 cup bbq sauce and 1/3 cup apple juice. 14 cup apple juice should be poured around each rib. Fold the foil over, then place the meat side down on the grill. Cook for an additional 2 hours after increasing the temperature to 300° f.

6. Remove the ribs from the barbecue, baste with bbq sauce, and return to the grill for another 10 to 15 minutes. Allow to rest for 15 minutes before slicing and serving sweet.

Nutrition:

protein 23g

fat   10g

calories   180g

carbs 0g

34. BEEF PLATE RIBS WITH SMOKED HOMEMADE BBQ SAUCE

Preparation Time: 10 minutes

Cooking Time: 6 hr 30 minutes

Servings: 2

Ingredients:

- 1 1/3 cup apple cider vinegar
- 4 lbs beef plate ribs
- 1/3 cup beef stock
- 1/2 tsp black pepper
- 1/4 tsp cayenne pepper
- 4 garlic cloves, peeled and smashed
- 2 tbsp honey
- 1/2 tsp kosher salt
- 1/4 cup molasses
- Tbsp olive oil
- 2 tsp paprika
- Tt pit boss beef and brisket rub
- 1 tbsp spicy brown mustard
- 2 lbs tomato, cubed

- 1 white onion, quartered

Instructions:
1. These massive smoked beef plate ribs will be a show stopper at your next barbecue. Beef plate ribs are sliced from the lower rib cage and have a nice coating of fat-laced beef on top.
2. Switch on your pit boss grill and choose the smoke setting. Set up a gas or charcoal grill for low, indirect fire.
3. Remove the top portion of the fat cap from the rib rack to prepare the ribs. Season with beef brisket rub after rubbing with mustard. Inject beef stock into the flesh, between the bones, and around the sides.
4. Place the rib rack in the middle of the grill and close the sear slide. Boost the temperature to 250 degrees fahrenheit. Ribs can be smoked for 3 hours.
5. Meanwhile, make the bbq sauce by lining a sheet tray with foil and layering tomatoes, onion, and garlic. Drizzle with olive oil and season with 14 teaspoon salt and 14 teaspoon black pepper to taste. Place in a smoke cabinet for 2 hours.

6. In a grill-safe pan, combine a quart of apple cider vinegar and water. Place the rib rack on the right side of the grill, followed by the other pan in the middle. Boost the temperature to 275°f.

7. Place the tomatoes for the smoke cabinet in a blender. Combine paprika, cayenne pepper, 1/4 teaspoon cinnamon, 1/4 teaspoon black pepper, 1/3 cup apple cider vinegar, molasses, and honey in a mixing bowl. Blend until the mixture is smooth and there are no lumps. Place the sauce in a cast iron pan and place it on the grill. As the ribs continue to cook, simmer the sauce for 1 hour, stirring regularly. When the sauce is finished, spoon it over the ribs and set aside before the ribs are done.

8. Cook the ribs for another 2-3 hours, or before the internal temperature exceeds 204°f and a metal skewer slides through like butter.

Nutrition:

protein 23g

fat 10g

calories   180g

carbs 0g

35. REVERSE SEARED PICANHA STEAK

Preparation Time: 10 minutes

Cooking Time: 2 hr 30 minutes

Servings: 2

Ingredients:

1. Olive oil
2. 3 lbs picanha steak, top sirloin cap, fat cap removed
3. Tt pit boss chop house steak rub

Instructions:

- With this simple and tasty picanha steak, you can turn your backyard into a brazilian steakhouse.
- Start your pit boss and preheat it to 225°f. Set up a gas or charcoal grill for low, indirect fire.
- Season both sides of the steak liberally with chop house, insert the temperature probe, and put the steak directly on the grill grate.

- Cook for 1 12 to 2 hours, or until internal temperature reaches 125°f to 130°f.
- Remove the steak from the grill and preheat the kc combo griddle to medium-high heat. On the griddle, heat the olive oil and sear the steak for 2 minutes per side on both sides.
- Enable the steak to rest for 10 minutes on a cutting board after removing it from the griddle. Serve steak cut against the grain.

Nutrition:

Protein 23g

Fat   10g

Calories   180g

Carbs 0g

36. NEXT LEVEL SMOKED PORCHETTA

Preparation Time: 10 minutes

Cooking Time: 1 hr 30 minutes

Servings: 2

Ingredients:

- 1 tbs ancho chili powder
- 1/2 cup brown sugar
- 3 tbs grilling seasoning
- 1 tbs chopped italian parsley
- 1/2 cup maple syrup
- 1 tsp dry oregano
- 1 tbs chopped oregano, leaves
- 1/2 pork, belly (skinless)
- 1 whole pork, tenderloins
- 6 slices prosciutto, sliced
- 1 tbs chopped rosemary, fresh

- 1 tbs chopped sage, leaves
- 1/2 cup sugar, cure

Instructions:

1. Rub on the sugar cure on both sides. (you can cure pork belly without using sodium nitrite (in the cure mix), but it is much better if you do, so i strongly advise you to do so.)
2. Whisk together brown sugar, maple syrup, ancho chili powder, and oregano in a small mug. Slather on both sides of each slice of pork belly.
3. Refrigerate the pork bag (if you can find a 2 gallon or larger one) or container. Per 24 hours, rotate and flip.
4. After 3 days, cut the pork belly and thoroughly rinse each slice.
5. Because of the sugar cure, the porchetta (or bacon) would be too salty if not thoroughly rinsed.
6. Place the skin side of the pork belly on a big cutting board.
7. To make the seasoning to penetrate, lightly score the meat side with diamond cuts.
8. Season lightly with grilling seasoning, then powder well with the herb mixture.
9. Place the prosciutto on top of the pork tenderloin, then the pork belly.

10.   Season the tenderloin lightly, then roll it firmly in the pork belly.

11.   Hook it up securely with cooking twine.

12.   Grilling seasoning should be applied gently but uniformly to the outside of the pork belly.

13.   Set smoker to 250°f with apple wood pellets (recommended).

14.   Smoke for 6 hours, or before the internal temperature exceeds 175°f.

15.   Enable for a 20-minute rest period after removing from the oven. After it has cooled, thinly slice it and fry it in a hot skillet.

16.   Allow it to cool for another 15 minutes.

Nutrition:

Protein 23g
Fat 10g
Calories 180g

37.   STANDING RIB ROAST

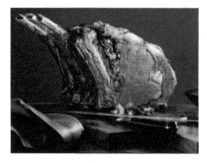

Preparation Time: 10 minutes

Cooking Time: 2 hr 30 minutes

Servings: 2

Ingredients:

- 1 tbsp cracked black pepper
- 1/2 tbsp granulated garlic
- 1/2 tbsp granulated onion
- 2 tbsp kosher salt
- 1 tbsp olive oil
- 2 tsp oregano, dried
- 1/2 tbsp parsley, dried
- 5 1/2 lbs prime rib roast, bone-in
- 2 tsp smoked paprika

Instructions:

1. A holiday feast isn't complete until it has a wonderfully tender standing rib roast. This prime rib, the king of all beef cuts, is given the boss care by being rubbed in a savory herb crust and then smoked low and slow for a kiss of wood-fired spice. Roast for a few minutes on high to make the fat and crisp the crust before slicing into a finely juicy and unusual roast fit for a king.

2. In a glass baking dish, place the roast. Combine the salt, pepper, granulated garlic, granulated onion, parsley, oregano, and smoked paprika in a shallow mixing cup. Cover and refrigerate the roast overnight after seasoning it with the spice mix.

3. Take the roast from the refrigerator one hour before serving, cover it, and set it out to come to room temperature.

4. Start your pit boss pellet grill on smoke mode and leave the lid open for 10 minutes before preheating to 225° f. Set up a gas or charcoal grill for low, indirect fire.

5. Place the seasoned roast in a cast iron skillet, drizzle with olive oil, and barbecue. 1 hour 45 minutes, or before the internal temperature reaches 120° f, smoke the roast. Enable the roast to rest for 15 minutes after removing it from the grill.

6. Double the grill temperature to 450°f, then return the roast to the grill for another 10 to 15 minutes. Allow the roast to rest for 15 minutes before slicing and serving.

Nutrition:

Protein 23g

Fat 10g

Calories 180g

Carbs 0g

38.   TIP BURNT ENDS

Preparation Time: 10 minutes

Cooking Time: 5 hr 30 minutes

Servings: 2

Ingredients:

- 1/2 cup bbq sauce
- To taste, beef & brisket rub
- 1 1/2 tbsp brown sugar
- 1 1/2 tbsp butter, cubed
- 1/2 cup dr. Pepper soda
- 1/2 tbsp honey
- 2 tbsp mustard
- 2 lbs tri tip steak
- 1/2 tbsp worcestershire sauce

Instructions:

1. With these tri tip burnt ends, you will enjoy beefy nuggets without having to smoke an entire brisket. The tri tip roast split, also known as santa maria steak, is heavily marbled and has a tender, beefy taste comparable to brisket. The tri tip is slathered with mustard and seasoned with beef & brisket rub before being smoked low and slow until soft and smoky.

2. Start your pit boss on smoke mode and leave the lid open for 10 minutes before setting it to 225° f. Set up a gas or charcoal grill for low, indirect fire.

3. Rub the mustard all over the tri tip before seasoning with the beef & brisket rub.

4. Place the tri tip directly on the grill grates and smoke for 2 1/2 hours, or until the internal temperature exceeds 165° f.

5. Cover the tri tip in pit boss butcher paper after removing it from the barbecue. Return the tri tip to the grill and continue to smoke for another 2 to 3 hours, or until the internal temperature exceeds 200° f.

6. Remove the tri tip from the grill and set aside for 30 minutes to rest, or set aside and refrigerate overnight.

7. Boost the temperature of the grill to 275° f.

8. Cube the tri tip into 1/2 to 3/4-inch cubes, then put in a big cast iron skillet.

9. In a container or mixing cup, combine the bbq sauce, dr. Pepper, sugar, and worcestershire sauce, and pipe over the cubed tri tip. Dot with honey, then dust with brown sugar.

10. Place the skillet on the grill grate and cook it over indirect fire. Cook for 1 1/2 to 2 hours, flipping the bits halfway through. The sauce would have depleted, coated, and charred the tri tip. Remove from the grill and serve while still hot.

Nutrition:

Protein 23g

Fat   10g

Calories 180g

Carbs 0g

39. BEEF CALDERETA STEW

Preparation Time: 10 minutes

Cooking Time: 3 hr 40 minutes

Servings: 2

Ingredients:

- 1/2 cup cheddar cheese, grated
- 2 lbs, cut into 1 1/2" cubes chuck roast
- 4 garlic cloves, chopped
- 1 tsp kosher salt
- 2 tbsp olive oil
- 2 large yukon gold potatoes
- 5 chopped serrano peppers
- 2 tbsp tomato paste
- 2 cups tomato sauce
- 2 cups water

Instruction:

1. This flavorful smoked beef caldereta stew is a tasty alternative to conventional beef stew. Caldereta is a common filipino dish served on special occasions and holidays, made with smoky chunks of chuck roast simmered in a bold and spicy tomato, onion, and pepper sauce.
2. Place the beef in a cast iron skillet and place it in the smoking drawer. Check that the sear slide and side dampers are open, then raise the temperature to 375°f to ensure that the cabinet retains a temperature between 225°f and 250°f (if cooking on a separate pit boss pellet grill, set the temperature to 225°f).
3. Smoke the beef for 1 1/2 hours, then turn it over and smoke for another 1 1/2 hours.
4. Place the cast iron dutch oven on the burner, directly over the blaze. Combine the olive oil, tomatoes, and carrots in a mixing bowl. Cook, stirring regularly, for 3 to 5 minutes. Cook for 2 minutes, or until the leeks and garlic are fragrant.
5. Remove the skillet from the smoking cabinet and apply the beef to the potato mixture.

6. Combine tomato sauce, tomato paste, water, and serrano peppers in a mixing bowl. Bring to a boil, then remove from heat and cover with a cap. Set the temperature to 275°f and let the stew simmer for 1 hour, or until the beef and potatoes are tender.
7. Gently whisk in the liver and cheese until the sauce thickens and the cheese melts.
8. Combine the bell peppers and olives in a mixing bowl. Cook for an extra 2 minutes, stirring occasionally. Season with salt and pepper and eat immediately.

Nutrition:

Protein 23g

Fat   10g

Calories   180g

Carbs 0g

40.   BALSAMIC SOY FLANK STEAK

Preparation Time: 15 minutes

Cooking Time: 30 minutes

Servings: 2

Ingredients

- 1½ lb. flank steak
- ½ onion, chopped
- 3 cloves garlic, chopped
- ¼ C olive oil
- ¼ C balsamic vinegar
- ¼ C soy sauce
- 1 TB Dijon mustard
- 1 TB dried rosemary
- 1 tsp salt
- ½ tsp black pepper

Instructions:

1. In a mixing bowl, combine the onion, garlic, olive oil, balsamic vinegar, soy sauce, Dijon, rosemary, salt, and pepper to prepare the soy balsamic marinade.
2. Place the steak in a large zip-top bag with the marinade and shake well. Refrigerate the bag for at least an hour or overnight to marinate.
3. Preheat the oven to 350 degrees Fahrenheit. Remove the steak from the bag and brush off any excess marinade, reserving the marinade.
4. Cook the steak for 8 to 10 minutes per side on the Pitboss (depending on desired level of doneness). Brush the steak with the reserved marinade every few minutes while it cooks. When the steak is done, remove it from the Pitboss and set it aside to rest for 5 minutes on a chopping board.
5. Using a sharp knife, slice the cooked flank steak thinly across the grain. This is crucial for a tender steak. Serve as is, or slice and add to a salad or use in fajitas or beef tacos.

Nutrition:

Protein 45g

Fat   31g

Calories 112g

Carbs 0g

41.   MOINK BALLS

Preparation Time: 15 minutes

Cooking Time: 30 minutes

Servings: 2

Ingredients

- 2 lbs. ground beef
- ¾ C fresh breadcrumbs
- 2 large eggs
- 2 tsp minced garlic
- 1 lb. slices of bacon, cut in half
- 1/3 C Pitboss AP Rub
- 1 C Pitboss BBQ Sauce

Instructions:

1. In a large mixing bowl, combine the ground beef, breadcrumbs, eggs, and garlic. Combine the ingredients in a mixing bowl and roll into 1 inch diameter balls with your palms.

2. Wrap half a piece of bacon around each meatball and fasten with a toothpick. If you want to save some toothpicks, you may put several of these on a prepared skewer. Using a good amount of the rub, coat the whole surface. Preheat your Pitboss to around 275 degrees Fahrenheit.

3. You may cook them at a lower temperature if you have time, or a higher temperature if you need them done quickly.

4. Cook until the meatballs have reached an internal temperature of 160°F and the bacon has crisped. If you're using store-bought meatballs, you'll only need to cook them until the bacon is done.

5. Coat the moink balls with your barbecue sauce during the last 10 minutes of cooking. Cut the barbecue sauce with a little grape jelly if you want your moink balls to have a sweeter finish. You may sprinkle the moink balls with the remaining dry rub once they've been removed from the grill.

Nutrition:

Protein 23g

Fat 10g

Calories 180g

Carbs 0g

42. FILET MIGNON

Ingredients

- Filet Mignon to your liking
- Your Favorite Steak Seasoning
- A couple of onions
- Garlic Cloves
- Rosemary
- A little (A lot) of butter

Instructions:

1. First and foremost, we purchased two gorgeous Filets from our neighborhood grocery shop. We cut them as little as possible, but they still had a lot of silver skin and fat to get rid of. I put a small layer of Moore's Marinade on them after they were cut to help the rub stay. I used a generous quantity of black pepper and a modest layer of Beef rub to season them. The beef rub and black pepper complement each other beautifully and bring out the taste of the meat.

2. We'll leave the steaks on the counter for approximately an hour to allow the rubs to do their job. I used a cooling rack to keep the steaks out of the seasoning, which appears to help the filets have a more consistent crust and color.

3. I'm going to fire up the Pitboss while the steaks are resting. With amazing results, you may cook these steaks on any grill you have. I'm simply trying to demonstrate that just because you have a pellet doesn't mean you can't cook a fantastic steak. Of course, I set the Pitboss to 485 degrees because I knew the grates will be well over 600 degrees.

4. I'm going to create the onion sauce while the grill is heating up. I grabbed two sweet onions and peeled off the outer skin and the steam. The stem was then removed by making a tiny pocket in the onion. In each, I put a single beef bouillon cube and a dab of butter. The onions, garlic cloves, rosemary, and six butter pads were then placed in a small dutch oven with the cover on. I'll bake it for approximately one hour at 400 degrees. You may perform the same thing with a tiny foil pack or any other container. The onions should be cooked until they are completely soft. It should take around an hour to complete.

5. It's time to start cooking these filets. This cook is as straightforward as they get. I just did the 2 minute twist, 2 minute flip, I cooked these filets to 122 degrees for a medium rare finish. Allowing them to relax for a few minutes is always a good idea. I melt a tiny amount of butter over them to slow down the cooking process.

6. I worked on the onion sauce while the meat rested. In the dutch oven, everything should be excellent and soft. This makes it simple to integrate and make a delicious sauce. I massaged the sauce with a potato masher until it was uniformly thick.

7. The sauce can be served on the side or poured over the steaks. The filets are delicious, and the sauce just adds to the deliciousness!

Nutrition:

Protein 23g

Fat 10g

Calories 180g

Carbs 0g

43.   DINO BONES

Preparation Time: 15 minutes

Cooking Time: 30 minutes

Servings: 2

INGREDIENTS

BRAISE

- 1 Cup Beef Broth or Stock
- 1 Cup Red Wine
- ¼ Cup Worcestershire Sauce
- 2 Tbsp. Butter

SPRITZ

1. 1 Cup Apple Cider Vinegar
2. 1 Cup Apple Juice

Instructions:

- To begin, score the raw ribs and cut away any fat or uneven meat. Pour olive oil over the membrane side of the meat once it has been trimmed. Then, evenly coat the ribs with our Pitboss Grills Beef Rub.
- To make the braise, mix beef broth, red wine, Worcestershire sauce, and butter in a deep-dish baking pan. To make cooking spritz, mix apple cider vinegar and apple juice in a small dish or spray bottle.
- Preheat the Pitboss or Pitboss to 250°F and set the beef ribs on the rack directly. Spray the spritz mix on the ribs every hour. Allow for three hours on the grill.
- Remove the ribs from the oven and set them flesh side down in the braising liquid. Wrap the dish in tin foil and return it to the grill for another 2 to 2 12 hours, or until the interior temperature reaches 200 degrees.
- Remove the ribs off the grill and turn them over so the meat is facing up. Allow to cool before adding the meat rub.
- Cut, serve, and have a good time!

Nutrition:

Protein 23g

Fat 10g

Calories 180g

Carbs 0g

44. BACON EXPLOSION

Preparation Time: 15 minutes

Cooking Time: 30 minutes

Servings: 2

Ingredients

1. 2 packages thick cut bacon
2. 1 package of Italian sausage or brats
3. ¼ C Fromaggio blend cheese (Asiago, Parmesan, Romano)
4. 3 to 6 jalapeños depending on size
5. 1 package cream cheese
6. ½ bottle BBQ Sauce
7. 1 C Pitboss AP Rub

Instructions:

- *Step 1* – Jalapenos should be washed, capped, and cored. Using a gadget like the "Pepper Whipper" makes this procedure go much faster. The Pepper Whipper is the transparent plastic gadget on the chopping board if you've never seen one before. They're cheap, simple, and straightforward to use, and you'll need one if you do a lot of A.B.T.s.

- *Step 2* – To make mixing simpler, place cream cheese in a bowl and either microwave for a few seconds to soften it or let it out on the counter for 20 to 30 minutes. In a stand mixer on the low speed, combine 14 cup of mixed cheese, 1.5 tablespoons AP Rub, and 3 tablespoons Smokin Sauce with cream cheese.

- *Step 3* – Transfer the cheese mixture to a zip-top plastic bag. Remove one corner of the bag from the cheese mixture and pipe it into the jalapenos. Make sure the cheese reaches the very bottom of each jalapeo.

- *Step 4* – To make a bacon weaving, lay the bacon out on a cutting board. Apply AP Rub on the finished weave.

- *Step 5* – Remove the casings from the brats, combine the meat, and spread evenly over the bacon weave. Drizzle Smokin' Sauce over the sausage after it has been dusted with AP Rub.
- *Step 6* - Cut one jalapeno's tip off. Place it in the center of the weave/sausage canvas, with a jalapeno on either side. This will result in a very long jalapeo.
- *Step 7* – Form a roll by wrapping the weave and sausage around the jalapenos. Add additional AP Rub to the mix.
- *Step 8* – Smoke on a 250°F Pitboss until the interior temperature reaches at least 145°F, or until the firmness and color you choose. To ensure that the bacon is thoroughly cooked, aim for more direct heat or cooking on the side of the pit with the highest heat. Brush with Smokin' Sauce during the last 15 minutes of cooking and again right before removing from the pit.
- *Step 9* – Allow for at least 25 minutes of cooling time before slicing to allow the cream cheese to resolidify. Then relax and enjoy yourself.

Nutrition:

Protein 23g

Fat   10g

Calories 180g

Carbs 0g

45. PITBOSS JERKY

Preparation Time: 26 minutes

Cooking Time: 42 minutes

Servings: 2

Ingredient

MARINADE

1. 2 TBS Ancho Chile powder
2. 1 TBS Onion Powder
3. 1 TBS Garlic Powder
4. 1 TBS Black Pepper
5. 1 TBS Pitboss Beef Rub
6. 1-2 cup Honey -optional
7. 1/4 cup Worcestershire Sauce
8. 1/2 cup Soy Sauce, Tamari or Panzu
9. 3 TBS Pitboss Beef Rub
10.   1 TSP Red Pepper Flake -optional

Instructions:

- This recipe yields around 2 pounds of sliced beef. Your butcher may slice the meat for you. If you're not using presliced beef, slice it against the grain into 18-14 inch pieces. Slicing will be easier if you chill the meat for 15-20 minutes before slicing.

- In a mixing dish, combine all ingredients except Pitboss Beef Rub. Combine the ingredients in a zip-top bag and add the meat slices. Marinate for at least 6 hours or overnight. Drain the steak thoroughly after removing it from the marinade. As you place the slices on the grill, dust them with Pitboss Beef and Red Pepper Flakes (optional).

- Preheat the grill to 200°F and smoke the slices with a strong pellet like hickory until they crack but do not break when bent. However, doneness is a question of personal choice. The humidity in the air and the thickness of the beef slices will dictate how long this procedure takes. At around the 2-hour mark, check and rotate the jerky to achieve even dehydration of the meat. Allow the jerky to cool before storing it in an airtight container. Consider putting your jerky in the refrigerator if you live in a humid area.

Nutrition:

Protein 65g

Fat   10g

Calories 180g

Carbs 34 g

46.   BUFFALO CANDIED BACON

Preparation Time: 30 minutes

Cooking Time: 20 minutes

Servings: 2

Ingredients

1. 1 lb thick-sliced bacon
2. 1/4 cup Frank's hot wing sauce
3. 1/2 cup brown sugar
4. 1/4 tsp cayenne pepper

Instructions:

- So, I've got a pound of thick-sliced bacon, and I'm going to show you what it looks like here. I usually use pepper bacon, but I didn't have any on hand, and I'm not going out in the snow.

- A quarter cup of Frank's spicy wing sauce, half a cup of brown sugar, and a quarter teaspoon of cayenne pepper have been combined.

- I mixed it up and brushed it on with the back of a spoon because it's really thick on both sides of this bacon, put it on a sheet pan with foil because it's very messy, and I'm going to put it on the Pitboss that looks like it's heated up to about 350 for about 15 minutes, then flip it over for another 15 minutes, and just watch it closely because it'll candy up really nice.
- For my buffalo bacon candy, I cooked it for approximately 15 minutes on each side at 375 degrees on the Pitboss. It's a fantastic tailgate accessory. I'm going to bring this in, let it cool for about 10 minutes so it can solidify up and get crispy, and then we'll eat it. Have fun!

Nutrition:

Protein 23g

Fat 10g

Calories 180g

Carbs 0g

47.   Smoked Italian Meatballs

Prep time 15 minutes

Cook time 30 minutes

Serving: 2

Ingredients

- 2 lbs ground beef
- 2 white bread slices
- a half-cup whole milk
- 1/2 teaspoon onion powder 1 teaspoon salt
- a half teaspoon minced garlic
- 2 tsp. Italian seasoning
- 1/4 teaspoon black pepper, ground

Instructions

1. Combine the white bread, milk, salt, onion powder, chopped garlic, Italian seasoning, and powdered black pepper in a mixing bowl. Mix in the ground beef with your hands until it is evenly distributed. The meatballs will be a little gooey.

2. Preheat your Traeger on smoke for 4-5 minutes with the lid open, or until the fire is created.

3. Line a large baking sheet with parchment paper, then roll the meatballs into golfball-sized balls and set them on the sheet.

4. Close the cover of the grill and place the baking sheet on it. 35 minutes of smoking Flip the meatballs once, then switch the Traeger to 325 degrees Fahrenheit and cook for an additional 25-30 minutes, or until the internal temperature of the meatballs reaches 160 degrees Fahrenheit.

5. Serve immediately!

Nutrition:
Calories: 453
Fat:27.07g
Carbs: 17.4g
Protein: 10.1g
Fiber: 5.1g

48. Grilled Bacon

Traeger Grilled Bacon is easy, and makes the BEST bacon ever!

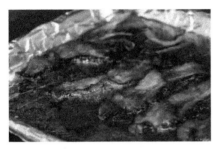

Prep Time 15 Minutes

Cook Time 25 Minutes

Total Time 40 Minutes

Serving: 3

Ingredients

- 1 pound thick-cut bacon

Instructions

1. Preheat your grill to 375°F according to the manufacturer's instructions.
2. Line a large baking sheet with parchment paper and arrange thick sliced bacon in a single layer on the sheet.
3. Bake at 375°F for 20 minutes. Close the cover and flip the bacon over. Cook for 5-10 minutes more, or until the bacon is no longer floppy.

Nutrition:
Calories: 315
Fat: 0.07g
Carbs: 17.4g
Protein: 4.1g
Fiber: 5.1g

PORK RECIPES

49.   SMOKED PORK LOIN

Preparation Time: 10 minutes

Cooking Time: 3 hr

Servings: 2

Ingredients:

- 1 tbsp olive oil
- Pit boss pulled pork rub
- 3 lbs pork loin, center-cut

Instructions:

- This smoked pork loin has just three ingredients and is a quick and convenient bbq favorite to have on hand. The pork loin roast, a leaner and less expensive cut of pork, becomes tender and juicy when smoked low and slow on the pellet grill. Through scoring the exterior of the loin and liberally seasoning it, the outer fat will make down into a delectable outer layer.
- Pre-heat your pit boss pellet grill to 250°f. Set up a gas or charcoal grill for low, indirect fire.
- Cross-hatch the fat cap of the loin, then drizzle with olive oil and season with pit boss pulled pork rub.
- Place the pork directly on the grill grates. 1 12 to 2 hours, or before internal temperature exceeds 145°f.
- Remove the pork loin from the gills and set aside for 15 minutes to rest before slicing and serving wet.

Nutrition:

Protein 23g

Fat 10g

Calories 180g

Carbs 0g

50.   PORK AND GREEN CHILI TAMALES

Preparation Time: 10 minutes

Cooking Time: 5 hr

Servings: 2

Ingredients:

1. 1 boneless, netted pork roast
2. 1 cup, fresh cilantro, chopped
3. 3 cloves garlic, peeled
4. 20 dried cornhusks
5. 1 tbsp lime juice
6. ¼ cup olive oil
7. 1 onion, quartered
8. 4 - 6 cups prepared masa harina tamale dough
9. 3 – 4 serrano peppers, deseeded
10.   1 tbsp sweet heat rub
11.   1 lb. Tomatillos, husked and washed

Instructions:

1. This smoked pork and green chili tamales are authentic south of the border comfort fare. Soft masa, smooth monterey jack cheese, and tender smoked pork fill these typical tamales, which are topped with a zesty green chili sauce.

Create tamales

2. Place a corn husk on a work surface to start assembling tamales. Spread 2-3 teaspoons tamale dough on the greater end of the husk and spread into a 14" thick rectangle, leaving a thin border around the side. On top of the dough, place a big tablespoon of the filling. Fold over the sides of the husk to cover the filling, then fold up the bottom of the husk and secure closed by tying a thin strip of husk around the tamale.

3. Place the tamales in a large metal colander over a large stockpot filled with water to prepare. Cover and set aside for 1 hour to steam.

4. Begin by soaking the corn husks in a pan of water. Soak for 2–4 hours, or overnight if necessary.

5. Remove the tomatillos from their shells and put them in a grill basket with a few deseeded serranos, garlic cloves, and 1 onion cut into quarters.

6. Set the temperature on your pit boss grill to 400°f. If you're using a gas or charcoal barbecue, set it to medium-low heat and load it with smoke chips for 15 minutes. Place your vegetables in the grill basket and barbecue them over an open flame on your pit boss until they are charred.

7. Cover the tomatillos, peppers, garlic, and onions in a bowl with plastic wrap and set aside for 10 to 15 minutes, or until cool enough to touch.

8. Season the pork roast liberally with sweet heat rub and grill for 1 hour at 350°f, or until the roast has developed a good crust on the outside.

9. When the pork roast is frying, in a food processor, combine a handful of cilantro, roasted vegetables, 1 tbsp sweet heat rub, 1 tbsp lime juice, and 14 cup olive oil. In a food processor, pulse until the mixture is uniform. Set aside some time

10.   Switch the heat down to 275°f after the pork roast has been grilled for an hour. Place the roast in a pan with around a cup of water, cover with aluminum foil, and cook for another 4 hours, or until the roast is tender enough to shred. Toss the shredded pork with the chile verde sauce to mix.

11. Place a corn husk on a work surface to begin assembling the tamales. Spread 2-3 teaspoons tamale dough on the greater end of the husk and spread into a 14" thick rectangle, leaving a thin border around the side. On top of the dough, place a big tablespoon of the chili and pork filling. Fold over the sides of the husk to cover the filling, then fold up the bottom of the husk and secure closed by tying a thin strip of husk around the tamale.

12. Place the tamales in a large metal colander over a large stockpot filled with water to prepare. Cover and set aside for 1 hour to steam. After the tamales have been steamed, remove them from the steamer and grill them at 350°f for 10-20 minutes, or until the corn husks have charred marks.

Nutrition:

Protein 23g

Fat   10g

Calories   180g

Carbs 0g

51.   STUFFED PORK SHOULDER

Preparation Time: 10 minutes

Cooking Time: 5 hr 20 minutes

Servings: 2

Ingredients:

- Aluminum foil aluminum foil
- 1 diced apple
- 1 cup broth, chicken
- 2 tbsp butter, salted
- 1 diced onion
- 1 pork shoulder or pork butt roast
- 1 box or bag of stovetop stuffing mix
- Champion chicken seasoning

Instructions:

- Look no further than this stuffed pork shoulder for a spectacular, show-stopping main course! This dish, filled with apples, onions, and stuffing, will astound and entertain your dinner guests.

- Cook the pork shoulder. Place the pork shoulder on a cutting board and, using a sharp knife, trim and scrape any very fatty parts of the pork shoulder. After that, butterfly the shoulder. Begin by carefully cutting a slit horizontally through one side of the pork shoulder and begin to slice nearly all the way to the right side, rolling the shoulder as you cut and spreading the meat like a novel, until the pork shoulder is one long strip.

- Begin making the stuffing by melting 2 tbsp salted butter in a medium-sized saucepan. Cook for about 5 minutes, stirring sometimes, with the onion and apple. 2 tablespoons champion chicken seasoning add 1 cup of chicken broth, then a bag of stuffing mix. Allow to minimize and combine thoroughly before removing from fire. Place in a bowl and set aside.

- Place some stuff on the roast after the pork shoulder has been butterflied, making sure to leave enough room to roll and tie the roast.

- Starting at one end of the pork shoulder, roll it up into a tight spiral and place it on the cutting board, seam side down. Cut four even lengths of butcher's twine and wiggle them under the pork shoulder, two inches apart. Place the roast on a sheet pan and tie it up securely.
- Set the temperature on your pit boss wood pellet grill to 250°f. If you're using a gas or charcoal barbecue, set the temperature to medium-low. Cook for 3-4 hours, or until the pork shoulder reaches an internal temperature of 180°f and is very tender, in the aluminum pan in the middle of the grill.
- Remove the pork shoulder from the grill and set aside for 15 minutes before slicing and serving.

Nutrition:

Protein 23g

Fat 10g

Calories 180g

Carbs 0g

52. PORK WITH SWEET POTATO, FENNEL & MUSTARD GRAVY

Preparation Time: 10 minutes

Cooking Time: 6 hr 30 minutes

Servings: 2

Ingredients:

1. 4 bay leaves
2. 2 jalapeno peppers
3. 1 six bone rack of pork
4. 1 cup salt
5. Salt & freshly ground black pepper
6. 2 tbsp smokey apple chipotle rub
7. 10 thyme, fresh sprigs
8. 1 gallon water

Pickled fennel ingredients

- 2 fennel bulbs, shaved thin on a mandolin
- 1 tbsp pickling spice
- 1 cup cider vinegar
- 1/2 cup sugar
- 2 tbsp salt
- 1 cup water

Caramelized sweet potato puree

1. 2 medium sweet potatoes, medium dice
2. 2 tbsp olive oil
3. Salt & freshly ground black pepper (to taste)
4. 2 cups water, divided
5. 1/2 cup whole milk
6. 1/4 cup heavy cream

Mustard gravy

- 1 tbsp olive oil
- ¼ cup shallot, minced finely
- ¼ cup bourbon
- 1 ¼ cups heavy cream
- 2 tbsp dijon mustard
- 2 tbsp whole grain mustard
- 1 tbsp italian parsley, minced
- Salt & freshly ground black pepper (to taste)

Instructions

1. Micro arugula greens

2. Best wood pellets for rack of pork

3. We consider using apple hardwood pellets for this recipe for a milder taste.

4. To prepare the rack of pork, follow these steps: in a big stock pot, combine the salt, water, bay, thyme, and jalapeo; bring to a boil and cook for 10 minutes, or until the salt is dissolved.

5. Remove from heat and set aside to cool entirely before adding the pork to the brine and brining overnight. Rinse after removing from the brine. Pat dry and season with salt and pepper and apple chipotle seasoning.

6. Smoke the pit boss pellet grill. Place the rack of pork on the smoker with a probe inserted and cook for 5 to 6 hours, or until the internal temperature reaches 140°f.

7. Increase the temperature to 450°f and remove the heat mask.

8. Sear the pork on both sides, then transfer to a cutting board and tent with foil for 20 minutes before slicing in between each bone and serving.

9. To make the pickled fennel, follow these steps: in a mixing dish, combine the fennel and the olive oil. Toast the pickling spice in a small saucepan over medium low heat for around 2 minutes, or until fragrant.

10. Get the cider vinegar to a boil over high pressure. Get the sugar, salt, and water to a boil.

11. Cook for 10 minutes on medium high heat to allow the flavors to meld. Put aside to cool after straining over the fennel. Once cold, cover and refrigerate until ready to use.

12. To make the caramelized sweet potato puree, heat the olive oil in a big skillet over high heat until it shimmers, then add the sweet potatoes and brown on all sides.

13. After the sweet potatoes are caramelized, add 1 cup of water and simmer until it has evaporated, then repeat with the remaining water.

14. Heat the milk and cream in a saucepan over low pressure. When the sweet potatoes are soft, combine them with the milk mixture in a blender and blend until creamy, being vigilant not to overprocess and make the potatoes into glue.

15. To make the mustard gravy, heat the olive oil in a big saucepan over medium-high heat, then add the shallots and cook until translucent but not browned.

16. Cook until the whiskey is almost fully reduced. Cook for 8 to 10 minutes, stirring often, until the sauce thickens and coats the back of a spoon.

17. Season with salt and pepper and stir in the parsley.

18. To make the fried shallots, place the shallots in a small bowl and cover with milk; soak for at least 1 hour.

19.   Move the shallots to a big ziplock bag and apply the rice, salt, and pepper. Seal the bag and shake vigorously to cover all of the shallots in flour. Remove the bag from the oven and shake off the extra flour.

20.   In a large pot, heat the oil to 350°f. Fry the shallots until golden brown, then transfer to a paper towel-lined tray. Season with salt and pepper.

21.   To plate and bring it all together: spread the puree in the center of the plate, followed by a small pinch of the pickled fennel on one side of the puree. Place the pork on top of the fennel. Cover with the fried shallots and micro arugula and spoon over the gravy.

Nutrition:

protein 23g

fat 10g

calories 180g

carbs 0g

53. ALMIROLA'S PIT STOP PORK SLIDERS

Preparation Time: 10 minutes

Cooking Time: 1 hr

Servings: 2

Ingredients:

- 1 bottle bbq sauce
- Coleslaw, prepared
- 12 kaiser rolls
- 8-10lbs pork butt roast, bone-in
- 5 oz sugar
- 1 cup yellow mustard

Instructions:

1. Pulled pork sandwiches are a crowd favorite when it comes to feeding a small army of people with tasty and high-quality barbecue. Pork butt is slow-cooked on the pit boss pellet grill, then shredded and mixed with tangy barbecue sauce before being piled onto a fluffy kaiser roll and served with creamy coleslaw for a thoroughly satisfying sandwich.

2. Preheat the pit boss grill to 225°f. Remove the pork roast from its wrapping and put it on a cookie sheet while the grill is heating. Yellow mustard can be rubbed all over the pork roast.

3. In a mixing cup, combine the bbq sauce and honey. Rub the whole mixture over the roast, causing the rub to blend into the beef.

4. Heat the roast in the smoker for 6 hours.

5. After 6 hours, cut the roast and roll it in tin foil twice. Turn the grill to 250°f and continue to cook the roast for another 2 hours, or until it is probe tender (an internal temperature of 204°f). Let the pork butt for up to an hour to rest in the foil before pulling.

6. Cut each kaiser roll in half, then combine the pulled pork with more barbecue sauce and layer it on each half of the roll. Serve with coleslaw and green onions on top. Don't combine any of the pulled pork with the barbecue sauce so that you can include the leftover pulled pork in other recipes. Serve immediately and enjoy!

Nutrition:

Protein 23g

Fat 10g

Calories 180g

Carbs 0g

54. PORK BELLY

Preparation Time: 10 minutes

Cooking Time: 1 hr

Servings: 2

Ingredients:

- Peanut oil
- Pit boss mandarin habanero spice
- 13 lbs pork, belly (skin and fat)
- Salt
- Sweet barbecue sauce

Instructions:

1. Pork ribs it's no longer there about bacon. The boom of pellet grilling has resulted in legions of home cooks popularizing the decadently flavored pork cut.
2. Set up the pork belly for smoking

3. Place the pork belly on a clean work surface, meat side down. Rate the top of the pork belly with a very sharp chef's knife, carving vertical lines across the skin and fat.

4. Season the skin with a generous amount of oil, followed by salt.

5. Turn the pork belly so that the meat side is facing up. Rub in the mandarin habanero seasoning. Allow it to sit in the refrigerator for at least 15 minutes to allow the seasonings to sink into the beef.

6. Start the grill on "smoke," leaving the lid open, until a fire forms in the burn pot (3-4 minutes). Preheat the oven to 250°f.

7. Place the pork belly, meat side down, on the preheated grill grates. Continue to smoke until the internal temperature reaches 195°f (this normally takes about 6 hours).

8. Flip the pork belly so that the beef hand is facing up in the flame broiler. Brush the bbq sauce on top (on meat side). Cook for about 5 minutes, or until the fat side is crispy.

9. Remove the pork belly from the barbecue with your grill gloves and seal in aluminum foil for 15 minutes, or until it's cold enough to tear apart with your meat claws. Alternatively, cut into cubes with a knife. Serve immediately.

Nutrition

Protein 23g

Fat 10g

Calories 180g

Carbs 0g

55. CUBAN STUFFED PORK LOIN

Preparation Time: 10 minutes

Cooking Time: 50 minutes

Servings: 2

Ingredients:

- 6 slices bacon
- 6 deli ham slices
- 6 dill pickles, spears
- To taste, pit boss gsp rub
- To taste, pit boss pit boss bbq rub
- 4 lbs pork loin
- 1 red onion, sliced
- To taste, stone ground mustard
- 6 swiss cheese slices

Instructions:

- The almirola family cuban stuffed pork loin, named after a recipe from pit boss ambassador aric almirola's ancestry, is a different twist on both the traditional smoked pork loin and the popular cuban sandwich.
- If necessary, butterfly the pork loin and pound it flat. Season both sides with pit boss gsp rub.
- In one line, spread mustard.
- Over the mustard, layer the ham, pickles, cheese, and onion. Add more mustard if desired.
- Place aside the rolled-up loin to be wrapped in butcher's twine.
- Place two slices of bacon on top of the twine. Place the pork loin on top, long side up. Place two more slices on top of the loin, followed by one on either foot. Butcher twine can be used to tie the loin.
- Season the loin on both sides with pit boss pit boss bbq rub.
- Start your pit boss lockhart platinum series pellet/ smoker combo grill and set the temperature to smoke mode with the lid open.
- Preheat the oven to 250° f until the fire is lit. Set up a gas or charcoal grill for low, indirect fire.

- When the grill is hot, put the loin on it, insert a meat probe, and close the lid. Enable it to cook until the internal temperature reaches 145°f.
- Remove from the grill and set aside for 10-15 minutes before slicing and serving.

Nutrition:

Protein 23g

Fat 10g

Calories 180g

Carbs 0g

56.　PORK BELLY BANH MI

Preparation Time: 10 minutes

Cooking Time: 8 hr 20 minutes

Servings: 2

Ingredients:

1. 2 carrots, sliced
2. 1 tbsp cilantro, minced
3. 1 tbsp honey
4. 2 kirby cucumbers, sliced thin
5. 1 lime, zest & juice
6. 2 tbsp pickling spice
7. 1 tbsp ponzu
8. 2 lbs pork belly
9. 1 cup rice wine vinegar
10. 　2 tbsp salt
11. 　4 sandwich buns
12. 　1 small daikon radish, sliced thin

13.   To taste, smoky salt & cracked pepper rub

14.   2 tbsp soy sauce

15.   1/2 cup sriracha hot sauce

16.   4 cloves star anise

17.   1/2 cup sugar

18.   1 cup water

Instructions:

1. Prepare to make one of the best sandwiches you've ever had! These vietnamese-inspired bbq pork belly banh mi sandwiches, created by former master chef champion shaun o'neale, are packed with luscious smoked and braised pork belly, crunchy fresh veggies, homemade pickles, and a zippy sriracha lime sauce, all nestled in a robust ciabatta bun. The pork belly is grilled on the grill for a little kick of wood-fired spice before being drizzled in a soft and tangy asian sauce.

2. Season the belly generously with the pit boss smoky salt and cracked pepper rub 30 minutes before putting it on the smoker. Prepare to make one of the best sandwiches you've ever had! These vietnamese-inspired bbq pork belly banh mi sandwiches, created by former master chef champion shaun o'neale, are packed with luscious smoked and braised pork belly, crunchy fresh veggies, homemade pickles, and a zippy sriracha lime sauce, all nestled in a robust ciabatta bun. The pork belly is grilled on the grill for a little kick of wood-fired spice before being drizzled in a soft and tangy asian sauce.

3. Season the belly generously with the pit boss smoky salt and cracked pepper rub 30 minutes before putting it on the smoker.

4. Start your pit boss on smoke mode and leave the lid open for 10 minutes before preheating to 240° f. Set up a gas or charcoal grill for low, indirect fire.

5. Place the pork belly on the smoker, with a tin pan underneath to collect the drippings. Smoke for 7 hours, or before the internal temperature reaches 195 degrees. Remove the pork and set aside for 30 minutes to relax.

6. To make the homemade pickles, toast the pickling spice and star anise in a shallow sauce pan. When the mixture is fragrant, apply the vinegar and bring to a boil for 3 minutes. Return to a boil and simmer for 5 minutes after adding the water, sugar, and salt. Immediately strain the liquid and spill it over the vegetables, making sure they are fully submerged. When cold, place in the refrigerator.

7. To make the sriracha lime sauce, follow these steps: in a mixing cup, whisk together the sriracha, lime, soy sauce, honey, cilantro, and ponzu.

8. Assemble the sandwiches by layering sliced pork belly and homemade pickles on a roll, then cover with the sriracha lime sauce.

Nutrition:

Protein 23g

Fat 10g

Calories 180g

Carbs 0g

57.   HANGING ST. LOUIS-STYLE RIBS

Preparation Time: 10 minutes

Cooking Time: 3 hr 20 minutes

Servings: 2

Ingredients:

- 1 1/3 cup apple juice
- 1 2/3 cup bbq sauce, divided
- Tt pit boss pulled pork rub
- 4 half racks spare ribs, st. Louis style

Instructions:

7. With these succulent hanging st. Louis-style ribs, you can channel your inner pitmaster. The fat and juices run down the length of the rack when hanging and smoked vertically in the pit boss, making it super juicy and soft.

8. Preheat the pit boss to 250 degrees fahrenheit. Set up a gas or charcoal grill for low, indirect fire.

9. Strip the back membrane from the rib racks with a sharp knife and pat dry with a paper towel. Cut rib racks in two, then generously season with pulled pork rub.

10. Insert a hanging hook under the top rib, then transfer the racks to the smoking drawer. Smoke for a total of 2 1/2 hours.

11. Take the ribs out of the smoking cabinet and place them on heavy duty foil. Brush thinned bbq sauce on both sides of ribs after combining 2/3 cup bbq sauce and 1/3 cup apple juice. 14 cup apple juice should be poured around each rib. Fold the foil over, then place the meat side down on the grill. Cook for an additional 2 hours after increasing the temperature to 300° f.

12. Remove the ribs from the barbecue, baste with bbq sauce, and return to the grill for another 10 to 15 minutes. Allow to rest for 15 minutes before slicing and serving sweet.

Nutrition:

protein 23g

fat 10g

calories 180g

carbs 0g

58.   PORK BELLY BURNT ENDS

Preparation Time: 10 minutes

Cooking Time: 4 hr 20 minutes

Servings: 2

Ingredients:

- 2/3 cup bbq sauce
- 2 tbsp butter, melted
- 2 tbsp honey
- 2 tbsp olive oil
- Tt pit boss blackened sriracha rub
- 3 lbs pork belly, skin removed

Instructions:

1. The ultimate meat candy treat are these pork belly burnt ends.
2. Preheat your pit boss to 225°f. Set up a gas or charcoal grill for low, indirect fire.
3. Place the pork belly in a big mixing bowl and cut it into 2-inch cubes.
4. Drizzle olive oil over the pork belly, then season generously with blackened sriracha.

5. Place the seasoned pork belly on a wire rack on the grill grate. 3 hours in the oven
6. Switch the pork belly from the wire rack to a foil-lined aluminum pan or a plastic foil pan.
7. Whisk together the bbq sauce, melted butter, and sugar, and then spill over the bacon.
8. Toss to spray, then place the pan on the grill rack and cover with aluminum foil.
9. Cook for an additional 1–12 hour, or until the internal temperature exceeds 200° f.
10. Remove the foil and put the pork belly in the middle of the grill in a cast iron skillet.
11. To crisp up the bacon, open the sear slide and cook for another 5 to 7 minutes, turning halfway.
12. Remove the pork belly from the grill and eat while still high.

Nutrition:

protein 23g

fat 10g

calories 180g

carbs 0g

59. PULLED PORK POUTINE

Preparation Time: 10 minutes

Cooking Time: 1 hr 30 minutes

Servings: 2

Ingredients:

- 2 tbsp apple cider vinegar
- 1/2 cup bbq sauce
- 1 1/2 cups beef stock
- 2 tbsp butter
- For assembly, cheese curds
- 2 cups chicken stock
- 2 tbsp flour
- For assembly, french fries
- 3 garlic cloves, minced
- 1 tbsp olive oil
- 2 1/2 lbs pork shoulder roast, bone-in
- To taste, pulled pork rub
- For assembly, sliced scallions
- 1/2 yellow onion, minced

- 1/2 yellow onion, sliced

Instructions:

- Crispy french fries are topped with traditional pit boss pulled pork, fluffy cheese curds, and a homemade bbq sauce-infused gravy.
- Start your pit boss pellet grill on smoke mode and leave the lid open for 10 minutes before preheating to 225° f. Set up a gas or charcoal grill for low, indirect fire.
- Season the pork shoulder with a pork rub, then place it fat side up on the grill grate. Smoke the pork shoulder for two and a half hours.
- In a dutch oven, combine chicken stock, vinegar, and sliced onion. Cover and raise the grill temperature to 325° f after adding the smoked pork shoulder to the dutch oven. Cook the pork shoulder for 1/2 hours, or until tender.
- When the pork is juicy, remove it from the grill and let it sit for 20 minutes before shredding.

- When the pork is resting, prepare the gravy by heating a cast iron skillet over high heat. In a pan, heat the butter and olive oil, then sauté the onion and garlic for 2 minutes, stirring frequently. Cook for 1 minute after adding the flour. Stir in the beef stock slowly until it thickens. Simmer for 3 minutes after adding the bbq sauce. Remove from the grill and set aside until ready to assemble.
- Lay out a layer of french fries, then layer gravy, pulled pork, cheese curds, more gravy, and scallions. Serve hot.

Nutrition:

Protein 23g

Fat 10g

Calories 180g

Carbs 0g

60. CURRY KETCHUP PORK RIBS

Preparation Time: 10 minutes

Cooking Time: 1 hr 20 minutes

Servings: 2

Ingredients:

1. 1 tsp chili powder
2. 1 tbsp curry powder
3. 1/2 tsp ground mustard
4. 2 tsp honey
5. To taste, kansas city barbecue rub seasoning
6. 1 cup ketchup
7. 2 pork back rib racks, membrane removed
8. 2 tsp smoked paprika
9. 2 tsp worcestershire sauce

Instructions:

1. With these curry ketchup pork ribs, you can add a new twist to your weekend rib game. Baby back ribs are seasoned with BBQ rub before being smoked and rolled until tender. In the last hour of Instructions, a richly spiced homemade curry ketchup is basted on to add moisture and earthy and warm curry taste.

2. Set your pit boss grill to smoke mode and leave the lid open for 10 minutes before preheating to 225° f. Set up a gas or charcoal grill for low, indirect fire.

3. Season both sides of the rib racks with kansas city barbeque rub and place them on a sheet tray. Place the ribs on the grill and smoke for 1 hour.

4. In the meantime, make the curry ketchup: whisk together ketchup, curry powder, smoked paprika, chili powder, powdered mustard, worcestershire sauce, and honey in a mixing cup. Place aside.

5. Rotate the rib racks and raise the temperature to 250 degrees fahrenheit. Cook for an additional hour before removing the ribs from the grill and placing them on butcher paper. Cover the ribs in paper after brushing them with sauce.

6. Place the ribs back on the barbecue. Cook for another hour, or until the potatoes are tender.

7. Remove the ribs from the oven, peel back the butcher paper, and baste with the leftover curry ketchup. Return the racks to the grill, raise the temperature to 275 f, and cook for an additional 15 minutes. Remove the ribs from the oven, peel back the butcher paper, and baste with the leftover curry ketchup. Return the racks to the grill, raise the temperature to 275 f, and cook for an additional 15 minutes.

8. Remove the ribs from the grill and set aside for 10 minutes before slicing and serving wet.

Nutrition:

Protein 23g

Fat   10g

Calories 180g

Carbs 0g

61.   TRI TIP BURNT ENDS

Preparation Time: 10 minutes

Cooking Time: 5 hr. 30 minutes

Servings: 2

Ingredients:

- 1/2 cup bbq sauce
- To taste, beef & brisket rub
- 1 1/2 tbsp brown sugar
- 1 1/2 tbsp butter, cubed
- 1/2 cup dr. Pepper soda
- 1/2 tbsp honey
- 2 tbsp mustard
- 2 lbs tri tip steak
- 1/2 tbsp worcestershire sauce

Instructions:

1. With these tri tip burnt ends, you will enjoy beefy nuggets without having to smoke an entire brisket. The tri tip roast split, also known as santa maria steak, is

heavily marbled and has a tender, beefy taste comparable to brisket. The tri tip is slathered with mustard and seasoned with beef & brisket rub before being smoked low and slow until soft and smoky.

2. Start your pit boss on smoke mode and leave the lid open for 10 minutes before setting it to 225° f. Set up a gas or charcoal grill for low, indirect fire.

3. Rub the mustard all over the tri tip before seasoning with the beef & brisket rub.

4. Place the tri tip directly on the grill grates and smoke for 2 1/2 hours, or until the internal temperature exceeds 165° f.

5. Cover the tri tip in pit boss butcher paper after removing it from the barbecue. Return the tri tip to the grill and continue to smoke for another 2 to 3 hours, or until the internal temperature exceeds 200° f.

6. Remove the tri tip from the grill and set aside for 30 minutes to rest, or set aside and refrigerate overnight.

7. Boost the temperature of the grill to 275° f.

8. Cube the tri tip into 1/2 to 3/4-inch cubes, then put in a big cast iron skillet.

9. In a container or mixing cup, combine the bbq sauce, dr. Pepper, sugar, and worcestershire sauce, and pipe over the cubed tri tip. Dot with honey, then dust with brown sugar.

10.Place the skillet on the grill grate and cook it over indirect fire. Cook for 1 1/2 to 2 hours, flipping the bits halfway through. The sauce would have depleted, coated, and charred the tri tip. Remove from the grill and serve while still hot.

Nutrition:

Protein 23g

Fat 10g

Calories 180g

Carbs 0g

62. PORK BUTT WITH SWEET CHILI INJECTION

Preparation Time: 10 minutes

Cooking Time: 5 hr 30 minutes

Servings: 2

Ingredients

- To taste, blackened sriracha rub seasoning
- 1/2 tbsp blackened sriracha rub seasoning (for injection)
- 1/4 cup butter, melted
- 2 cups chicken stock
- 1/2 cup chicken stock (for injection)
- 1 tbsp ginger root, sliced thin
- 1/2 lime, juiced
- 1 tbsp olive oil
- 5 lbs pork butt, bone-in
- 1 red onion, sliced
- 1/4 cup rice vinegar
- 1/2 tbsp sugar, granulated

- 2 tbsp sweet chili sauce

Instructions:

- With this smoked pork butt with sweet chili injection, you can amp up your pulled pork. Injecting liquid into pork distributes tasty flavor throughout the meat while both adding moisture and protecting it from drying out.
- Place the pork butt on a baking sheet and pat dry with a paper towel.
- Prepare the injection solution as follows: in a glass measuring cup, whisk together all of the ingredients (1/2 cup chicken stock, 1/4 cup melted butter, 1/4 cup rice wine vinegar, 1/2 tbsp blackened sriracha rub seasoning, 1/2 lime juice, 1/2 tbsp granulated sugar).
- Inject the solution into the pork butt with a beef syringe, 1/2 inch apart.
- Cross-hatch the fat cap, then rub sweet chili sauce on the outside of the pork ass, and season with blackened sriracha. Allow for 30 minutes at room temperature.
- Start your pit boss and set the temperature to smoke mode with the lid open.
- Preheat the oven to 250° f until the fire is lit. Set up a gas or charcoal grill for low, indirect fire.

- Smoke the pork shoulder for 2 hours on the grill grate.
- On the barbecue, place a dutch oven or a large cast iron skillet. Heat the olive oil, then add the sliced onion and ginger, followed by the pork ass. Cover with a tight-fitting lid or foil after adding the chicken stock.
- Boost the temperature to 325° f and cook for 3 hours, or until the pork is tender. Remove the pork from the dutch oven and place it on a sheet tray or cutting board to rest.
- Pull the pork and eat it warm with the braising jus.

Nutrition:

Protein 23g

Fat 10g

Calories 180g

Carbs 0g

63.   CIDER BRINED GRILLED PORK STEAK

Preparation Time:20 minutes

Cooking Time: 33 minutes

Servings: 2

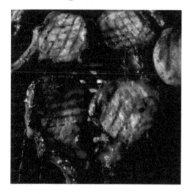

Ingredients

1. 4 pork steaks
2. 1/3 C sea salt
3. ¼ C Pitboss AP Rub
4. 1 C maple syrup
5. ¼ C Pitboss BBQ Sauce
6. 2 tsp dried thyme
7. 1½ C apple cider
8. 1½ C ice water
9. 2 tsp hot sauce
10.   1 C water

Instructions:

- Combine 1 cup water, salt, and 1/3 cup maple syrup with dried thyme in a small pot. Cook over medium heat until the salt has dissolved and the water has reached a boiling temperature.
- Remove the pan from the heat. Stir in the cider, ice water, and 1 teaspoon of spicy sauce until the ice melts. Refrigerate the brine until it reaches a temperature of 45 degrees. Put the pork steaks in a zip-top bag, add the brine, and close the bag. Refrigerate for 2 hours to let flavors to meld.
- Combine the remaining maple syrup and spicy sauce with the barbecue sauce in a small dish and set aside. Preheat your Pitboss Grill to 300°F.
- Using paper towels, blot the pork steaks dry after removing them from the brine. Grill the meat until the first side has nice grill marks, then flip. Internal temperature should be between 145 and 160 degrees. Brush the pork steaks with the syrup mixture every 3 minutes throughout the last 10 minutes of cooking.
- Allow 5 minutes for the meat to rest before serving.

Nutrition:

Protein 63g

Fat   10g

Calories 210g

Carbs 0g

64. HOT BACON EXPLOSION

Preparation Time: 15 minutes

Cooking Time: 30 minutes

Servings: 2

Ingredients

8. 2 packages thick cut bacon

9. 1 package of Italian sausage or brats

10.   ¼ C Formaggio blend cheese (Asiago, Parmesan, Romano)

11.   3 to 6 jalapeños depending on size

12.   1 package cream cheese

13.   ½ bottle BBQ Sauce

14.   1 C Pitboss AP Rub

Instructions:

- *Step 1* – Jalapenos should be washed, capped, and cored. Using a gadget like the "Pepper Whipper" makes this procedure go much faster. The Pepper Whipper is the transparent plastic gadget on the chopping board if you've never seen one before. They're cheap, simple, and straightforward to use, and you'll need one if you do a lot of A.B.T.s.

- *Step 2* – To make mixing simpler, place cream cheese in a bowl and either microwave for a few seconds to soften it or let it out on the counter for 20 to 30 minutes. In a stand mixer on the low speed, combine 14 cup of mixed cheese, 1.5 tablespoons AP Rub, and 3 tablespoons Smokin Sauce with cream cheese.

- *Step 3* – Transfer the cheese mixture to a zip-top plastic bag. Remove one corner of the bag from the cheese mixture and pipe it into the jalapenos. Make sure the cheese reaches the very bottom of each jalapeo.

- *Step 4* – To make a bacon weaving, lay the bacon out on a cutting board. Apply AP Rub on the finished weave.

- *Step 5* – Remove the casings from the brats, combine the meat, and spread evenly over the bacon weave. Drizzle Smokin' Sauce over the sausage after it has been dusted with AP Rub.

- *Step 6* - Cut one jalapeno's tip off. Place it in the center of the weave/sausage canvas, with a jalapeno on either side. This will result in a very long jalapeo.
- *Step 7* – Form a roll by wrapping the weave and sausage around the jalapenos. Add additional AP Rub to the mix.
- *Step 8* – Smoke on a 250°F Pitboss until the interior temperature reaches at least 145°F, or until the firmness and color you choose. To ensure that the bacon is thoroughly cooked, aim for more direct heat or cooking on the side of the pit with the highest heat. Brush with Smokin' Sauce during the last 15 minutes of cooking and again right before removing from the pit.
- *Step 9* – Allow for at least 25 minutes of cooling time before slicing to allow the cream cheese to resolidify. Then relax and enjoy yourself.

Nutrition:

Protein 23g

Fat   10g

Calories   180g

Carbs 0g

65.   PORK BUTT THROWDOWN

Preparation Time: 23 minutes

Cooking Time: 20 minutes

Servings: 2

Ingredients

1. 8lbs – 10lbs. Pork butt

Instructions:

- Butt pork should be trimmed and scored. Use salt or rub to season. Smoke until the interior temperature reaches 195 degrees Fahrenheit at 225 degrees Fahrenheit. Serve with a pull.

Nutrition:

Protein 50g

Fat   70g

Calories 230g

Carbs 70g

66.   PULLED PORK NACHOS

Preparation Time: 35 minutes

Cooking Time: 20 minutes

Servings: 2

PORK SHOULDER

2. Pork Shoulder

3. Mustard

4. Pitboss All Purpose Rub

5. Apple Cider Vinegar

6. Beer

7. Brown Sugar 1/2C.

PICO DE GALLO

1. 1 Red Onion

2. 3 Cloves Garlic

3. Cilantro 1 Bunch

4. 4 Limes

5. Pinch of salt

6. 3 Tomato

7. Cumin

PICKLED JALAPENOS

- 1C. Vinegar
- 1C. Water
- 2 Cloves Garlic
- 2 Tbsp. Sugar
- 1 Tbsp. Salt
- Jalapenos

RANCH

1. 2 Lemons
2. 1 Qt. Buttermilk
3. 1 Qt. Sour Cream
4. 1 Jar Mayonaise

NACHO TOPPINGS

- Shredded Cheese
- Tortilla Chips
- Black Beans

Instructions:

For the pulled pork:

1. Allow the pork shoulder to come to room temperature after removing it from the fridge. Set your Pitboss Grill to 275°F because this pork butt is going to be hot and quick. (This will be the top of the line when it comes to smoking meat.) Apply mustard liberally on the whole shoulder. Apply dry rub liberally on the outside of the shoulder; the mustard will keep it in place.

NOTE: You can mix together the cider, beer, and brown sugar (recipe above) in a glass dish to use for spraying the meat regularly while it cooks; this is absolutely optional.

2. Place the shoulder on the prepared grill for three hours to smoke. If you opt to use the spray every 30 minutes, do so. After three hours, remove the shoulder from the grill and cover with butcher paper or foil. Cook the shoulder for another two hours on the grill. Remove the shoulder and the foil or butcher paper from the grill. Return the shoulder to the gill and cook until it reaches 205 degrees on the inside. Remove the pork from the oven for the last time and set aside for thirty minutes before shredding.

For the Jalapenos:

3. In a sauce pan, combine all ingredients (except the jalapenos) and bring to a boil. Cut the peppers into slices and put them in a glass container. Cover the jalapenos with the boiling pickling liquid and let aside for 10 minutes.

For the Nachos:

4. To create the salsa, mix the cilantro, onions, tomatoes, garlic, cumin, and the juice of two limes in a bowl. Place a substantial number of chips on a party tray

and top with the beans, salsa, pulled pork, cheese, and pickled jalapenos. To melt the cheese, place the prepared nachos in the oven for a few minutes; garnish with the remaining limes and ENJOY!

Nutrition:

Protein 63g

Fat 50g

Calories 193g

Carbs 0g

67. SIMPLE PULLED PORK

Preparation Time: 10 minutes

Cooking Time: 30 minutes

Servings: 2

Ingredients

1. 1 8 to 10-lb Boston pork butt
2. ¾ C salt
3. ¼ C black pepper
4. 1/3 C Pitboss AP Rub
5. Aluminum foil

Instructions:

- Begin with your butt of Boston pork. You'll want to look for one with beautiful marbling and symmetry.
- Rinse the meat in the sink after removing it from the packaging. Allow it to dry completely before flipping it fat-cap up. Cut a diamond design into the fat cap using a knife. Cuts should be made only through the fat cap and into the flesh below.
- After that, take your salt can and spread it all over the meat. The meat should be salt-coated thoroughly. Replace the pepper and repeat the process. If you're in

a rush, combine the salt and pepper and massage it on. Allow your meat to come to room temperature while your Pitboss wood pellet grill warms up to 225°F.

- If you're in a hurry, set the pit to 275 degrees Fahrenheit. By cooking hotter and faster, you can save a number of hours on the cooking time. Although there won't be as much smoke penetration, it'll still be a good sandwich. Place your meat fat-side up on the wood pellet grill. Before you even open the pit door, let it cook for at least 4 hours.

- It will be near to time to wrap at 4 to 5 hours if you are cooking at 275 degrees. If you want your beef to have more color while it's cooking at 225 degrees, cook it for another 1 to 2 hours before wrapping it. It is critical to achieve a strong seal while wrapping. 2 pieces of foil, long enough to completely encase your meat Wrap the first sheet around the butt in the middle of the foil, crimping tightly, then repeat with the second sheet. You want a tight seal to prevent any rendered fat from escaping. If you move this foil pack about too much, it will split and create a massive mess on your barbecue.

- Cook the butt for another 2 hours before testing the internal temperature. Make use of a good thermometer. In all areas of the butt, the internal temperature should be at least 195 degrees.

- When the Pitboss reaches the desired temperature, gently remove the foil wrapper. Because the contents are boiling hot, you should wear insulated gloves. Place the foil package in a pan and rest the meat in the oven for a couple of hours if you are not in a rush. This will give the meat even more time to break down.

- Open the package and remove the meat when you're ready to pull it. The meat should be more than fall-apart tender at this time. You should be able to squish the meat into small bits using insulated rubber gloves and then pull it correctly with extra time. Place the meat in a big mixing basin when it's been removed, and then sprinkle the AP Rub on top. Then add around 2 cups of the rendered fat you've preserved.
- Toss the meat thoroughly and serve with your favorite slaw or a wonderful vinegar sauce on top.

Nutrition:

Protein 23g

Fat 10g

Calories 180g

Carbs 0g

68. SMOKED TROUT

Preparation Time: 10 minutes

Cooking Time: 2 hr 10 minutes

Servings: 2

Ingredients:

1. 2 tbsp brown sugar
2. 1 ½ tsp kosher salt
3. 1 tsp dried oregano
4. ½ tsp dried thyme
5. ½ tsp onion powder
6. ½ tsp chili powder
7. ¼ tsp freshly ground black pepper
8. 4 trout filets – skin on one side, (2 lbs)
9. Lemon wedges

Instructions:

1. Preheat the pit boss pellet grill to 225°F.
2. While a well-handled fish filet should be free of pin bones, I still look for them by running my fingertips along the center of each filet. They are limited in

number, and one or two are frequently ignored. Tweezers or fine needle-nose pliers can be used to remove any pin bones you find.

3. To prepare the rub, combine the brown sugar, salt, oregano, thyme, onion powder, chili powder, and pepper. Apply the rub to the tops of each fish filet.
4. Close the lid and place the prepared filets on the pit boss's bottom rack. Smoke the fish until it reaches an internal temperature of 140 degrees Fahrenheit. This will take between 1 1/2 and 2 hours, depending on the thickness of the fish filets.

Nutrition:

protein 23g

fat 10g

calories 180g

69. Smoked Pork Shoulder

Prep Time: 15 minutes

Cook Time: 8 hours

Resting Time: 20 minutes

Total Time: 8 hours 45 minutes

Ingredients

1. 8 lb bone-in pork shoulder these may also be labeled as pork butt
2. olive oil
3. water

DRY RUB

- 1/4 cup light brown sugar packed
- 2 Tbsp black pepper coarsely ground
- 2 Tbsp kosher salt
- 1 Tbsp paprika
- 1 Tbsp garlic powder
- 1 Tbsp dried minced onions
- 1 tsp cayenne pepper

SPRITZ

1. 1/4 cup apple juice
2. 1/4 cup apple cider vinegar

Instructions

Prepare The smoker

1. Fill the smoker's hopper with wood pellets. I generally use applewood, but pecan or cherry would also work.
2. Start the smoker for 5-10 minutes on the smoke setting. Raise the temperature to 250°F.
3. Fill an 8x8" baking dish or another baking dish halfway with water and set aside for later use. I like to use a foil dish for this since I don't mind if it gets splattered.

Prepare the pork shoulder

1. In a small bowl, mix all of your ingredients (brown sugar, pepper, salt, paprika garlic, chopped onion, and cayenne) using a fork.
2. Place the pork shoulder on a baking pan and massage it with olive oil all over. Seasonings should be sprinkled over it and rubbed in (every inch of the shoulder should be covered). There's no better tool for this than your hands, so if you're wary of handling raw meat, put on a pair of disposable gloves.

Smoke the pork

1. Place a baking dish filled with water on the grate on one side of the smoker.

2. Set aside a small spray bottle filled with apple juice and apple cider vinegar. Every hour, you'll open the smoker and thoroughly spray the pork shoulder.

3. Close the cover and place the pork shoulder on the grate. During the first several hours of smoking, keep the smoker temperature between 250 and 275 degrees Fahrenheit. Smoke for 4 hours, spritzing every hour with the spray bottle.

4. Using a meat thermometer, check the internal temperature of the pork shoulder. The pork should be AT LEAST 145 F degrees at this point.

5. Spray the pork shoulder again and carefully cover it in aluminum foil or peach paper.

6. Return the pork to the smoker and reduce the temperature to 225 degrees Fahrenheit. Smoke the pork for another 4 hours, but do not spritz during this time.

7. Using a meat thermometer, check the internal temperature of the pork shoulder. You want your pork shoulder to be around 200 degrees Fahrenheit. 195-205 F degrees is an excellent temperature range for creating delicious pulled pork!

8. Remove the pork from the smoker and set aside for at least 20 minutes, but no more than 2 hours. Keep the pork well wrapped, and I like to place mine in either a clean, empty cooler or my oven (turned off).

Nutrition:
Calories: 303
Fat: 0.07g
Carbs: 17.4g
Protein: 12.1g
Fiber: 5.1g

70.   Apple Bourbon Pulled Pork Sandwiches

Prep Time: 5 minutes

Cook Time: 7 hours

Total Time: 7 hours 5 minutes

Ingredients

- 2 to 3 pounds boneless pork loin or shoulder
- 1 pound Campbell's Apple Bourbon Pulled Pork Slow Cooker
- Sauce pinch brown sugar
- optional splash apple cider vinegar

Instructions

1. Place the meat in the bottom of the slow cooker after patting it dry with a paper towel.
2. Sauce should be poured over the meat.
3. Cook on LOW for 7-8 hours (or HIGH for 4-5 hours).
4. Shred the pork with two forks and combine with the remaining sauce.
5. Stir in the brown sugar and vinegar, if using.

Nutrition:

Protein 23g

Fat 10g

Calories 180g

71. Grilled Pork Ribs

Prep time 15 minutes

Cook time 4 hours

Total time 4 hours 15 minutes

Ingredients

- two racks of baby back ribs
- 1 cup homemade bbq rub (or your favorite store-bought type)
- 1 bottle hard apple cider (about 12 oz.)
- 1 batch homemade barbecue sauce or your preferred canned variety

Instructions

1. Set your grill to smoke (or 180-200 degrees if it does not have a smoke setting).
2. After removing the membrane from the rib, slather it with the barbecue rub.
3. Smoke for 2 hours at a temperature of 180-200 degrees.

4. Remove the ribs from the grill and set them in an Instant Pot with a trivet in the bottom to protect the meat from falling into the liquid. Pour in just enough hard cider to generate pressure but not enough to cover the ribs.

5. Set the pressure cooker to high pressure and the timer to 30 minutes. Allow it to release pressure naturally for 10-15 minutes before releasing the excess and removing the ribs.

6. Preheat your grill to 325° (or close, precise temperature isn't crucial) and lay the ribs on it. Coat with BBQ sauce and bake for an hour, flipping and re-coating with sauce as needed.

7. Remove from the grill and serve!

Nutrition:
Calories: 753
Fat: 40.07g
Carbs: 17.4g
Protein: 14.1g
Fiber: 5.1g

72. Mustard Pork Tenderloin

Prep time 10 minutes

Cook time 15 minutes

Total time 25 minutes

Ingredients

- 1 tenderloin of pork
- 1 and 1/2 tbsp Dijon mustard
- 1 and 1/2 tbsp. cooking oil
- 1 and 1/2 tbsp. white vinegar
- 1 tsp red pepper flakes
- 1 tsp paprika, chopped
- 14 tsp of salt
- 1/2 teaspoon dried parsley flakes
- a half teaspoon onion powder
- 1/2 teaspoon garlic granules
- 1/4 teaspoon black pepper, ground

Instructions

1. Preheat your pellet grill to 350°F according to the manufacturer's instructions.
2. Combine all of the mustard sauce ingredients and spread them all over the pork tenderloin.
3. Cook for 15-20 minutes, rotating every 5 minutes, or until the internal temperature reaches 150°.

Nutrition:
Calories: 87
Fat: 6.07g
Carbs: 17.4g
Protein: 4.1g
Fiber: 5.1g

73.   Shortcut Smoked Pulled Pork

Prep Time: 1 hour

Cook Time: 10 hours

Resting Time: 30 minutes

Total Time: 11 hours 30 minutes

Ingredients

- 2 pound roast pork shoulder
- Spiceology Shoulder Rub in copious quantities.
- 2 tbsp of kosher salt
- 2 cups apple juice (or hard cider)
- 2 quarts barbecue sauce

Instructions

1. Set your pellet grill to smoke mode or a temperature of 180-190 degrees Fahrenheit, or as near as you can go. You want to hit this with a lot of smoke.

2. Grill your pork roast after coating it with the Shoulder Rub and salt.

3. Smoke for 3-4 hours, turning many times during.

4. Remove the roast from the smoker and place it in the slow cooker. Cover and leave the apple juice or hard cider to simmer overnight. If you have an Instant Pot, set it at high pressure for 60 minutes with 2 cups apple juice or hard cider. Allow the pot to naturally release pressure for at least 15 minutes after the cycle has completed.

5. Your pork should be very soft and easily shreddable.

6. If it isn't, re-seal the cooker and continue to pressure cook for another 20-30 minutes (depending on how close to shreddable it is when you test it.) Allow it to NPR (natural pressure release) and repeat until the meat is soft and shreddable.

7. Shred the meat, remove the skin, fat, and any other pieces you find in there, and generously coat with barbecue sauce before serving or smoking for more smoky flavor. Place the shredded pork in a grill-safe container, slather with your preferred BBQ sauce, and return to the smoker for 30-40 minutes at 200°F.

Nutrition:
Calories: 249
Fat: 16.07g

Carbs: 17.4g
Protein: 4.1g

74. Bbq Potatoes With Pulled Pork

Active: 45 mins

Total: 50 mins

INGREDIENTS

- 4 Russet potatoes, large
- 1 pound bacon, thinly sliced
- Sour Cream, 8 oz.
- 2 cups shredded chesse
- 2 cups Monterey Jack cheese, shredded
- 1 pound of butter
- 1 bunch finely sliced green onions
- 2 pound pulled pork
- Killer Hogs Hot Rub, 2 tbsp.
- Killer Hogs AP Seasoning, 2 tsp.
- Killer Hogs The BBQ Sauce, 1/4 cup

Instructions

1. Cook the bacon until it is crispy, then cut it. Keep the bacon grease aside.

2. Preheat the pellet grill to 350°F for indirect grilling.
3. Wash the potatoes and wipe them dry with a paper towel.
4. Drizzle bacon grease over potatoes and season with Killer Hogs Hot Rub.
5. Place the potatoes on the grill and cook until they are soft. (When a skewer easily glides in, they're done)
6. Cut the tops off each potato and dump the insides into a large mixing basin. Combine the butter, sour cream, half of the cheese, Killer Hogs AP Seasoning, bacon, and green onion in a mixing bowl (reserve a little bacon and green onion for garnish).
7. Stir everything together, then put the mixture back into each hollowed-out potato.
8. Drizzle with Killer Hogs BBQ Sauce and top with a generous mound of pulled pork.
9. Return to the pit for 10 minutes, or until the cheese melts, then top with the remaining cheese.
10. Serve garnished with the leftover green onion and crumbled bacon.

Nutrition

183 Calories

6.7g Total Fat

15.5g Protein

75.   Pulled Pork On A Pellet Grill

Active: 35 mins

Total: 35 mins

Serving: 3

INGREDIENTS

1. 8–10lb pork butt
2. 2 Tablespoons Killer Hogs AP seasoning
3. 2 Tablespoons Killer Hogs The BBQ Rub

Instructions

- Season the pork butt with AP and The BBQ Rub on all sides.
- Refrigerate the pork butt for at least 2 hours on a wire cooing rack.
- Preheat a pellet grill to 200°F for low and slow cooking.
- Place the pork butt fat side down on the frying grate.

- Smoke for 8 hours at 200°F, then increase to 220°F for cooking.
- Continue to cook until the internal temperature reaches 190°F or a probe thermometer slides in easily.
- Take the pig butt from the grill and set it aside to rest for 15 minutes before removing it.

Nutrition:
Calories: 261
Fat: 19.07g
Carbs: 17.4g
Protein: 12.1g
Fiber: 5.1g

76.   Grilled Bone-in Pork Chops

Traeger Grilled Pork Chops are a perfect way to use those amazing bone-in chops you find, and keep them tender and juicy and full of flavor.

Prep Time: 5 Minutes

Cook Time: 30min

Total Time: 35 Min

Serving: 5

Ingredients

- 6 thick cut pork chops
- generous amounts bbq rub

Instructions

1. Preheat pellet grill to 450°. Place seasoned pork chops on grill, and close lid. Cook 6 minutes per side, or until internal temps reach 145°.

2. Remove from heat and let sit for 5-10 minutes before serving.

Nutrition:
Calories: 398
Fat: 19.07g
Carbs: 17.4g
Protein: 6.1g
Fiber: 8.1g

77.   Traeger Pulled Pork

This Traeger Pulled Pork takes a while to get on the table, but the long cook is mostly hands off, and totally worth it.

Prep Time: 10 Minutes

Cook Time: 9hrs

Total Time: 9hours 10 Min

Serving: 5

Ingredients

1. 8 pound bone-in pork shoulder roast
2. copious amounts of BBQ Rub
3. 3 cups dry hard apple cider

Instructions

- Preheat your Traeger according to the manufacturer's recommendations. Set the grill to "smoke."

- Apply bbq rub liberally to the exterior of the shoulder on both sides. Smoke the shoulder for 4-5 hours over the grill grates. Make sure your pellets are stirred every hour or so to avoid tunneling. Flip the roast every hour or so with care.
- Increase the heat on the grill to 225 degrees Fahrenheit and continue to cook. After 3 hours on the grate, transfer the shoulder to a foil pan and pour the hard cider into the pan's bottom.
- A temperature of 200 degrees is ideal for a pig roast. The roast will "stall" for a long time before that, but keep cooking and don't turn up the heat!
- Remove the roast from the grill when it reaches 200 degrees, cover loosely with foil, and set aside to rest for 1 hour.
- Remove the fat/skin layer from the roast after 2 hours.

Nutrition:

Calories: 912
Fat: 65.07g
Carbs: 17.4g
Protein: 24.1g
Fiber: 5.1g

78. Pigs In A Blanket

Easy Traegerized Pigs in a Blanket are wrapped in biscuit dough, cooked on the Traeger, and are an easy kid-friendly dinner that is a great option for an easy lunch or dinner.

Prep Time: 10 Minutes

Cook Time: 15min

Total Time: 25 Min

Serving: 2

Ingredients

1. 1 package hotdogs, cut into thirds
2. 1 package refrigerated biscuit dough

Instructions

- Line a baking pan with parchment paper and warm your Traeger to 350°F according to the manufacturer's instructions.

- Cut both the hot dogs and the biscuits into thirds, then wrap the biscuit dough around the hot dog pieces and place on a parchment-lined cookie sheet.
- Close the lid and place the sheet on the grill. Cook the biscuits for 20-25 minutes, or until golden brown and cooked through.

Nutrition:
Calories: 267
Fat: 22.07g
Carbs: 17.4g
Protein: 9.1g
Fiber: 5.1g

79.   Grilled Stuffed Pork Tenderloin

This impressive pork tenderloin is butterflied, stuffed with two different kinds of cheeses and fresh spinach, and then wrapped in a bacon weave and cooked on the Traeger grill.

Prep time: 20 mins

Cook time: 30 mins

Resting time: 10 mins

Total time: 1 hr

Ingredients

- 1 pork tenderloin
- 1 cup fresh spinach leaves
- 3-4 ounces cheddar cheese
- 3-4 ounces provolone cheese
- 1 pound this sliced bacon

Rub

1. 1 teaspoon salt

2. 1/2 teaspoon black pepper

3. 1/2 teaspoon garlic granules

4. 1/2 teaspoon onion powder

5. 1 tblsp. Paprika

6. 1 teaspoon flakes of red pepper

7. A quarter teaspoon of cumin

Instructions

1. Preheat your grill to 325 degrees Fahrenheit.

2. Begin by butterflying the tenderloin and flattening it out on a chopping board or another level surface.

3. Stack your spinach leaves flat on top of each other the entire length of the tenderloin in the centre.

4. Arrange the cheese pieces next to and on top of the spinach.

5. Begin rolling the tenderloin on one side until all of the spinach and cheese are included. The spinach and cheese should be completely coated and stuffed into the rolled-up tenderloin.

6. Combine all of the rub's components, mix thoroughly, and evenly apply to the exterior of the tenderloin.

7. Begin wrapping the bacon around the exterior of the tenderloin in a lattice pattern until it is completely coated. Make sure the bacon ends are all on the side of the tenderloin that will be pressed against the cooking surface.

8. Place the tenderloin in the center of the rack and cook for about an hour, or until the flesh reaches a temperature of 145°.

9. After the tenderloin has completed cooking, remove it from the grill and let it rest for 8-10 minutes before chopping into it.

Nutrition:
Calories: 616
Fat: 4.07g
Carbs: 17.4g
Protein: 4.1g
Fiber: 5.1g

80. PULLED PORK NACHOS

Preparation Time: 10 minutes

Cooking Time: 1 hr

Servings: 2

Ingredients:

- ½ cup apple cider
- ½ avocado, diced
- 2 tbsp cilantro, chopped
- ¼ cup crema
- 2 tbsp jalapeno, chopped
- 1 cup marble jack, grated
- 2 tbsp pit boss sweet heat rub
- 2 lbs pork shoulder
- 1 cup queso fresco, crumbled
- ¼ cup red bell pepper, chopped
- 1 tsp red chili flakes
- 2 tbsp red onion, chopped
- 2 tbsp scallions, chopped
- 10 oz. Tortilla chips

- 1 cup water

Instructions:

1. These crowd-pleasing pulled pork nachos are brimming with melt-in-your-mouth smoked pork shoulder and all the fixings. The pork is smoked low and slow before being shredded and piled high on tortilla chips with gooey cheese, onions, avocado, and a fiery lime crema.

Nutrition:

Protein 37g

Fat   10g

Calories 192g

Carbs 0g

81.   CURRY KETCHUP PORK RIBS

Preparation Time: 10 minutes

Cooking Time: 1 hr 20 minutes

Servings: 2

Ingredients:

10.   1 tsp chili powder

11.   1 tbsp curry powder

12.   1/2 tsp ground mustard

13.   2 tsp honey

14.   To taste, kansas city barbecue rub seasoning

15.   1 cup ketchup

16.   2 pork back rib racks, membrane removed

17.   2 tsp smoked paprika

18.   2 tsp worcestershire sauce

Instructions:

2. With these curry ketchup pork ribs, you can add a new twist to your weekend rib game. Baby back ribs are seasoned with BBQ rub before being smoked and rolled

until tender. In the last hour of Instructions, a richly spiced homemade curry ketchup is basted on to add moisture and earthy and warm curry taste.

3. Set your pit boss grill to smoke mode and leave the lid open for 10 minutes before preheating to 225° f. Set up a gas or charcoal grill for low, indirect fire.

4. Season both sides of the rib racks with kansas city barbeque rub and place them on a sheet tray. Place the ribs on the grill and smoke for 1 hour.

5. In the meantime, make the curry ketchup: whisk together ketchup, curry powder, smoked paprika, chili powder, powdered mustard, worcestershire sauce, and honey in a mixing cup. Place aside.

6. Rotate the rib racks and raise the temperature to 250 degrees fahrenheit. Cook for an additional hour before removing the ribs from the grill and placing them on butcher paper. Cover the ribs in paper after brushing them with sauce.

7. Place the ribs back on the barbecue. Cook for another hour, or until the potatoes are tender.

8. Remove the ribs from the oven, peel back the butcher paper, and baste with the leftover curry ketchup. Return the racks to the grill, raise the temperature to 275 f, and cook for an additional 15 minutes. Remove the ribs from the oven, peel back the butcher paper, and baste with the leftover curry ketchup. Return the racks to the grill, raise the temperature to 275 f, and cook for an additional 15 minutes.

9. Remove the ribs from the grill and set aside for 10 minutes before slicing and serving wet.

Nutrition:

Protein 23g

Fat 10g

Calories 180g

82.   GRILLED PORK STEAK

Preparation Time:20 minutes

Cooking Time: 33 minutes

Servings: 2

ingredients

11.	4 pork steaks
12.	1/3 C sea salt
13.	¼ C Pitboss AP Rub
14.	1 C maple syrup
15.	¼ C Pitboss BBQ Sauce
16.	2 tsp dried thyme
17.	1½ C apple cider
18.	1½ C ice water
19.	2 tsp hot sauce
20.	1 C water

Instructions:

1. Combine 1 cup water, salt, and 1/3 cup maple syrup with dried thyme in a small pot. Cook over medium heat until the salt has dissolved and the water has reached a boiling temperature.
2. Remove the pan from the heat. Stir in the cider, ice water, and 1 teaspoon of spicy sauce until the ice melts. Refrigerate the brine until it reaches a temperature of 45 degrees. Put the pork steaks in a zip-top bag, add the brine, and close the bag. Refrigerate for 2 hours to let flavors to meld.
3. Combine the remaining maple syrup and spicy sauce with the barbecue sauce in a small dish and set aside. Preheat your Pitboss Grill to 300°F.
4. Using paper towels, blot the pork steaks dry after removing them from the brine. Grill the meat until the first side has nice grill marks, then flip. Internal temperature should be between 145 and 160 degrees. Brush the pork steaks with the syrup mixture every 3 minutes throughout the last 10 minutes of cooking.
5. Allow 5 minutes for the meat to rest before serving.

Nutrition:

Protein 63g

Fat 10g

Calories 210g

Carbs 0g

83. PULLED PORK QUESO DIP

Preparation Time: 10 minutes

Cooking Time: 3 hr 20 minute

Servings: 2

Ingredients:

- 1/2 bunch cilantro, chopped
- 3 ears corn, grilled and removed from the cobb
- 1/2 block cream cheese, room temperature
- 3 tbsp cumin
- 3 grilled jalapenos, diced and seeded
- 2 tbsp lime zest
- 1 lime, juiced
- 16 ounces mexican cheese, shredded
- 16 ounces pepper jack cheese, 1" cubes
- Tt pit boss pulled pork rub
- 4 lbs pork shoulder, bone in
- 1/2 yellow onion, diced

Instructions:

1. Queso is a favorite in every home, which is what inspired this pulled pork edition.
2. Set your pit boss grill to smoke mode and turn it on. Enable the grill to run for 10 minutes with the lid open.
3. When the grill is heating up, put the pork shoulder to room temperature.
4. Remove the silver skin and score the fat hat.
5. Coat with mustard and season with pit boss pulled pork rub on both sides.
6. Preheat your barbecue to 250°f.
7. Place the pork shoulder on the grill and smoke it until the internal temperature reaches 165°f. (approximately 2 - 3 hours)
8. Remove from the oven and seal in peach butcher paper. Return to your pit boss and raise the temperature to 275°f. Smoke until the internal temperature reaches 205°f. Pull for thirty minutes and then rest.
9. Prepare your queso dip while you're waiting.
10. Prepare the vegetables and herbs for queso by chopping all of the cheese into 1" cubes.
11. Pork can be shredded.

12. In an aluminium pan, combine all of the queso ingredients (2-3 inch deep pan). Continue to keep the pork warm but do not apply it yet.

13. Smoke for 10-15 minutes in the boss at 250°f. Have an eye on it to combine it as the cheese begins to turn into a gooey substance. When fully molten, remove it and prepare a cast iron skillet and pork.

14. Apply a thin coat of olive oil or butter to the bottom of the cast iron and place 1 pound of pulled pork on top.

15. Pour gooey queso over the pulled pork in the cast iron skillet. Attach 3/4 bag of mexican cheese quickly.

16. Return to the pit boss at 250°f before the cheese is fried on top.

17. Remove the cast iron skillet with care and grab a couple bags of chips to enjoy!

Nutrition:

protein 23g

fat 10g

calories   180g

carbs 0g

84. BRISKET TATER TOT NACHOS

Preparation Time: 10 minutes

Cooking Time: 3 hr

Servings: 2

Ingredients:

- Your favorite bbq sauce
- 1 12 lb brisket
- 1, skiced jalapeno pepper
- ¼ cup pit boss beef and brisket rub
- ¾ cup sharp cheddar cheese, shredded
- ⅓ cup sour cream
- 32 oz. Tater tots, frozen

SMOKED CHUCK ROAST

Ingredients

- 3 cups beef stock, divided
- 1, 3 lb chuck roast
- 3 tbsp pit boss sweet heat rub
- 1 yellow onion

Instructions

1. Any time of year, this tender, melt-in-your-mouth smoked chuck roast is a delicious pick. Beef chuck is an easily available cut that is less expensive than brisket and simpler to master than brisket. We slow smoke it on the pellet grill like a conventional brisket, crunch it with foil, and shred it into juicy, smoky morsels. Serve on bread to make pulled beef sandwiches, or eat it straight from the grill.

How to smoke a chuck roast

1. A chuck roast can be smoked in the same way as a brisket is. Smoke directly on the grill grates at 225°F for about 3 hours. Spray with beef stock or your favorite juice combination every hour or so. Then, put the roast in a pan with the liquid and return to the grill at 250°F until the internal temperature reaches 165°F. Finally, tent the roast with foil and cook until it is probe tender (about 200°F internal temperature).

2. In a 9x13 baking dish, place the chuck roast. Season generously with pit boss sweet heat rub and massage to evenly coat both sides.
3. Refrigerate overnight, foil-wrapped.
4. The next day, remove the chuck roast from the refrigerator and leave it aside to come to room temperature.
5. For smoking, preheat the pit boss to 225° F. Make sure your barbeque is on low heat, whether it's gas or charcoal.
6. Before placing the roast directly on the grill grate, insert a temperature probe into the thickest portion of the roast. Close the lid and leave it to burn for 3 hours.
7. Spray the roast with 1 cup beef stock every hour.
8. Slice the onion and place it in a 9x13 aluminum pan. Place the roast on top of the onions and pour the remaining cup of liquid over it.
9. Cook for another 2 1/2 to 3 hours, or until the internal temperature surpasses 165°f, at a temperature of 250°f.
10. Cover the roast with aluminum foil and continue cooking for another 2 12 to 3 hours, or until the internal temperature reaches 200°f.
11. Take the chuck roast from the grill.
12. Allow for a 15-minute rest before taking the roast from the pan and shredding with meat claws. Serve with some of the remaining cooking liquid on top of the shredded roast to enhance moisture and flavor.

Nutrition:

Protein 23g

Fat 10g

Calories 350g

85.   HOMEMADE HOT DOGS

Preparation Time: 10 minutes

Cooking Time: 1 hr

Servings: 2

Ingredients:

- 1/3 lbs binder flour
- 1 tbsp black pepper
- 2 tsp coriander
- 1 3/4 cup distilled ice water, divided
- 1 tbsp garlic powder
- 7 1/2 lbs ground beef
- 5 lbs ground pork
- 2 tsp mace
- 3 1/2 oz maple cure
- 1/4 cup mustard powder
- 3 tbsp paprika
- 1/4 cup salt
- 24 - 26 mm sheep casings, pre-flushed

Instructions:

1. Nothing beats the sizzle and snap of a freshly grilled hot dog. Homemade hot dogs are simple to make with the right equipment and will fill your fridge with tasty franks to last you the whole summer.

2. Cover sheep casings in warm water in a glass bowl or measuring cup and soak for 1 hour.

3. Whisk together paprika, mustard powder, black pepper, garlic powder, coriander, mace, and salt in a shallow cup. Place aside.

4. Combine ground beef and ground pork in a big mixing bowl. By side, combine the ingredients, then apply the maple cure and 3/4 cup plus 2 tablespoons of chilled ice water. In a medium mixing dish, combine seasoning and binder flour, then add 34 cup plus 2 tablespoons water. Combine for the beef combination.

5. Hand-mix the meat mixture for 5 minutes, or until the meat is tacky. Divide the mixture into two wide mixing cups. One bowl should be refrigerated while the other bowl's mixture is stuffed.

6. Prepare the sausage stuffer and wrap a 12 inch horn in sheep casing. Place a sheet tray with a little water on it underneath the stuffer's nozzle and begin filling the casings.

7. If the casings are complete, twist them off to the desired length. Refrigerate for at least 24 hours.

8. Preheat your pit boss platinum series lockhart to 250°f. Set up a gas or charcoal grill for low, indirect fire. Pull both side handles open to raise the amount of smoke and temperature in the smoking cabinet.

9. Remove hot dogs from the smoking cabinet and serve hot with your choice toppings, or put in an ice water bath for 15 minutes, then dry at room temperature before refrigerating or freezing for later use.

Nutrition:
Calories: 164
Fat: 3.07g
Carbs: 17.4g
Protein: 4.1g
Fiber: 5.1g

86.   SMOKED PIGS IN A BLANKET

Preparation Time: 15 minutes

Cooking Time: 30 minutes

Servings: 2

Ingredients

- Beef Franks, Or Any Cooked Sausage
- 1 Can of Crescent Rolls
- 3 Tbsp. Mustard
- Pitboss Grills All Purpose Rub

Instructions:

1. Preheat the smoker to 350 degrees, or according to the Instructions:s on the crescent roll container. The temperature on the can is the one you should use; several types differ!

2. Roll out the crescent rolls on a level surface and season with mustard and a sprinkle of rub to taste. Here, a little goes a big way.

3. Fold over the sausage in the centre of the prepared roll until it is completely wrapped. It's ok if the sausage ends protrude.

4. Place the pigs in a blanket on a sheet tray coated with nonstick oil and smoke for 20—25 minutes, or until the pastry is done to your liking.

Nutrition:

Protein 23g

Fat 10g

Calories 180g

Carbs 0g

87.   PULLED PORK EGGS BENEDICT

Preparation Time: 10 minutes

Cooking Time: 1 hr

Servings: 2

Ingredients:

- 2/3 cup apple cider vinegar
- 2 sticks butter
- 6 cups chicken broth
- 2 egg yolks
- 8 eggs
- 4 english muffins
- 2/3 cup ketchup
- 1 tsp lemon juice
- 1 cup maple chipotle rub seasoning
- 7 lbs pork shoulder
- To taste, salt & pepper

Instructions:

1. Who's up for a nice time?! This pulled pork eggs benedict with our maple chipotle rub is made with a thinly toasted english muffin, a generous scoop of pulled pork, and a poached egg drenched in hollandaise.

2. Preheat your pit boss pellet grill to smoke and leave the lid open for 10 minutes before turning it off. Preheat a gas or charcoal grill to medium/high heat.

3. Combine the chicken broth, ketchup, apple cider vinegar, and 4 teaspoons of maple chipotle seasoning in a mixing dish. Set aside after thoroughly whisking together.

4. Season the pork shoulder with the remaining 3/4 cup maple chipotle. Season the pork shoulder on all sides, then put it on the grill and sear on all sides until golden brown, about 10 minutes.

5. Place the pork shoulder in the disposable aluminum pan after removing it from the grill. Pour the combination of chicken broth and water over the pork shoulder. It can come around a third to a quarter of the way up the side of the pork shoulder. Wrap aluminium foil closely across the pan's rim.

6. Reduce the temperature of your pit boss grill to 250 degrees fahrenheit. Grill the foil pan for four or five hours, or until the pork is tender and falls off the bone.

7. Enable the pork to cool slightly after removing it from the grill. Remove around a cup of the liquid from the pan, then shred the pork and cover with the reserved liquid. Place aside.

8. To make the hollandaise, set up a pot of boiling water on the stovetop and put the two yolks in a bowl that will rest on top of the boiling water without touching it.

9. Heat the yolks over boiling water, whisking vigorously, until they thicken and form a ribbon-like stream when raised with the whisk.

10. In a measuring cup, melt the fat. Place the bowl containing the egg yolks on a flat surface that will not slip or roll.

11. Slowly drizzle the butter onto the eggs while whisking briskly and continuously. When more butter is added into the yolks, the sauce can thicken.

12. Season with lemon juice, salt, and pepper to taste.

13. Bring 4" of water up the side of a sauce pot to a boil. Poach the 8 eggs with vinegar and salt, if necessary.

14. Toast the english muffins before assembling the benedicts.

15. Top the benedicts with hollandaise sauce and a dash of maple chipotle. Have fun!

Nutrition:

Protein 23g

Fat 10g

Calories 180g

Carbs 0g

88. GROUND PORK BURGERS

Preparation Time: 10 minutes

Cooking Time: 1 hr

Servings: 2

Ingredients:

- 1 avocado, sliced
- 1/2 cup bacon bits
- 1 tbsp cilantro, chopped (for mayo)
- 2 tbsp cilantro, chopped (for salsa)
- 1 piece green leaf lettuce
- 2 lbs ground pork
- 4 hamburger buns
- To taste, hickory bacon rub seasoning
- 1 jalapeño, minced
- 1/2 lime, zest and juice (for mayo)
- 1/2 lime, zest and juice (for salsa)
- 1/3 cup mayonnaise
- 2 nectarines, diced
- 1/2 red onion, minced

Instructions:

1. Don't let beef burgers steal the show; these smoked ground pork burgers are juicy, fluffy, and bursting with mouthwatering bbq taste. Smoking the burger not only provides wood-fired flavor, but it also helps the fat to slowly render, resulting in a juicy and crisp burger that pairs well with every topping.

2. Set your pit boss to smoke and start cooking. Set up a gas or charcoal grill for low, indirect fire.

3. In a mixing cup, combine ground pork and bacon bits, then season with hickory bacon. Form into 4 patties, making an indent in the center of each. Place aside.

4. To make the salsa, combine the nectarines, jalapeo, red onion, lime zest and juice, and cilantro in a mixing cup. Refrigerate after covering with plastic wrap.

5. To make the mayonnaise, add the mayonnaise, lime zest and juice, and cilantro in a mixing cup. Refrigerate after covering with plastic wrap.

6. Place the pork patties on the grill rack over indirect heat. Cook for another 20 to 25 minutes, or until the internal temperature hits 150° f, after covering and smoking for 30 minutes. Open the sear slide and grill for 2 minutes, rotating and tossing every now and then. Remove the burgers from the grill and set aside for 5 minutes before serving hot.

Nutrition:

Protein 23g

Fat 10g

Calories 180g

Carbs 0g

89.   HAWAIIAN PULLED PORK SLIDERS

Preparation Time: 10 minutes

Cooking Time: 2 hr

Servings: 2

Ingredients:

- ½ cup apple cider vinegar
- 1 package of cabbage
- 2 tbsp minced cilantro
- 1/3 cup green onions, diced
- 1 tbsp mango magic
- 1 ½ cup mayonnaise
- 1 cup pineapple, diced
- 1 lbs pulled pork
- 8 hawaiian rolls

Instructions:

1. Are you about to have a hawaiian-style grilling party?
2. In a big mixing cup, combine all of the coleslaw ingredients and place in the refrigerator for at least 2 hours.
3. Reheat the pulled pork on the grill or in the oven.
4. Serve alongside the pulled pork on hawaiian rolls.

Nutrition:

protein 23g

fat 10g

calories 180g

carbs 0g

90. PULLED PORK SANDWICH WITH PRETZEL BUN

Preparation Time: 10 minutes

Cooking Time: 5 hr

Servings: 2

Ingredients:

- ⅓ cup apple cider vinegar
- 1 ½ cups bbq sauce, divided
- 1 qt. Chicken stock
- ⅓ cup ketchup
- 3 tbsp pit boss pulled pork rub, divided
- 1, 4 lb. Pork shoulder, bone in
- 4 pretzel buns

Instructions:

1. Preheat the pit boss to 400 degrees fahrenheit. Set the barbecue to medium-high heat whether you're using a gas or charcoal grill. Combine the apple cider vinegar, chicken stock, ketchup, and 1 tablespoon of pit boss pulled pork rub in a mixing bowl. Set aside after thoroughly whisking together.

2. Season the pork shoulder on both sides with the remaining 2 teaspoons of pulled pork seasoning, then put on the grill and sear until golden brown, about 10 minutes.

3. Place the pork shoulder in the disposable aluminum pan after removing it from the grill. Distribute the sauce over the pork shoulder. It can come around a third to a quarter of the way up the side of the pork shoulder. Wrap aluminium foil closely across the pan's rim.

4. Reduce the temperature of your pit boss barbecue to 250 degrees fahrenheit. Grill the foil pan for 4 to 5 hours, or until the pork is tender and falls off the bone.

5. Enable the pork to rest for 15 minutes after removing it from the grill. Remove around a cup of the liquid from the pan, then shred the pork and cover with the reserved liquid. Set aside 3 1/2 to 4 cups of the pulled pork for sandwiches and the rest for later use.

6. When the pork is resting, heat 1 cup of bbq sauce in a skillet to a boil. Stir in the reserved shredded pork. Divide the pork into four pretzel buns, cover with more bbq sauce, and dig in!

Nutrition:

Protein 23g

Fat 10g

Calories 180g

Carbs 0

91.   ITALIAN VENISON SAUSAGE SANDWICHES

Preparation Time: 10 minutes

Cooking Time: 5 hr. 20 minutes

Servings: 2

Ingredients:

- 1 tsp black pepper, ground
- 1 tbsp butter
- 1 tbsp competition smoked rub
- 1/4 cup distilled ice water
- 1 tsp fennel seed, cracked
- To taste, fresh basil
- 6 hoagie rolls, sliced lengthwise
- 32-35 mm hog casings
- 1 cup marinara sauce
- 1 tbsp olive oil
- 1 tsp oregano, dried
- 1/2 tsp paprika
- 1 tsp parsley, dried
- 1 lb pork, ground

- 12 slices provolone cheese
- 1 red bell pepper, sliced thin
- 2 red onions, sliced thin
- 1/2 tsp red pepper flakes, crushed
- 1 lb venison, ground

Instructions:

1. Make the most of your trophy quest with these delectable homemade italian venison sausage sandwiches. This recipe begins of homemade sausage links made with ground venison, bacon, and an italian spice mixture made from scratch. The sausages are smoked to perfection before being stuffed into a hearty hoagie roll with sautéed peppers, tomatoes, marinara, and melty provolone cheese.

2. Cover hog casings in warm water in a glass bowl or measuring cup and soak for 1 hour.

3. Whisk together competition smoked, parsley, black pepper, red pepper flakes, oregano, fennel, and paprika in a small bowl.

4. Combine ground venison and ground pork in a big mixing dish. By side, combine the ingredients, then apply the seasoning and chilled ice water. Mix the paste by hand for 1 minute, or until the seasoning is evenly distributed.

5. Prepare the sausage stuffer by wrapping one hog casing around a 1 to 14-inch horn. Place a sheet tray with a little water on it underneath the stuffer's nozzle and begin filling the casing.

6. If the casing has been packed, twist it off into desired lengths, poke it to remove any air bubbles, seal it in plastic wrap, and place it in the refrigerator overnight.

7. Start your pit boss on smoke mode and leave the lid open for 10 minutes before preheating to 200° f. Set up a gas or charcoal grill for low, indirect fire.

8. Pull both side handles open to raise the amount of smoke and temperature in the smoking cabinet. The aim is to keep the temperature between 150 and 160° f.

9. Hang the connected sausage with s-hooks from the top shelf, taking caution not to overlap the ties for even smoking. Smoke for 3 hours, then raise the grill temperature to 225° f, which raises the temperature of the smoking cabinet to 170° f, and continue smoking the sausage for another 1 to 2 hours, or until the internal temperature exceeds 155° f.

10. Remove the hoagie rolls from the smoking cabinet and place them in the upper cabinet to stay warm. Place aside a portion that has been sliced with scissors.

11. In the meantime, heat a cast iron skillet on the gill. Button the sear slide open. Sauté peppers and onion in olive oil and butter for 3 minutes. Slide the pan to the left and sear the sausages for 1 minute over an open flame.

12. Put 2 slices of provolone in each roll while the peppers and onion are grilling, then keep warm in the cabinet.

13. Sausage sandwiches are served hot with marinara, provolone cheese, sautéed bell peppers and onions, and fresh basil. Alternatively, put the sausages in an ice water bath for 15 minutes, then dry at room temperature before refrigerating or freezing for later use.

Nutrition:

Protein 23g

Fat 10g

Calories 180g

Carbs 0g

92.   BBQ SPAGHETTI

Preparation Time: 15 minutes

Cooking Time: 30 minutes

Servings: 2

Ingredients

- 2 pound pulled pork
- 1 sliced small onion
- 1 chopped Green Bell Pepper
- 5 minced garlic cloves
- 1 tin Petite Diced Tomato (14oz).
- 1 tin of tomato sauce (14oz).
- 12 cup Killer Hogs The Barbecue Sauce
- 12 cup Vinegar Sauce Killer Hogs
- Spaghetti Pasta 8 oz.
- 2 tbsp tomato paste
- 2 tbsp. olive oil
- 3 tbsp. Killer Hogs The BBQ Rub
- 1 tablespoon dried oregano
- 1 tablespoon dried parsley
- 1 teaspoon basil (sweet)
- 1 tsp fresh marjoram
- 1 tsp of Kosher salt
- 1 teaspoon ground black pepper

Instructions:

1. In a large saucepan, heat the olive oil over medium heat. 3-4 minutes, or until onion and bell pepper are soft. Cook for another 1-2 minutes after adding the minced garlic.

2. Stir in the tomato sauce, diced tomatoes, tomato paste, BBQ sauce, Vinegar Sauce, spices, and 12 pound pulled pork; cover and cook over very low heat for 45 minutes to an hour, stirring regularly.

3. Drain the pasta after cooking it according to the package recommendations. Return the pasta to the boiler pot and melt 2 tablespoons of butter over medium heat. Stir for about 1 minute, or until the butter has melted.

4. Take the pasta from the fire and pour the sauce over it. Place on a large serving plate and gently toss to incorporate. Drizzle with more BBQ sauce and top with the leftover pulled pork.

Nutrition:

Protein 23g

Fat 10g

Calories 180g

Carbs 0g

93.   APPLE BOURBON BBQ BEANS

Preparation Time: 15 minutes

Cooking Time: 30 minutes

Servings: 2

Ingredients

- Baked Beans, 2 cans (28oz ea).
- 3 diced Gala apples
- 1 medium diced onion
- 3 seeded and sliced jalapeño peppers
- 3 minced garlic cloves
- 6 thick-cut bacon pieces, chopped
- 1 pound of jerked pork
- Killer Hogs The BBQ Sauce, 8 oz.
- 1 pound brown sugar (divided).
- Four Roses Bourbon, 2 oz.
- 1 teaspoon Dijon mustard
- 3 tbsp. Killer Hogs The BBQ Rub
- 1 tbsp. Killer Hogs AP Rub

Instructions:

1. For indirect cooking, prepare a Big Green Egg or another grill. Maintain a 3000°F grill temperature. For smoke, add cherry wood pieces to the heated coals.

2. In a large sauté pan, cook bacon for 8 minutes, or until fat has rendered but the bacon is still soft and not crispy. On a paper towel, drain the bacon. 1 TBS bacon fat is set aside for sautéing.

3. Sauté the onion in the pan for 2-3 minutes. Continue to sauté for 2 minutes after adding the jalapeño and garlic. Season with a sprinkle of AP rub and the diced apple. Cook for 2-3 minutes after adding 12 cup of brown sugar to the apple mixture. Stir everything together, then pour in the bourbon. Reduce the liquid to half its original volume and pour into a small basin.

4. Fill a dutch oven iron pot halfway with beans. Combine the apple mixture, pulled pork, bacon, BBQ Sauce, Dijon Mustard, the remaining brown sugar, and spices in a large mixing bowl. Stir to mix and set on the barbecue grill, uncovered.

5. Cook for 2 hours, stirring regularly, before serving.

Nutrition:

Protein 23g

Fat 10g

Calories 180g

Carbs 0g

94. BRUNSWICK STEW – MISSISSIPPI STYLE.

Preparation Time: 15 minutes

Cooking Time: 30 minutes

Servings: 2

Ingredient

- 1 Whole Chicken (pulled)
- 2lb. Pulled Pork
- 32oz Chicken Stock
- 28oz Can Diced Tomatoes
- 28oz Can Tomato Puree
- 1 Lg Sweet Onion (chopped)
- 6 Cloves Chopped Garlic
- 1/2 Cup Worcestershire Sauce
- 2 Sticks Butter
- 1 16oz Frozen Package Sweet Corn
- 1 16oz Frozen Package Butter Beans
- 1 16oz Frozen Package Diced Potatoes
- 1 Bottle of Killer Hogs BBQ Sauce (or your fave BBQ sauce)

- 2 Mustard – 2 T. Killer Hogs Rub (or your fave BBQ Rub)
- Kosher Salt
- 1 Black Pepper
- 1t Cayenne Pepper To star

In a big stock pot, I boiled the whole chicken to make my own chicken stock. I put the chicken in a stock pot with cold water and added 1 teaspoon Kosher salt, 1 teaspoon black pepper, 2 bay leaves, 2 course chopped carrots, 1 quartered onion, and 3-4 split garlic cloves.

Instructions:

1. Bring to a boil, then lower to a low heat and simmer until the chicken is cooked through. After removing the chicken, the liquid was strained through a mesh strainer. The stock was then returned to the stock pot and decreased for 20 minutes. When the chicken stock was finished, I poured it into a large container. You may substitute bottled chicken stock for homemade stock, but nothing surpasses the flavor of homemade stock in soups and stews. While my stock was depleting, I grabbed my chicken and prepared all of my other things. It was now time to make the stew! In a large stockpot, I melted two

sticks of butter and added the chopped onions and garlic. Sautéing time: 8 minutes

2. After that, I cooked for another 6-8 minutes with the Worcestershire sauce, salt, pepper, rub, and cayenne pepper. Then I added my pulled pork, chicken, mustard, and Killer Hogs BBQ Sauce. I combined everything, double-checked that the meat was well coated, and cooked it for 5 minutes.

3. Then I mixed in the Tomato Puree and Diced Tomatoes from both cans. I also added 32 ounces of pre-made chicken stock. I brought it all to a boil and let it simmer for an hour.

4. Then came the Sweet Corn, Butter Beans, and Diced Potatoes (NOTE: If you dice your own potatoes using raw potatoes, you will need to add them to the pot when adding the chicken stock). They'll take a little longer to tenderize.) After I've added all of the vegetables, I let it boil for about 2 hours.

5. If required, add extra chicken stock. However, keep in mind that this is a thick stew rather than a soup. After it's been simmering on the stove for a while and become all lovely, it's ready to eat. You may serve it whatever you like, but in my family,

we like to serve it with homemade cornbread on the side.

Nutrition:

Protein 23g

Fat 10g

Calories 180g

TURKEY, RABBIT AND VEAL RECIPES

95. Chicken Chili Recipe

Prep Time: 10

Cook Time: 30 minutes

Serve: 3

Ingredients

- 2 tblsp. Melted butter
- 1 sliced onion
- 1 sliced poblano pepper
- 1 chopped jalapeo
- 5–6 garlic cloves, minced
- 2–4 ounces green chiles, diced
- 32 ounces of chicken broth
- Malcom's bonafide chili seasoning, 2 tblsp.
- 8 ounces softened cream cheese
- 2 cups shredded monterrey jack cheese
- Cream of chicken soup (in a can).

- Bush's white chili beans, 2 cans
- 1 litre heavy cream
- A pinch of salt (optional).
- 1 teaspoon freshly ground black pepper (optional).
- 2 pound cooked chicken

Instructions

1. Cook onion and peppers in butter for 2-3 minutes over medium heat. Continue to sauté for 1-2 minutes after adding the garlic.

2. Combine the broth, canned green chilies, and Malcom's Bonafide Chili Seasoning in a large mixing bowl. Cook for 15-20 minutes on a low heat.

3. Combine the cream of chicken soup, cream cheese, and jack cheese in a mixing bowl. Continue to cook, stirring periodically, until the cheese has melted.

4. Stir in the heavy cream and chili beans once the cheese has melted. Return to a low simmer after tasting for seasoning. Before serving, add the chicken and cook it through (10-15 minutes).

Shredded cheddar, sour cream, avocado slices, cilantro, sliced jalapeo, and spicy sauce are all good garnish alternatives.

To smoke chicken: season it with 1 tablespoon Bonafide Chili Seasoning and smoke it until the breast temperature reaches 165 degrees. Chicken should be shredded and set aside for later.

Nutrition:
Calories: 574
Fat: 31.07g
Carbs: 17.4g
Protein: 14.1g
Fiber: 5.1g

96.   Macrib Sandwich

Now this is how you do a rib sandwich the right way!

Prep Time: 10 Minutes

Cook Time: 20min

Serving: 5

Ingredients

- 1 pound slab Loin Back Ribs
- 2 tbsp Killer Hogs AP seasoning
- 2 tbsp. Killer Hogs The BBQ Rub
- a third cup of brown sugar
- 1 pound of butter (split in half lengthwise).
- Killer Hogs Vinegar Sauce, 3/4 cup
- 1/2 cup Killer Hogs The Barbecue Sauce
- 1 fresh loaf of French bread
- 1/2 finely sliced onion
- Several dill pickles in the shape of hamburgers.

Instructions

1. Set up the barbecue smoker for indirect cooking at 275°F using pecan wood for smoke.

2. Make a small incision along each bone and remove the membrane from the rear side of the ribs. (I also removed the end bones from the rack of ribs, leaving around ten bones.)

3. Season each side with AP seasoning, then drizzle with mustard. Dust the pork with The BBQ Rub after patting the spices into it. Allow the ribs to sit meat side up for 15 - 20 minutes until the smoker stabilizes.

4. Place the ribs on the smoker for 2 hours to cook.

5. Wrap the ribs as follows: Spread out the brown sugar, then the butter, sprinkle with 1/4 cup of Vinegar sauce, and arrange the ribs flesh down. Wrap the foil tightly around the ribs and return them to the smoker.

6. Cook for another 1 hour 45 minutes, or until the ribs are tender. Open the foil and remove the ribs from the cooker. Remove each bone with care (they should pop out cleanly at this stage).

7. Place the ribs on a cooling rack lined with foil to cool. Brush the reverse side with the leftover sauces. Brush the ribs with sauce after flipping them over, flesh side up.

8. Set the cooling rack on top of the pit and glaze for 15- 20 minutes.

9. Cut the French bread in half lengthwise and smear with a little amount of butter. Toast for 2—3 minutes on broil - don't walk away!

10. To make the sandwich: Drizzle the bottom half of the toast with part of the 50/50 sauce. Serve with finely sliced onion and pickles on top. Drizzle with additional sauce and serve the ribs on top. To serve, add the top half of the bread and cut it into quarters.

Nutrition:
Calories: 112
Fat: 1.07g
Carbs: 17.4g
Protein: 2.1g
Fiber: 5.1g

97.   Pan Fajitas

Prep time: 20 minutes

Cook time: 25 minutes

Total time: 45 minutes

Ingredients

- 2 pounds finely sliced chicken breast
- 1 big chopped onion
- 1 big seeded and sliced red bell pepper
- 1 big seeded and sliced orange bell pepper
- 1 teaspoon of salt
- a half teaspoon onion powder
- 1/2 teaspoon garlic granules
- 2 tbsp Chile Margarita Seasoning from Spiceologist
- 2 tablespoons olive oil

Instructions

1. Preheat your grill (or oven) to 450°F according to the manufacturer's instructions.

2. Combine the oil and spices in a mixing bowl. Combine the chicken and peppers in a mixing bowl.

3. Line a big sheet pan with nonstick foil and set it on your grill that has been preheated (or oven). Allow the pan to heat up for about 10 minutes within the grill (or oven).

4. Open the grill and arrange the peppers and veggies in a single layer on the pan. Close the grill and continue to cook for 8 to 10 minutes, or until the chicken is no longer pink.

5. Remove off the grill with care and serve with warm tortillas and all of your favorite toppings!

Nutrition:
Calories: 211
Fat: 6.07g
Carbs: 17.4g
Protein: 4.1g
Fiber: 5.1g

98. Grilled Chicken

Prep time 5 minutes

Cook time 15 minutes

Serving: 3

Ingredients

- Whole chicken weighing 5 pounds
- Chicken Rub
- 1/2 cup oil

Instructions

1. Preheat your grill for 4-5 minutes on "smoke" with the lid open. Set the temperature to high, then close the lid and warm for another 10-15 minutes, or until the temperature reaches 400-450 degrees.

2. Tie your chicken's legs together using baker's twine. Coat the chicken with the chicken rub after rubbing it with oil. Place your chicken breast side up on the grill.

3. 70 minutes on the grill do not turn on the grill for the next 70 minutes. (if you have a thermometer, put it in straight away so you can check the interior temperature for doneness! open the grill if it gets 165° before the 70-minute mark.)
4. Check the chicken's internal temperature to ensure it is at least 165°. If it hasn't reached 165° yet, keep it on the grill for a few minutes more.
5. Remove the chicken from the grill and set aside for 15 minutes to rest. Slice and serve!

Nutrition:
Calories: 935
Fat: 53.07g
Carbs: 17.4g
Protein: 14.1g
Fiber: 5.1g

99.   Marinated Grilled Chicken Kabobs

Prep time 45 minutes

Cook time 12 minutes

Total time 57 minutes

Serving: 4

Ingredients

Marinade:

- a half-cup olive oil
- 2 tbsp of white vinegar
- 1 tablespoon lemon juice
- 1 1/2 tablespoons sea salt
- 1 tsp coarsely ground pepper
- 2 teaspoons chopped fresh chives
- 1 1/2 tablespoons chopped fresh thyme
- 2 teaspoons chopped fresh Italian parsley
- 1 teaspoon minced garlic

Kabobs:

- 1 red, 1 orange, and 1 yellow bell pepper
- 1 1/2 pounds boneless, skinless chicken breasts, cut into 2" pieces
- 10-12 crimini mushrooms, medium

Serve with:

- naan bread

Instructions

1. Toss the chicken and mushrooms in the marinade after mixing together all of the marinade ingredients. Refrigerate the marinade for 30 minutes. Soak the kabob skewers in boiling water while the meat is marinating.
2. Remove from the refrigerator and begin constructing your kabobs. Preheat your Traeger to 450 degrees Fahrenheit.
3. Grill the kabobs for 6 minutes on one side, then turn and cook for another 6 minutes on the other. Set aside after removing from the grill.
4. Place the naan bread on the grill for 1-2 minutes to warm it up.
5. Serve with a dollop of fresh caesar dressing.

Nutrition:
Calories: 165
Fat: 2.07g
Carbs: 17.4g

Protein: 4.1g
Fiber: 5.1g

100. Grilled Chicken Wings Recipe

Prep time 10 minutes

Cook time 35 minutes

Serving: 2

Ingredients

- 6-8 pounds chicken wing segments (about a pound per person for a meal-sized portion)
- 4 tbsp BBQ Seasoning
- a third of a cup of canola oil

Instructions

1. In a large mixing bowl, combine the oil and spices, then toss in the chicken wing segments. Stir to coat evenly with oil and spices.
2. With the lid open, set your Traeger to smoke for 4-5 minutes. Preheat the grill for 15 minutes by turning the thermostat to 350 degrees Fahrenheit and closing the lid.

3. Arrange the wings on the grill in an equal layer. Close the lid and cook for 45 minutes, or until the chicken is cooked through and the skin is crispy.

4. Remove from the heat and mix with your preferred barbecue or buffalo sauce. Serve immediately!

Nutrition:
Calories: 490
Fat: 0.07g
Carbs: 17.4g
Protein: 33.1g
Fiber: 5.1g

101. Spicy Candied Bacon

Prep time 5 minutes

Cook time 35 minutes

Total time 40 minutes

Ingredients

- 1 pound center-cut bacon
- 1/2 cup dark brown sugar
- 1/2 cup real maple syrup
- 1 tablespoon sriracha hot sauce
- 1/2 teaspoon cayenne pepper

Instructions

1. In a small mixing dish, combine the brown sugar, maple syrup, spicy sauce, and cayenne. Whisk everything together until it's smooth.
2. Preheat your grill to 300°F according to the manufacturer's recommendations.

3. Preheat the oven to 350°F. Line a baking sheet with parchment paper. Brush both sides of the bacon with the sugar mixture and arrange it in a single layer.

4. Cook the pans in the grill(or your oven) for 20 minutes. Then flip the bacon over and cook for the remaining 15 minutes (or until the bacon looks cooked and the sugar is melted and delicious, your mileage may vary by 3-4 minutes either way.)

5. Remove from the grill or oven and leave aside for 10-15 minutes to allow the "candy" to settle before removing from the pan. Do not place directly on paper towels, otherwise you will get paper towel candied bacon, which no one loves.

Nutrition:
Calories: 458
Fat: 10.07g
Carbs: 17.4g
Protein: 4.1g
Fiber: 5.1g

102. Bacon Sausage Bites

Total Time

Prep: 20 Min. + Chilling Bake: 35 Min.

Ingredients

- 1 package smoked sausage
- 1 pound thick-cut bacon
- 2 cups brown sugar

Instructions

1. Cut the sausage into thirds and wrap with bacon slices. Teethpicks are used to keep it all together.
2. Place the sausages in a prepared baking sheet and sprinkle with brown sugar.
3. Preheat your grill (or over) to 300°F according to the manufacturer's directions. For 30 minutes, place the sausages inside.
4. Remove from the oven and set aside for 10-15 minutes before serving warm.

Nutrition:
Calories: 132

Fat: 30.07g
Carbs: 17.4g
Protein: 4.1g
Fiber: 5.1g

103. Yaki Udon

Prep time 10 mins

Cook time 10 mins

Total time 20 mins

Ingredients
- 1 pound of fresh Udon noodles
- 2 cups cooked protein, such as cut pork chops, chicken breasts, shrimp, or other seafood
- 3 cups fresh veggies, such as green beans, broccoli, pea pods, and other similar items
- 3 tablespoons oil (to stir-fry).

Sauce
- 1/2 cup soy sauce
- 1/2 cup House of Tsang General Tsao Sauce
- 1/4 teaspoon fresh ginger
- 2 tablespoons sriracha

Instructions

1. Set aside the sauce ingredients after mixing them together.

2. To prepare udon for stir-frying, follow the package guidelines.

3. Heat a portion of your oil in a wok over high heat. Add your meat and vegetables once it has been pre-heated. Stir continuously until well hot.

4. Continue to stir fry the udon noodles, using additional oil as needed. Cook for around 2-3 minutes.

5. Stir in the sauce for an additional 1-2 minutes in the wok. Serve right away.

Nutrition:
Calories: 504
Fat: 0.07g
Carbs: 17.4g
Protein: 4.1g
Fiber: 5.1g

104. Salsa Verde

Prep time 10 minutes

Cook time 40 minutes

Total time 50 minutes

Ingredients

- 3 seeded big anaheim peppers
- 2 big seeded pasilla peppers
- 6 medium hulled and halved tomatillos
- 1 seeded jalapeno
- 1/2 medium diced yellow onion
- 3 garlic cloves, diced
- 1 cup cilantro, coarsely chopped
- 1/2 cup chicken broth
- 1 medium lime, squeezed
- 1 teaspoon of salt
- 1 tbsp of canola oil

Instructions

1. Place the seeded peppers, tomatillos, onion, and garlic on a baking sheet coated with parchment paper or a silicone baking mat.

2. Preheat your Traeger according to the manufacturer's instructions and set the temperature to 225 degrees Fahrenheit. Allow 30 minutes to cook with the baking sheet inside. (If you don't have a Traeger, you can roast them in the oven.)

3. Take the meat out of the Traeger and set it aside to cool for a few minutes. In a blender, combine all of the ingredients and puree until smooth.

4. In a medium sauce pan, heat the canola oil over medium heat. Pour in the salsa verde and give it a good swirl. Bring to a low simmer, then decrease heat to medium-low and cook for 10-15 minutes, stirring regularly.

Nutrition:
Calories: 25
Fat: 0.07g
Carbs: 17.4g
Protein: 1g
Fiber: 5.1g

105. Grilled Bacon

Prep time 15 minutes

Cook time 25 minutes

Total time 40 minutes

Ingredients

1. 1 pound bacon {thick cut}

Instructions

1. Preheat your grill to 375°F according to the manufacturer's instructions.
2. Line a large baking sheet with parchment paper and arrange thick sliced bacon in a single layer on the sheet.
3. Cook for 20 minutes on the grill at 375°F. Close the cover and flip the bacon over. Cook for 5-10 minutes more, or until the bacon is no longer floppy.

Baked bacon hardens up and cools somewhat after it comes off the grill. If you try to get it to the exact ideal doneness ON the grill, it is easy(ish) to overcook. Pull it a minute or two early than you expect. You can always cook it a little longer, but if you go a couple minutes too long, all you'll have are bacon pieces. (Not that bacon bits are inherently bad.)

Nutrition:
Calories: 315
Fat: 10.07g
Carbs: 17.4g
Protein: 4.1g
Fiber: 5.1g

106. Smoked Turkey

Prep time 15 minutes

Cook time 4 hours

Ingredients

- 1 10-13 pound turkey, thawed, rinsed, and patted dry
- 1/4 cup olive oil
- 2 teaspoons ground poultry seasoning
- 1 1/2 teaspoons salt
- 2 teaspoons Traeger Chicken Rub

Instructions

1. Rub in the oil and spices after mixing them together. You want it all Extra points if you get some between the skin and the breast.
2. Place the turkey, breast up, on a rack to lift it off the bottom of the pan.
3. Preheat the Traeger to 250 degrees Fahrenheit according to the manufacturer's instructions. Place the

uncovered turkey and pan on the grill. Close the grill cover and set your timer for 2 hours, since you don't want to peek before that.

4. After two hours, raise the temperature to 325°F and cover the turkey.
5. Cook for another 2-4 hours (depending on the size of your turkey) or until the internal temperature reaches 165°F.
6. Remove off the grill, carve, and use the drippings to make gravy!

Nutrition:
Calories: 418
Fat: 4.07g
Carbs: 17.4g
Protein: 4.1g
Fiber: 5.1g

107. Buffalo Chicken Recipe

Prep Time 5 Minutes

Cook Time 20 Minutes

Rest Time 5 Minutes

Total Time 30 Minutes

Ingredients

- 5 boneless-skinless chicken breasts
- 2 tablespoons Homemade BBQ rub
- 1/2 - 1 cup homemade Cholula buffalo sauce

Instructions

1. Preheat your grill to 400 degrees Fahrenheit and fire it up according to the manufacturer's instructions.

2. Season your chicken breasts by slicing them lengthwise into long strips and seasoning them with the barbecue rub.

3. Place the chicken on the grill and brush both sides well with the buffalo sauce.

4. Cook for 4 minutes with the grill closed, then open it up and spray both sides again before flipping the chicken over.

5. Continue turning and coating the chicken every 4-5 minutes until the internal temperature reaches 165 degrees.

6. Remove and serve warm, or preserve for future meals!

Nutrition:
Calories: 176
Fat: 4.07g
Carbs: 17.4g
Protein: 4.1g
Fiber: 5.1g

108. Stuffed Peppers

Prep Time 15 Minutes

Cook Time 40 Minutes

Ingredient

- 3 bell peppers, sliced in half and seeded
- 1 pound lean ground beef
- 1 medium onion, chopped
- 1/2 teaspoon red pepper flakes
- 1/2 teaspoon salt
- 1/4 teaspoon pepper
- 1/2 teaspoon onion powder
- 1/2 teaspoon garlic powder
- 1/2 cup white rice
- 15 ounce can stewed tomatoes
- 8 ounces tomato sauce
- 1 1/2 cups water
- 6 cups shredded cabbage
- 2 cups shredded cheddar cheese

Instructions

1. Arrange the peppers on a baking sheet and set away. Set your pellet grill to 325°F according to the manufacturer's instructions.
2. Brown the ground beef and onions in a large pan over medium-high heat with the red pepper flakes, salt, pepper, onion powder, and garlic powder.
3. When the meat has finished cooking, add the rice, stewed tomatoes, tomato sauce, water, and shredded cabbage. Cook, covered, over medium-low heat until the rice is soft and the cabbage is tender.
4. If there is any extra water after the rice has been cooked, increase the heat to medium-high and let it simmer for a few minutes.
5. Fill the waiting cups with the meat mixture that you produced with the bell peppers. Top with cheese and cook for about 30 minutes on a preheated pellet grill.
6. Take out and enjoy!

Nutrition:

Calories: 422

Total Fat: 22g

Saturated Fat: 11g

109. Lamb Chops

Tender lamb chops seasoned with Greek herbs and spices and topped with a delicious mint sauce.

Prep: 5 Min

Inactive: 1 Hr 20 Min

Cook: 5 Min

Ingredients

Lamb

- A total of 16 lamb chops
- Avocado oil (2 tblsp.)
- Greek freak seasoning, 2 tblsp.

Mint Sauce

- 1 cup olive oil, 10-12 garlic cloves, 1 teaspoon salt
- 1 tsp. black pepper, freshly ground
- 1/4 teaspoon oregano, dried
- a quarter-cup of lemon juice
- 1 tablespoon mint, chopped
- 1 tablespoon Italian parsley, chopped

Instructions

1. Marinate the lamb chops for around 30 minutes in a baggie with 1/4 - 1/3 cup of the mint sauce.
2. Remove the raw lamb from the marinade and discard the remaining sauce.
3. Preheat your pellet grill to 450°F and season your lamb chops with Greek Freak seasoning before placing them on the grill.
4. Cook for 3-4 minutes each side on each side, then set aside to rest.

Nutrition:
Calories: 362
Fat: 26.07g
Carbs: 17.4g
Protein: 12.1g

110. Beer Can Chicken

Prep Time 10 Mins

Cook Time 90 Mins

Total Time 100 Mins

Ingredients

- 1 4-5 pound chicken
- 1/2 cup dry chicken rub
- 1 can beer

Instructions

1. Preheat your grill for 4-5 minutes on "smoke" with the lid open. Preheat the oven to high, then shut the lid and cook for another 10-15 minutes, or until it reaches 450 degrees.

2. Pour half of the beer into your mouth, then bury the open can in the chicken where the sun doesn't shine. Push it down there and prop it up with the legs like a tripod.

3. Cook until the internal temperature reaches 165 degrees.

4. Remove the chicken from the grill with care and set aside to rest for 15 minutes. Slice and serve!

Nutrition:
Calories: 882
Fat:14.07g
Carbs: 17.4g
Protein: 4.1g
Fiber: 5.1g

111. Berbere Chicken Wings

Grilled Berbere Chicken Wings are super flavorful, easy to make, and coated in the most flavorful coconut sauce. You're going to love it! You've got to try it!

Prep Time 10 Minutes

Cook Time 45 Minutes

Total Time 55 Minutes

Ingredients

- 1 pound of chicken wings
- Salt
- 2 tablespoons berbere seasoning
- 1/2 teaspoon black pepper

Sauce

- 1 teaspoon salt
- 1 tablespoon sugar
- 1 small onion
- 1 head broccoli
- 1 can coconut milk

- 3 tablespoons berbere seasoning

Garnish
- Cilantro

Instructions

1. Preheat your pellet grill to 350 degrees Fahrenheit, as directed by the manufacturer.
2. Toss the wings in the berbere, salt, and pepper. Place on a grill that has been preheated.
3. Grill the wings for 30-45 minutes, or until they reach an internal temperature of at least 165°F.
4. While the wings are cooking, make the sauce by whisking together all of the ingredients in a small saucepan and bringing to a boil while stirring. Take the pan off the heat and set it aside.
5. Toss the wings in the sauce after they're done and serve over rice with chopped cilantro on top.

Nutrition:
Calories: 399
Fat: 33.07g
Carbs: 19.4g
Protein: 4.1g
Fiber: 5.1g

112. Chicken Thighs

Prep time: 10 mins

Cook time: 1 hr

Total time: 1 hr 10 mins

Ingredients

- 8 chicken thighs
- 1/2 cup bbq rub
- 1/2 cup canola oil

Instructions

1. Preheat your pellet grill to 180-200°F, and if you have one, use the smoke setting.
2. Rub the chicken thighs liberally with the homemade rub or a dry rub of your choice.
3. Place the chicken skin-side up on the grill and smoke for 30-120 minutes. The flavor will become more powerful the longer you smoke, so adjust appropriately.

4. After the smoke period is over, preheat the grill to 325° and insert a temperature probe to monitor the temperature.
5. Cook the chicken until it reaches a temperature of 165°F on the inside. Remove the steaks from the grill.
6. Heat a cast-iron pan with approximately 1/4 inch of oil in the bottom on the burner.
7. Cook the chicken thighs in the pan skin-side down for 3-4 minutes, or until the skin is crispy.

Nutrition:
Calories: 283
Fat: 22.07g
Carbs: 17.4g
Protein: 4.1g
Fiber: 5.1g

113. Grilled Broccoli Chicken Divan

This cheesy broccoli chicken divan is super simple, baked on the pellet grill, and is a family favorite!

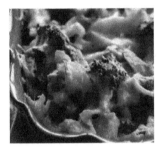

Prep time 10 minutes

Cook time 18 minutes

Total time 28 minutes

Ingredients

- One pound of egg noodles
- 2 big cubed chicken breasts
- A pinch of salt and pepper
- 1 tablespoon of oil
- 4 cups florets (broccoli)
- 1 can cream of chicken soup, condensed
-
- 1 can cream of mushroom soup, condensed
- A half teaspoon of onion powder

- A half-teaspoon of garlic powder
- A quarter teaspoon of black pepper
- 1 quart half-and-half
- 1 quart of chicken broth
- A half-cup of sour cream
- A quarter cup of white wine
- 4 cups shredded cheddar cheese
- Ritz crackers, crushed (optional).

Instructions

1. Preheat your pellet grill to 325°F, as directed by the manufacturer.
2. Bring a large pot of salted water to a boil, and half-cook the egg noodles while you finish the rest of the ingredients. Drain after half-cooking and rinse in hot water before setting aside.
3. Season the chicken with salt and pepper to taste. Cook until the exterior of the chicken is no longer pink in a nonstick pan over medium-high heat. It doesn't need to be entirely done at this stage because the grill/oven will continue cooking it. Remove the chicken from the pan, but save any liquids in the pan to add to the sauce.

4. Half-cook the broccoli florets by steaming them. You don't want them to be entirely raw, but you do want them to be crunchy. Remove the chicken and set it aside.

5. Whisk together the condensed soups, onion powder, garlic powder, pepper, half-and-half, chicken broth, sour cream, and white wine in a large mixing bowl. Mix until everything is well mixed, then add any pan drippings from the chicken.

6. Combine the noodles, chicken, broccoli, sauce, and half of the cheese in a 10x13 casserole pan that can be baked or grilled. I like enameled cast iron pans for this, but ordinary cast iron pans would suffice. Just be sure to coat it with cooking spray liberally.

7. If preferred, top with the remaining cheese and crumbled ritz (not seen).

8. Preheat oven to 325°F/350°F and bake for 45-60 minutes. Check to see if the chicken is fully done. If the top starts to brown too much, cover it with foil.

9. Serve immediately

Nutrition:
Calories: 548
Fat: 34.07g
Carbs: 17.4g
Protein: 16.1g
Fiber: 5.1g

114. Pellet Grill Jerk Chicken Thighs

The chicken thighs are marinated overnight in a homemade jerk marinade before being cooked on the pellet grill. It's flavorful, worth the effort, and all-around excellent.

Prep time 20 minutes

Cook time 1 hour

Total time 1 hour 20 minutes

Ingredients
- 6 skin-on chicken thighs
- 1/2 cup frying oil

Marinade for jerk chicken
- 4 garlic cloves
- 3 tblsp. extra virgin olive oil
- 2 tblsp soy sauce
- a quarter teaspoon of salt
- 1 1/2 teaspoon freshly ground black pepper

- 1 teaspoon all-spice powder
- a half teaspoon of cinnamon
- 1/2 teaspoon nutmeg powder
- 4-5 habanero/scotch bonnet peppers
- 1 tablespoon lime juice
- 1 tbsp. granulated brown sugar
- 1 medium onion
- 1 tablespoon green onion, chopped
- 2 teaspoon thyme leaves, fresh

Instructions

1. In a blender, mix all of the marinade ingredients and blend until smooth. In a large gallon-sized baggie, pour over the chicken thighs and chill overnight.
2. Preheat your grill to 375° (plus or minus 25°) and put the chicken skin side down on the grates. Allow 20-25 minutes for the chicken to cook, then gently turn and continue grilling until the internal temperature reaches 165°.
3. Take the steaks off the grill and inside the house.
4. Heat an oil-coated nonstick skillet over medium to medium-high heat. CAREFULLY place a couple of the chicken thighs, skin-side down, in the shimmering oil.
5. Remove the skin to a dish after 2-3 minutes of crisping.

6. Continue until all of the thighs' skin is crisped. Serve with rice and vegetables as a side dish.

Nutrition:
Calories: 619
Fat: 44.07g
Carbs: 17.4g
Protein: 24.1g
Fiber: 5.1g

115. CAJUN TURKEY CLUB

Preparation Time: 15 minutes

Cooking Time: 30 minutes

Servings: 2

Ingredients

- 1 3lbs Turkey Breast
- 1 stick Butter (melted)
- 8oz Chicken Broth
- 1 tbsp. Killer Hogs Chili Sauce
- Malcom's King Craw Seasoning, 1/4 cup
- Thick Sliced Bacon in 8 Pieces
- 1 pound of brown sugar
- Green Leaf Lettuce, 1 head
- Tomato (one) (sliced).
- 6 Toasted Bread Slicings
- Follow the instructions for 1/2 cup Cajun Mayo.
- Mayonnaise (Cajun).

- 1 cup mayonnaise
- Dijon Mustard, 1 tblsp.
- 1 Tablespoon Sweet Fire Pickles from Killer Hogs (chopped).
- Hourseradish, 1 tblsp.
- Malcom's King Craw Seasoning, 1/2 tsp
- 1 tablespoon of Killer Hogs Hot Sauce
- Season with a pinch of salt and black pepper to taste.

Instructions:

1. Preheat a pellet smoker to 325°F for indirect cooking with your choice wood pellets (I used a combination of Hickory, Maple, & Cherry)
2. In a mixing dish, combine the melted butter, chicken stock, spicy sauce, and 1 teaspoon Cajun Seasoning. Inject the mixture into the turkey breast evenly spaced injection holes.
3. Season the exterior of the turkey breast with Malcom's King Craw Seasoning and a spritz of vegetable frying spray.
4. Cook the turkey breast on the smoker until it reaches 165 degrees on the inside. To keep track of the temperature during the cooking process, use an instant read thermometer.

5. Combine brown sugar and 1 teaspoon King Craw in a small bowl. Cover the bacon with the sugar mixture on a frying rack (spray the rack with cooking spray to prevent sticking).
6. Cook the bacon for 12-15 minutes, or until it is brown. Flip the bacon halfway through to ensure even cooking.
7. Toasted bread, thinly sliced tomatoes, and rinsed/ dried lettuce leaves
8. Remove the turkey breast from the grill when it reaches 165 degrees and let it rest for 15 minutes. Remove the netting from the breasts and slice them thinly.
9. To create the sandwich, spread Cajun Mayo* over the bread and layer turkey breast, lettuce, tomato, and bacon strips on top. Repeat the process with another slice of bread. Slice the sandwich in half and serve with the top piece of bread spread with additional Cajun mayo.

Nutrition:

Protein 23g

Fat 10g

Calories 180g

Carbs 0g

116. HOT TURKEY SANDWICH

Preparation Time: 10 minutes

Cooking Time: 1 hr

Servings: 2

Ingredients:

- 8 slices bread, sliced
- 1 cup gravy, prepared
- 2 cups leftover turkey, shredded

Instructions:

1. Switch on your grill's flame broiler. Start the grill on "smoke," leaving the lid open, until a fire forms in the burn pot (3-7 minutes). Preheat the oven to 400°f.

2. Place the bbq grill mat on the grates of your preheated grill and thinly distribute the shredded turkey around the mat for about 10 minutes to reheat.
3. Make or re-heat the gravy. When the turkey has been reheated and the bread has been toasted, you can have the gravy warmed and ready.
4. To toast each slice of bread, place it over the flame broiler.
5. When all of your ingredients are hot, scoop 1/2 cup shredded turkey onto a piece of toasted bread, generously cover with gravy, and top with another piece of toasted bread.

Nutrition:

Protein 23g

Fat 10g

Calories 180g

Carbs 0g

117. TURKEY KOFTA KEBABS

Preparation Time: 25 minutes

Cooking Time: 20 minutes

Servings: 2

Ingredients

- 1 lb ground turkey
- ¼ cup minced onion
- 2 cloves garlic, minced
- 1 bundle fresh parsley or herbs (I used basil and oregano).
- 2 tblsp almond flour (if you are not eating Paleo you can do bread crumbs).
- ¼ tsp allspice
- ¼ tsp coriander
- ¼ teaspoon smoked paprika (normal paprika would suffice if you can't locate smoked paprika).
- ¼ tablespoons chipotle powder (or chili powder).
- to taste, sea salt and freshly ground pepper

- Soak bamboo skewers ahead of time.

Instructions:

1. Combine all of the ingredients in a mixing bowl and chill for at least 10 minutes to let the flavors to blend.
2. After that, pour into heaping tablespoon parts (about 1/8th cup size) and roll into little turkey logs or oval shapes.
3. As I was rolling them, I jokingly referred to them as "turkey turds."
4. Fill each skewer with two ovals. (Leave the skewers in the water for at least 30 minutes before using).
5. Preheat the grill to 350 degrees Fahrenheit, medium heat.
6. So the turkey doesn't stick, oil the grill grates. Grill the meatballs for 3-4 minutes on each side, or until they have lovely grill marks. When an internal thermometer reads 165°F, the kebabs are ready to be removed off the grill.

Nutrition:

Protein 49g

Fat   32 g

Calories 173 g

Carbs 0g

118. TURKEY ON THE GRILL

Preparation Time: 15 minutes

Cooking Time: 30 minutes

Servings: 2

Ingredients

1 stick butter, softened

1 large bunch rosemary, tarragon and thyme- leaves removed off the stems

Juice of 2 lemons

Sea salt, large pinch, large pinch

Fresh ground pepper, large pinch

1 turkey, spatchcocked with back bone removed (save yourself the trouble and have your butcher do this!)

Instructions:

1. If brining, brine for at least 24 hours and then pat dry.

2. With a stick blender, combine the butter, herbs, salt, pepper, and lemon juice in a small mixing dish.

3. After that, spread the turkey out on a large chopping board or dish. To place the butter, slide your fingers beneath the skin and detach it from the flesh. Slather butter below the breasts, legs, and anyplace else you can get butter under the skin to keep it wet (this is the unpleasant part, but the results are well worth it!).

4. Preheat your grill to 350 degrees Fahrenheit. Lightly oil the grill grates and, after they're nice and hot, cook the turkey for 8-10 minutes on each side, or until attractive char marks appear.

5. Remove the turkey from the oven and lay it on a grill-safe pan so that the fluids from the bird may be used to make gravy. ** Remove the pan from the oven and place it directly on the grill for the remaining 20 minutes to achieve char marks and crispy edges.

6. Return the turkey to the oven and cook until an internal thermometer, such as the ThermaPen or ChefAlarm, registers 170 degrees. This might take anywhere from 2 to 3 hours, depending on the size of the turkey. It took 2.5 hours to cook a smaller bird that weighed around 10 pounds.

Nutrition:

Protein 69g

Fat   25g

Calories 97g

Carbs 0g

119. BIG GREEN EGG BEER CAN TURKEY

Prep Time: 5 Minutes

Cook Time: 1hrs 15min

Total Time: 2hours 20 Min

Serving: 5

Ingredients

- 1 medium sized turkey
- 2 sticks of butter
- A big bouquet of herbs, such as rosemary, thyme, and sage.
- 2 tbsp. kosher salt
- 2 tbsp. freshly ground black pepper
- 2 oranges, one for filling the cavities and the other for zesting the compound butter
- 1 can of beer

EQUIPMENT YOU'LL NEED

- A meat thermometer or a smoker controller.

- A foil pan to set the turkey on so that any drippings may be caught.
- A plate setter is a person who sets the plates on the table.
- You'll need an immersion blender.

INSTRUCTIONS:

COMPOUND BUTTER

1. In a mixing dish, combine the butter sticks, grated orange zest, and herbs. To produce a compound butter, mix all of the ingredients in an immersion blender.
2. Take your compound butter and rub it into the skin's nooks and crannies as thoroughly as possible. This will infuse the bird with the herbiness and citrus flavor of the butter, while also keeping everything wet so it doesn't dry out.
3. Get the butter all over the place, and then put it on our sitting turkey.

BEER

You can't have beer can turkey unless you have beer! I'm using a seasonal pumpkin spice beer, which is ideal if you're making this around Thanksgiving. You may use anything you want since you'll be drinking the rest of it while you're cooking the turkey!

Then you'll pour this over your sitting turkey. The beer is responsible for keeping your turkey moist. We're essentially boiling this bird with beer.

TEMPERATURE

1. I'm utilizing the pit Boss, which is a pretty fantastic tool. It will regulate the temperature of my smoker, allowing me to do other things while my turkey cooks. It will also alert me when my turkey reaches a temperature of 165 degrees Fahrenheit on the inside. It's essentially the same as setting my smoker on autopilot so I can go handle my side dishes and other things while this chicken cooks.

Nutrition:

Protein 43g

Fat 10g

Calories 192g

Carbs 0g

120. LEMON SAGE SPATCHCOCKED TURKEY

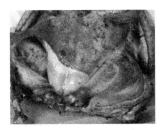

Prep Time: 20 Minutes

Cook Time: 45min

Serving: 5

Ingredients

- 1 stick butter, softened
- 1 large bunch fresh sage
- juice of 2 lemons
- sea salt, large pinch, large pinch
- fresh ground pepper, large pinch
- 1 organic young turkey, spatch cocked with backbone removed (save yourself the trouble and have your butcher do this!)

Instructions:

1. If brining, brine for at least 24 hours and then pat dry. (For a terrific all-purpose brine recipe, see the notes below.)

2. Using an immersion blender, combine the butter, herbs, salt, pepper, and lemon juice in a small mixing dish.
3. After that, spread the turkey out on a large chopping board or dish. To place the butter, slide your fingers beneath the skin and detach it from the flesh. Spread butter beneath the breasts, legs, and anyplace else you can get butter under the skin to keep it wet (this is the least enjoyable part, but the results are worth it!).
4. Preheat your grill to 350 degrees and divide it into two zones: direct and indirect. Grill the turkey on the indirect side, turning halfway through, until the internal temperature of the breast reaches 160 degrees. Depending on the size of your turkey, this might take up to two hours.
5. Finish the turkey on the direct side to get grill marks and crisp the skin, turning midway through, until an internal temperature thermometer reads 170 degrees; this will take 10-20 minutes, depending on the size of the bird.
6. Remove the turkey from the grill and tent it with foil for 10 minutes to absorb the juices. When you serve this with your favorite sides, you will be astounded by the luscious results!

Nutrition:

Protein 23g

Fat 10g

Calories 180g

121. CHICKEN THIGHS WITH GLAZED DELICATA SQUASH

Prep Time: 20 Minutes

Cook Time: 30 min

Serving: 5

Ingredients

- 1 18 X 12″ (half) sheet pan
- Boneless chicken thighs, 1 pound
- smoked paprika, 2 tbsp
- 1 teaspoon of salt (such as maldon, French grey, smoked, etc).
- 1 tbsp pepper, freshly ground
- ¾ lb delicate squash
- 1/2 lb turnips
- ½ tsp dried thyme OR a few sprigs of fresh thyme, leaves trimmed from stems
- 2 tbsp maple syrup

Instructions:

1. Before slicing the vegetables, give them a good rinse. Slice the turnips and delicate squash on a mandolin with the widest slice setting, about 1/4″ thick. It's critical to use a mandolin to ensure that the vegetables are thinly and consistently cut.

2. Preheat your pellet smoker to 350 degrees Fahrenheit on the smoking setting. In other words, the vents are designed to provide maximum ventilation.

3. Using parchment or foil, line a 12″ X 18″ sheet pan (parchment is better for the environment).

4. Place the chicken on one side of the pan and the squash and turnips on the other. Smoked paprika should be sprinkled over the chicken.

5. Season all of the ingredients with salt, pepper, and thyme. Drizzle the maple syrup over the squash.

6. Preheat the oven to 350°F and smoke the sheet pan meal for 30 minutes, or until the chicken reaches an internal temperature of 170°F. A Thermapen internal read thermometer is recommended.

7. Serve right away—that it's simple!

Nutrition:

Protein 63g

Fat 10g

Calories 210g

Carbs 0g

122. CILANTRO & GARLIC GRILLED CHICKEN WINGS

Prep Time: 15 Minutes

Cook Time: 35min

Serving: 5

Ingredients

- 1–2 tablespoon olive oil
- 3 stalks lemongrass OR 3 tablespoons lemon or lime zest (remove the outer layers of the lemongrass and chop up before putting into the food processor).
- 1 cup sprigs cilantro
- 8 peeled garlic cloves
- 1/2 teaspoon turmeric
- 1/2 teaspoon sea salt
- 1/2 teaspoon pepper (or to taste).
- 10–12 chicken wings (around 1.5 pounds) (if making two pounds go ahead and double ingredients for marinade).

Instructions:

1. The method of making spice paste!

2. Combine the olive oil, lemongrass/or zest, cilantro, garlic, turmeric, sea salt, and pepper in a food processor until well mixed; you want to make a spice "paste." Next, set aside about 2 tablespoons of the marinade to top the fish with before serving. Marinate the chicken wings for 30 minutes before cooking.

3. Preheat your grill to 350°F with a medium direct heat. I used my Green Mountain Grill Pellet Smoker, which I set at 375°F with the smoker holes open. Grill the wings for 15-18 minutes, turning halfway, or until an internal temperature of 170 degrees is reached with an internal read thermometer.

4. Pull the wings off and sprinkle with the leftover marinade once they've reached 170 degrees (I recommend using an internal read thermometer such as the thermapen to verify internal temp). Prepare yourself for an out-of-this-world taste combo! Enjoy!

Nutrition:

Protein 38g

Fat 10g

Calories 170g

123. PINEAPPLE GINGER GRILLED CHICKEN

Prep Time: 10 minutes + marinate time

Cook Time: 30 minutes

Total Time: 40 minutes

Ingredients

- 8 – 10 skinless chicken thighs
- 2 garlic cloves, minced or chopped
- 3 tsp ginger, grated or minced
- Pineapple juice, 1 cup
- 1.5 cups soy sauce (I use a low-sodium kind).
- Half cup of chopped cilantro
- Half cup of chopped mint
- Half cup of chopped basil

Instructions

1. Combine all of the ingredients in a big gallon bag. Give it a good shake to properly cover the chicken thighs. Refrigerate for at least an hour, preferably overnight, to marinate. Preheat your grill to 350 degrees (we use charcoal). Place the thighs, skin side up, on an indirect heat source. I let them cook for about 10-15 minutes before covering them with the vents open. After another 25 minutes, flip them over and cover them. Bring them to direct heat once they've reached an internal temperature of at least 165°F so they can obtain a good char. Allow for at least 10 minutes of rest before serving.

Nutrition:

Protein 36g

Fat 10g

Calories 189g

Carbs 0g

124. KATHY PULLIN'S TURKEY LASAGNA WONTON CUPS

Prep Time: 15 min

Cook Time: 45 min

Total Time: 1 hour

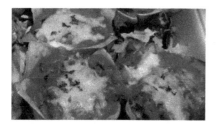

Ingredients

- 1 pound of ground turkey
- 6 ounces of diced pancetta
- 1/4 cup of diced onion
- 1/2 teaspoon Italian seasoning – pick your favorite
- 1/2 teaspoon of basil flakes
- 1/2 teaspoon parsley flakes
- 1 clove of garlic
- 8 ounces of ricotta cheese
- 8 ounces of shredded mozzarella
- 8 ounces of shredded Italian cheese
- 2 cups of marinara
- Salt and pepper
- Lots of wonton wrappers

Instructions:

1. Gather your ground turkey, pancetta, and onion first. Once you've gathered all of your ingredients, place them in a cast iron pan and cook them over hot coals until the turkey is well browned.

2. Once the turkey has begun to tan, mince the garlic clove and combine it with the Italian seasoning, 1/4 teaspoon basil, and 1/4 teaspoon parsley in a pan. When it's done simmering, season with a little of salt and pepper.

3. Is it a lovely, brown turkey? Toss everything into the container and set it aside.

4. This is when things start to become corny. Remove all of the ricotta, 6 ounces of mozzarella, and another 6 ounces of shredded Italian cheese from the fridge. In a separate bowl, combine all of the cheese with the remaining basil and parsley.

5. Place wonton wrappers in the center of each cupcake holder after greasing your preferred cupcake pan.

6. Scoop out a spoonful of the meat mixture and place it on the wonton wrapper, followed by a teaspoon of the cheese mixture. Do you have any extra space? That's on purpose. Add another spoonful of meat mixture and shredded cheese on top. (Repeat)

7. It's time to turn up the heat. Set your timer for 20 minutes and bake all of these savory wontons over hot coals at 350 degrees.

Nutrition:

Protein 39g

Fat 10g

Calories190g

Carbs 0g

125. ROSEMARY TURKEY BRINE RECIPE

Preparation Time: 15 minutes

Cooking Time: 30 minutes

Servings: 2

Ingredients

- 2 quarts + 4 cups Water
- 2 cups sea salt
- 1 ½ cup sugar
- 1 large orange, sliced
- 8 sprigs Rosemary
- 4 tbsp Peppercorns
- 4 Bay leaves
- Make the Rosemary Lemon Grilled Spatchcocked Turkey dish that follows with this recipe.

Instructions:

1. In a large 12-quart stock pot, combine all of the ingredients and bring to a low boil until the sugar and salt have dissolved. Submerge your turkey in the saucepan after the mixture has cooled. If your turkey won't fit in the cooler, I recommend using a trashbag-lined cooler to keep the bird and brine solution apart from the ice.

Nutrition:

Protein 36g

Fat 10g

Calories 126g

Carbs 0g

126. GRILLED ROSEMARY LEMON SPATCHCOCKED TURKEY

Preparation Time: 10 minutes

Cooking Time: 50 minutes

Servings: 2

Ingredients

- 1 13-pound turkey, spatchcocked (backbone removed) — if your turkey is larger, double the compound butter recipe.
- pound butter (room temperature).
- 2 lemons, zest
- 1 tablespoon sea salt
- 6 rosemary sprigs, stems removed

Instructions:

1. Overnight brine the turkey. The recipe for turkey brine may be found here. Remove the backbone from the turkey if it hasn't already been done (see Instructions:s in blog article; save yourself some time and have your butcher do it for you!).

2. With a stick blender, combine the butter, lemon zest, rosemary, and salt until a consistent consistency is achieved and all of the rosemary needles have been diced up.

3. Separate the skin from the meat of the turkey with your finger to create a pocket in which to insert the butter behind the skin. Gently work the butter into as many areas as possible underneath the skin of the bird. Repeat with the exterior of the bird, slathering it with butter as well.

4. On your grill, create direct and indirect zones with temperatures ranging from 375 to 400 degrees. If desired, add wood chips; cherry, maple, oak, and apple are all excellent choices for turkey. Remember, until the very end, you'll be smoking on the grill over indirect heat. Cook until an internal read thermometer reaches 160 degrees on indirect heat with the breast facing up. When the temperature reaches that point, move the turkey to the direct side of the grill and cook until the internal temperature of the breast reaches 165 degrees. Keep in mind that once you remove the bird from the grill, it will continue to cook. Before slicing into it, tent it with foil for 10 minutes to allow the fluids to disperse.

Nutrition:

Protein 39g

Fat 18g

Calories 205g

Carbs 60g

127. SMOKED CHICKEN STOCK

Prep Time: 15min

Cook Time: 24-48hrs

Total Time: 59 minute

Ingredients

- 1 large carrot split and cut to short lengths
- 2 med onions quartered with skin on
- 3 stalks celery cut to short lengths
- 2 tbs apple cider vinegar
- bones from one whole chicken raw. 2-4lbs.
- 1 gallon water

Instructions:

1. Preheat your smoker to roughly 220 degrees Fahrenheit. Roast the chicken bones for 20 minutes in a single layer on a sheet pan. Allow them to cook for another 20 minutes after turning them.

2. Raise the temperature of the smoker to 380°F and cook the bones until they are a beautiful golden brown. Add another 30-40 minutes to the cooking time.

3. Place the roasted bones in a stock pot or slow cooker once they've been browned. Stir in the Apple Cider Vinegar until well combined. Allow 30 minutes for the collagen and minerals to be drawn out of the bone.

4. Allow this mixture to simmer in your slow cooker or stock pot. For the first hour, use a slotted spoon to skim the froth from the soup. This will result in a clearer broth.

5. Add your vegetables halfway through the cooking process. The veggies are added afterward to avoid them becoming harsh during the extended stew period. When I have approximately 10 hours left on the simmer time, I add mine.

6. Strain the broth into a stock pot or other heat-resistant container using a mesh strainer. Place the container in an ice and water-filled sink. It's critical to chill the soup fast to avoid the formation of dangerous microorganisms.

7. Place in the fridge overnight once it has cooled. You'll also want to skim off any fat that rises to the surface of the soup.

8. The broth can be refrigerated for up to two days or frozen for up to three months.

Nutrition:

Protein 45g

Fat 15g

Calories 160g

Carbs 80g

128. ALABAMA WHITE SAUCE CHICKEN WINGS

Prep Time: 5 min

Cook Time: 30 min

Total Time: 35 minutes

Ingredients

- 1 / 4 cup mayonnaise
- 34 cup white vinegar, distilled
- a 12 cup apple juice
- 2 tsp hourseradish, prepared
- 1 tablespoon freshly grated black pepper
- One lemon's juice and zest
- 1 teaspoon sea salt
- a pinch of cayenne pepper
- 1 teaspoon sugar
- a dash of spicy sauce
- a pinch of smoked paprika, plus more for serving

Instructions:

Sauce

1. In a pint-sized mason jar, combine all ingredients, whisk to blend, then shake to thoroughly incorporate. It may be kept in the fridge for up to two weeks.

Grilling Instructions:

2. Set your pellet smoker to 350 degrees Fahrenheit. Allow chicken wings to simmer for around 25 minutes before turning up the heat to 400 degrees to produce crispy skin. Use a thermapen or an internal read thermometer (the Green Mountain Grill comes with one and will tell you!). That's one of my favorite characteristics of this grill!) to check internal temperature - remove the wings from the grill when they achieve an internal temperature of 170°F. Before serving, season with smoked paprika and sprinkle with sauce.

Nutrition:

Protein 23g

Fat 10g

Calories 180g

SMOKING RECIPES

129. SMOKED CHICKEN STOCK

Prep Time: 15min

Cook Time: 24-48hrs

Total Time: 59 minute

Ingredients

- 1 large carrot split and cut to short lengths
- 2 med onions quartered with skin on
- 3 stalks celery cut to short lengths
- 2 tbs apple cider vinegar
- bones from one whole chicken raw. 2-4lbs.
- 1 gallon water

Instructions:

1. Preheat your smoker to roughly 220 degrees Fahrenheit. Roast the chicken bones for 20 minutes in a single layer on a sheet pan. Allow them to cook for another 20 minutes after turning them.

2. Raise the temperature of the smoker to 380°F and cook the bones until they are a beautiful golden brown. Add another 30-40 minutes to the cooking time.

3. Place the roasted bones in a stock pot or slow cooker once they've been browned. Stir in the Apple Cider Vinegar until well combined. Allow 30 minutes for the collagen and minerals to be drawn out of the bone.

4. Allow this mixture to simmer in your slow cooker or stock pot. For the first hour, use a slotted spoon to skim the froth from the soup. This will result in a clearer broth.

5. Add your vegetables halfway through the cooking process. The veggies are added afterward to avoid them becoming harsh during the extended stew period. When I have approximately 10 hours left on the simmer time, I add mine.

6. Strain the broth into a stock pot or other heat-resistant container using a mesh strainer. Place the container in an ice and water-filled sink. It's critical to chill the soup fast to avoid the formation of dangerous microorganisms.

7. Place in the fridge overnight once it has cooled. You'll also want to skim off any fat that rises to the surface of the soup.

8. The broth can be refrigerated for up to two days or frozen for up to three months.

Nutrition:

Protein 45g

Fat 15g

Calories 160g

Carbs 80g

130. SMOKED CHICKEN CHILI

Prep Time: 30 minutes

Cook Time: 2 1/2 to 3 hours

Total Time: 3 to 3 1/2 hours

Ingredients

- 1 large chicken, gizzards removed for smoking

Dry rub ingredients:

- a quarter cup brown sugar
- smoked paprika, 1/4 cup
- 2 tsp kosher salt and 2 tbsp ground pepper
- 1 tbsp. cayenne pepper
- 2 tsp garlic powder
- 2 teaspoons onion powder

Chili:

- 2 tbsp extra virgin olive oil
- 1 onion, diced
- 3 garlic cloves, finely minced

- 1 chopped green bell pepper
- 2 celery stalks, finely chopped
- 1 tablespoon cumin powder
- 1 teaspoon smoked paprika
- 1 teaspoon chili powder
- 1 tbsp chile powder from New Mexico
- 1 teaspoon dried oregano
- 1 tsp ground black pepper
- 3 minced chipotle chilis, canned in adobo sauce
- 1 (15-ounce) can washed and drained kidney beans
- 1 (15-ounce) can washed and drained black beans
- 3 cups broth (chicken)
- three cups of water
- 5 fire-roasted tomatoes, blended
- 1 smoked shredded chicken entire

Instructions:

1. In a medium-sized mixing bowl, whisk together the dry rub ingredients until thoroughly blended. Remove from the equation.

2. Remove the gizzard and trim any excess fat. Rinse the chicken and wipe it dry with paper towels after cleaning it (including the cavity). Place the chicken on a baking sheet and chill uncovered for at least 20 minutes to dry while you prepare the smoker.

3. Turn on the grill to smoke and wait 4–5 minutes for the fire to begin going. Warm the grill to 225 degrees and keep it closed for 15 minutes to preheat.

4. Take the chicken out of the fridge and massage it with 1/4 cup olive oil all over. Season the chicken well with dry rub, including the cavity, and then set it breast side down in a grate. Then smoke it for 2 1/2 to 3 hours, or until a thermometer placed into the thickest portion of the breast registers 160 degrees F.

5. Take the chicken out of the smoker, shred it, and set it aside.

TO PREPARE CHILI

1. In a large dutch oven pot, heat the oil over medium-high heat.

2. Cook for 7 minutes, or until onion is soft, after adding the first 5 ingredients.

3. Mix together the remaining ingredients. Season with salt and pepper, cover, and cook on low heat for 30 minutes, or until the sauce thickens.

4. Sliced green onions, sliced jalapeos, shredded cheese, sour cream, chopped cilantro, a dash of lime, and a side of tortilla chips are some of my favorite toppings.

Nutrition:

Protein 31g

Fat 10g

Calories 192g

Carbs 0g

131. ORANGE OREGANO MAPLE SMOKED CHICKEN THIGHS

Preparation Time: 10 minutes

Cooking Time: 20 minutes

Servings: 2

Ingredients

- (2) Maple Grill Planks – soak for 30 minutes before use
- 4 chicken thighs

Seasoning paste:

- 2 oranges, zest
- 1 oregano bunch, leaves trimmed from stems
- 2 tablespoons freshly ground black pepper (I used smoked pepper).
- 2 generous tablespoons sea salt (I used smoked sea salt).
- 2 heaping teaspoons smoked paprika (if you don't have smoked paprika, normal paprika will suffice; nevertheless, smoked paprika makes a significant difference).

- 5 tbsp extra-virgin olive oil

Instructions:

1. Preheat your grill to 350°F and divide it into two cooking zones: direct and indirect. Before utilizing your grilling planks, make sure they've been soaked for at least 30 minutes. Following that, rinse and pat dry your chicken.

2. In a small mixing dish, combine the seasoning paste components. Next, slip your finger beneath the skin of the chicken (I know, it's not enjoyable, but it will seal in all the spices and moisture!)

3. Apply the paste to all four pieces of chicken, beneath and over the skin. Place two thighs on each maple grilling board (if maple is unavailable, cherry, hickory, or other woods will suffice).

4. Cook the planks for 25-30 minutes over indirect heat on a medium/hot grill, or until an internal read thermometer (such the ThermaPen, my favorite) registers 170 degrees (a few degrees under is okay).

5. Allow it rest for 10 minutes under foil before serving with your preferred side dish.

6. It was delicious when I served it with garlic kale.

Nutrition:

Protein 23g

Fat 10g

Calories 180g

Carbs 0g

132. SMOKED SEAFOOD CEVICHE

Preparation Time: 10 minutes

Cooking Time: 4 hr

Servings: 2

Ingredients:

- 1 Pound sea scallops, shucked
- 1 Pound shrimp, peeled and deveined
- 1 Tablespoon canola oil
- 1 lime, zested and juiced
- 1 lemon juice
- 1 orange, juiced
- 1 Teaspoon garlic powder
- 1 Teaspoon onion powder
- 2 Teaspoon salt
- 1/2 Teaspoon black pepper
- 1 diced avocado
- 1/2 red onion, diced
- 1 Tablespoon cilantro, finely chopped
- 1 Pinch red pepper flakes

Instructions:

1. Combine the lobster, scallops, and canola oil in a mixing cup.

2. When you're about to roast, preheat the grill to 180°F with the lid closed for 15 minutes.
3. Place the shrimp and scallops on the grill for 45 minutes to smoke. When they're smoking, cook the rest of the ingredients and combine them in a big mixing bowl.
4. When the shrimp and scallops are done smoking, increase the heat to 325°F and cook for an extra 5 minutes to ensure they are thoroughly cooked.
5. Allow the scallops and shrimp to cool before cutting them in half widthwise and combining them with the other ingredients in the dish.
6. Refrigerate the Ceviche for at least 2-3 hours to allow the flavors to meld. Serve with corn tortilla chips.

Nutrition:

Protein 23g

Fat 10g

Calories 180g

Carbs 0g

133. SMOKED LOBSTER MAC & CHEESE

Preparation Time: 10 minutes

Cooking Time: 30 minutes

Servings: 2

Ingredients

- 1.5lb Lobster Tails
- 8oz Elbow Macaroni
- 16oz Milk
- 1 stick Unsalted Butter
- 1/4 cup All Purpose Flour
- 1 cup Sharp Cheddar Cheese grated
- 1 cup Gruyere Cheese grated
- 1 cup Mozzarella Cheese shredded
- 1/2 cup Panko Bread Crumbs
- Juice from 1/2 Lemon
- 2 teaspoons Killer Hogs AP Rub
- 1 teaspoon Killer Hogs Hot Rub

- 1/2 teaspoon Old Bay Seasoning
- 1/2 teaspoon Ground Nutmeg
- 1/2 teaspoon White Pepper

Instructions:

1. At 300 degrees, prepare a pellet smoker or any grill/smoker for indirect cooking. Place lobster tails on the grill for 15-20 minutes, or until the flesh becomes opaque.
2. Prepare elbow macaroni as directed on the packet.
3. Melt butter in a medium sauce saucepan over medium heat. Whisk together the milk and flour until smooth and a simmer is attained.
4. Combine the Gruyere, Cheddar, and Mozzarella cheeses in a mixing bowl (reserve a little of each for topping). Stir until the cheese has melted.
5. Season with salt, pepper, and lemon juice. Keep heated until you're ready to mix the ingredients.
6. Cut the lobster tail into bite-size pieces. In a 5qt Dutch oven, combine the macaroni, lobster, and cheese sauce. Stir to blend, then taste to see if seasoning needs to be adjusted.
7. The remaining cheese and Panko bread crumbs should be sprinkled on top.
8. Place on the smoker for 25-30 minutes at 300 degrees, or until the top is brown.

Nutrition:

Protein 43g

Fat 10g

Calories 190g

Carbs 0g

134. WHOLE SMOKED GATOR

Preparation Time: 15 minutes

Cooking Time: 30 minutes

Servings: 2

Ingredients

- Whole alligator weighing 30 lbs (dressed).
- Malcom's King Craw Cajun Seasoning, 1/4 cup
- a quarter cup of Killer Hogs Hot Rub
- 1 bottle of Killer Hogs Barbecue Sauce
- 1 bottle Vinegar Sauce by Killer Hogs

Instructions:

1. Place the 30 pound entire gator in an empty cooler once it has been washed and dressed. Over the gator, pour the brine solution (recipe below). Depending on the size of the cooler you're using, 4 gallons should be plenty to cover the gator. Place a 20-pound bag of ice on top of the gator to keep it weighted down and cool during the brining procedure. Soak the gator in the brine for 24 hours.

2. Allow the gator to drain completely after removing it from the brine. To remove excess moisture, pat the exterior with a paper towel.

3. Split the tail muscles around the bone and trim away all the fat under and around the muscles by placing the gator backside up on the cutting board.

4. All sides of the gator should be seasoned with King Craw cajun flavor and Killer Hogs Hot BBQ Rub. Fill the hollow of the tail with the boudin cream cheese mixture (recipe below) and season the top with the same cajun and spicy rub. With a block of wood, prop the gator's jaws open (careful, the fangs are dangerous!)

5. Place the gator on a 275-degree barbeque pit and smoke it with pecan wood.

6. Cook for 4 1/2 hours or until the internal temperature of the tail reaches 165 degrees on an instant read thermometer.

7. Remove the gator from the pit and coat it with a 50/50 mixture of Killer Hogs BBQ sauce and Killer Hogs Vinegar sauce on the exterior.

Optional

1. I smoked a full chicken for 2 hours at 325 degrees on a pellet barbecue as a garnish. Remove the block of wood from the gator's mouth and place the chicken inside.
2. Caramelize the outside of the gator with a propane torch (don't do this at home unless you've worked with a torch before!!)
3. Steamed shrimp, corn on the cob, potatoes, and smoked sausage should be served alongside the gator (this was my touch for the people that might not like gator)

To serve:

1. Stuffing, tail muscles, tenderloin, leg meat, and jowls should all be removed.
2. Chop the meat into little pieces to make it easier to consume.
3. Place a small amount of the filling on a hot god bun and top with gator meat pieces.
4. Drizzle some barbecue sauce on top and enjoy!

Gator Brine Recipe

- 4 gallons water
- 4 cups sugar
- 4 cups salt
- 6oz Malcom's King Craw cajun seasoning
- 2oz cup dry Louisiana crawfish/crab boil seasoning

- 2oz Louisiana liquid crab boil

Juice from 2 lemons

- In a big boiler pot, pour one gallon of water. Sugar, salt, King Craw, dry crab boil, liquid crab boil, and lemon juice should all be added. Bring the mixture to a boil, then lower to a low heat and continue to stir frequently to dissolve the dry ingredients. Allow to cool to room temperature after removing from the heat. To expedite the process, add a few cubes of ice. In a big cooler, pour the remaining water over the gator. The brine should totally submerge the gator. Soak for at least 24 hours. A 20-pound bag of ice also helps to weigh the gator down.

Gator Stuffing Recipe

- 2 softened cream cheese blocks
- Casing removed from 1 pound of jalapeo pig boudin sausage
- 1 jar Hidden Valley Ranch Dressing
- Crumbled bacon, 8 slices
- 1 tsp. cajun seasoning (King Craw)

1. In a large mixing bowl, combine cream cheese, boudin, ranch dressing mix, bacon, and King Craw. Combine all ingredients in a large mixing bowl and chill until ready to use in the gator.

Nutrition:

Protein 23g

Fat 10g

Calories 180g

Carbs 0g

135. SMOKED BRUSSELS SPROUTS

Preparation Time: 15 minutes

Cooking Time: 30 minutes

Servings: 2

Ingredients

- 1 lb. brussels sprouts (serves approx. 4)
- 2 tbsp. olive oil
- 1/8 tsp. cracked pepper
- 1 tsp. garlic salt
- Kosher salt

Instructions:

1. Preheat your Pitboss, or Pitboss to 400°F. Wash brussels sprouts with water and snip off the base of each sprout as your Pitboss Grill warms up. Cut a little X in the bottom core of the brussels sprouts and place them in a large mixing bowl once the base has been removed. Using either flavored or ordinary olive oil, coat the sprouts.

2. To taste, season with black pepper, garlic salt, and kosher salt. Add a little additional salt to your Brussels sprouts since they need to be salty. Using nonstick cooking spray, coat your grilling rack and evenly distribute the brussels sprouts.
3. They'll go into the Pitboss for 30 minutes at 400 degrees. They'll turn up smoky, roasted, and bursting with flavor.

Nutrition:

Protein 23g

Fat 10g

Calories 180g

Carbs 0g

136. SMOKED CREAMED SPINACH

Preparation Time: 15 minutes

Cooking Time: 30 minutes

Servings: 2

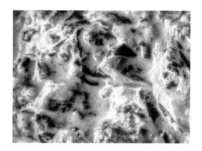

Ingredients

- 12oz bag frozen spinach
- 2 cups heavy cream
- 1/3 cup and 1 tablespoon butter
- 3 tablespoons and 1/2 teaspoon minced garlic
- 1/4 cup and minced white onion
- 9 slices shredded provolone cheese
- 3/4 cup and 2 teaspoons freshly grated Parmesan cheese
- Salt and pepper to taste

Instructions:

1. Thaw the frozen spinach, then press it against the edges of a tight mesh sieve to remove as much extra moisture as possible before setting it aside.
2. In a pan over medium heat, melt the butter. Cook, stirring often, until the garlic and onions are soft, about 5 minutes.
3. Stir in the heavy cream after adding the spinach. Stir in the provolone and parmesan cheeses until the cheeses have melted and coated the spinach. Preheat the grill to 350°F/400°F and whisk the mixture every 5 minutes until it has thickened. Season to taste with salt and pepper and serve immediately.

Nutrition:

Protein 27g

Fat 10g

Calories 368g

Carbs 0g

137. SMOKED IRISH SODA BREAD

Preparation Time: 15 minutes

Cooking Time: 30 minutes

Servings: 2

Ingredients

- ½ cup sugar
- 4 cup flour
- 2 tsp. baking powder
- 1 tsp. baking soda
- ¾ tsp. salt
- 1 cup raisins
- 1 tbsp. caraway seeds
- 2 eggs
- 1 ¼ cup buttermilk
- 1 cup sour cream

Instructions:

1. Preheat the grill to 350°F. Grease a 9-inch round cast-iron skillet or a 9-inch round baking or cake pan with cooking spray.

2. In a mixing bowl, combine flour (save 1 tablespoon), sugar, baking powder, baking soda, salt, raisins, and caraway seeds. In a small mixing bowl, whisk together the eggs, buttermilk, and sour cream. Stir in the liquid mixture just until the flour is moistened. Knead dough for 10 to 12 strokes in a bowl. It's going to be a sticky dough. Place the dough in the skillet or pan that has been prepped and press it down. Cut a 4 3/4-inch deep cut on the bread's top. Dust with the flour that was set aside.

3. Preheat the oven to 350°F and bake for an hour to an hour and a half. To test for doneness, use a toothpick. Allow to cool completely before transferring to a wire rack.

Nutrition:

Protein 23g

Fat 10g

Calories 180g

Carbs 0g

138. SMOKED ROSEMARY POTATOES

Preparation Time: 15 minutes

Cooking Time: 30 minutes

Servings: 2

Ingredients

- 4 Potatoes, Diced Large
- Olive Oil
- 3 Tbsp. Fresh Rosemary, Chopped
- 1 Tbsp. Salt
- 1 Tsp. Pepper

Instructions:

1. Preheat the Pellet Grill Pitboss to 425 degrees Fahrenheit.
2. In a mixing basin, toss the diced potatoes with the dry ingredients until well covered.

3. Place the potatoes on a tray in a uniform layer and grill for 45-60 minutes, or until done to your liking.
4. Take pleasure in your accompaniment!

Nutrition:

Protein 130g

Fat 10g

Calories 167g

Carbs 0g

139. BUTTER SMOKED CABBAGE

Preparation Time: 15 minutes

Cooking Time: 30 minutes

Servings: 2

Ingredients

- 1 cabbage
- 1 stick Kerrigold salted butter
- 2 tbsp. Pitboss AP Rub
- 2 tbsp. white balsamic vinega

Instructions:

1. One big cabbage leaf should be put aside once the cabbage has been cored.
2. Inside the core, layer butter and massage it in until it is completely filled. Make a well in the butter with your finger.
3. Fill the well with white balsamic vinegar. Place a cabbage leaf on top of the cabbage and secure it.
4. Smoke for 4 hours at 250°F. Wrap in tinfoil and smoke for 2 hours or until tender.

Nutrition:

Protein 23g

Fat 10g

Calories 180g

Carbs 0g

140. SMOKED BREAKFAST FRITTATA

Preparation Time: 20 minutes

Cooking Time: 30 minutes

Servings: 2

Ingredients

- 8oz baby spinach
- ¾ cup Portobello mushrooms
- 4 green onions
- ½ red bell pepper
- 8 eggs
- ¼ cup whole milk/heavy cream
- ½ cup shredded cheese
- 1/3 cup goat cheese
- 1 tbsp. Pitboss AP Rub

Instructions:

1. Fill a bowl halfway with spinach and sprinkle with oil or butter. Add the mushrooms once the mixture has been thoroughly broken down. Green onion, red bell pepper, and any other desired ingredients should be diced and added to the spinach-mushroom mixture.

2. Combine eggs, full milk/heavy cream, and Pitboss AP Rub in a separate bowl. Whisk until everything is fully combined.

3. Next, cover the bottom of a cast iron skillet with a thin coating of olive oil. Pour in the egg mixture and stir in the spinach. Once all of the ingredients are uniformly dispersed in the skillet, take goat cheese balls and equally distribute them throughout.

4. Preheat your Pitboss Grill to 375 degrees and cook the pan for 45 minutes. Sprinkle shredded cheese over the frittata just before serving. Remove off the grill and savor this morning's delicacy!

Nutrition:

Protein 23g

Fat 10g

Calories 180g

Carbs 0g

141. SMOKED SERRANO GUACAMOLE

Preparation Time: 15 minutes

Cooking Time: 30 minutes

Servings: 2

Ingredients

- 4 Serrano Peppers, Sliced Lengthwise
- 3 Ripe Avocados, Skinned & Pitted
- 1 Small Onion, Finely Diced
- 2 Tomatoes, Diced
- 1 Jalapeno, Seeds Removed and Diced
- 3 Garlic Cloves, Finely Diced
- 1 Lime, Juiced
- Half Bunch Cilantro, Freshly Chopped
- Salt to Taste

Instructions:

1. Preheat your Pitboss Grill to 225°F and cook your peppers for around 30 minutes. The idea is to flavor the pepper with smoke while not drying it off.

2. In a large mixing basin, combine the remaining prepared ingredients and stir until well combined. To add a little spice, garnish with smoked serrano peppers, and you're ready to dine. Serve with tortilla chips or on any dish that needs a touch of the south of the border. We also have a variety of salsa recipes on our website that you may use as an additional dip for the party!

Nutrition:

Protein 23g

Fat 10g

Calories 180g

Carbs 0g

142. SMOKED SAUSAGE AND POTATO SKILLET

Preparation Time: 15 minutes

Cooking Time: 30 minutes

Servings: 2

Ingredients

- Sausage links
- Small potatoes (whole)
- Celery
- Onion
- 1/2 cup broth
- Dash of Worchestershire
- 1 tbsp stone ground mustard
- Garlic salt to taste

Instructions:

1. In a cast-iron pan, add the sausage.
2. In a cast iron skillet, place the potatoes.
3. Celery and onion should be added at this point.
4. Toss in 1/2 cup stock and a pinch of Worchestershire sauce into the skillet.
5. Mix in 1 tablespoon stone ground mustard and season with garlic salt to taste.
6. Cook for 2.5 to 3 hours at 250°F.

Nutrition:

Protein 23g

Fat 10g

Calories 180g

Carbs 0g

143. SMOKED BREAD PUDDING

Preparation Time: 15 minutes

Cooking Time: 30 minutes

Servings: 2

Ingredient

BREAD PUDDING

- 8 stale donuts
- 3 eggs
- 1 cup milk
- 1 cup heavy cream
- 1/2 cup brown sugar
- 1 tsp vanilla
- 1 pinch salt

BLUEBERRY COMPOTE

- 1 pint blueberries
- 2/3 cup granulated sugar
- 1/4 cup water
- 1 lemon

OAT TOPPING

- 1 cup quick oats
- 1/2 cup brown sugar
- 1 tsp flour
- 2-3 tbsp room temperature butter

Instructions:

1. Preheat the Pitboss Grill to 350 degrees Fahrenheit.

2. Set aside your doughnuts after cutting them into 6 pieces each. In a mixing dish, whisk together the eggs, milk, cream, brown sugar, vanilla, and salt. Place the donuts in a greased 9x13 pan and pour the custard mixture over them. To ensure that the donuts are well covered and absorb the juices, press down on them.

3. Combine the oats, brown sugar, flour, and butter in a separate basin, mixing with your hands until the mixture clumps together like sand. When that's done, sprinkle it over the top of the bread pudding and grill it for 40-45 minutes, or until golden brown.

4. While the bread pudding is baking, put your blueberries in a pan and simmer them down until the juices start to flow. After that, add your sugar and water and stir thoroughly. Reduce the heat to medium-low and continue to simmer until the sauce thickens. When the mixture begins to thicken, zest your lemon and stir it into the blueberry compote, then cut your lemon in halves and squeeze the juice into the mixture. The result is a delightful, vibrant compote that complements the sweetness of the bread pudding well.

5. Around the 40-minute point, keep an eye on your bread pudding. The mixture will still wobble a little in the middle when you peel it off, but it will firm up as it cools. You may pull it out earlier if you like your bread pudding to be a little more moist, but the perfect bread pudding, in my opinion, will be a little darker with some caramelization but still juicy!

6. This is when I'd grab a pretty bowl, pour in a generous portion of bread pudding, top it with the compote, and a big scoop of vanilla bean ice cream, and watch people's faces light up. Not only is this a stunning meal, but the flavor is out of this world. It'll undoubtedly be a big hit in your house. Take a chance and you'll thank me afterwards!

7. And, as usual, don't forget to snap a photo of your creations and tag us in them! We'd love to highlight your work!

Nutrition:

Protein 23g

Fat 10g

Calories 180g

144. SMOKED CHEESECAKE WITH SMOKED CHERRY COMPOTE

Preparation Time: 15 minutes

Cooking Time: 30 minutes

Servings: 2

Ingredient

SMOKED CHERRY COMPOTE

- 5 oz pitted cherries
- 2 tbsp sugar
- 1 tbsp lemon juice
- 3 tbsp water
- 1 tbsp cornstarch

CHEESECAKE CRUST

- 1 c graham cracker crumbs
- 1/4 c melted butter
- 3 tbsp white sugar
- Pinch of salt

CHEESECAKE FILLING

- 1 pkg cream cheese
- 2 tbsp sour cream
- 2 tsp vanilla
- 1 egg
- 1/2 c white sugar
- 2 tsp lemon juice

Instructions:

1. Cheesecake with Smoked Cherry Compote
2. In a small metal pan, combine the cherries, lemon juice, and water. For 40 minutes, smoke at 240°F using Pitboss Competition mix.
3. Remove the meat from the smoker and set it aside to cool.
4. Once cool, place in a small saucepan with the smoked cherry combination and put to a low simmer.
5. Cornstarch should be added. Allow 10-15 minutes for cooling.
6. Crust for Cheesecake
7. Combine all ingredients in a medium mixing basin.
8. In the bottom of a spring form pan, place the graham crumb mixture.
9. Filling for Cheesecake
10. Preheat the smoker to 300 degrees.

11. Combine all ingredients in a medium mixing dish with a hand-held blender. Blend until the mixture is completely smooth.

12. Fill a 5-inch graham crusted pan halfway with the cheesecake mixture.

13. Smoke for about 1 1/2 hours at 300 degrees.

14. The centre of the cheesecake should be slightly jiggly but not moist.

15. Remove from heat and chill for 30 minutes in the refrigerator.

16. Add the cherry compote once it has cooled.

Nutrition:

Protein 23g

Fat 10g

Calories 180g

145. SMOKED FRUIT COBBLER

Preparation Time: 15 minutes

Cooking Time: 30 minutes

Servings: 2

Ingredients

- Four cups of fruit
- Two cups of sugar
- Cup and a half self-rising flour
- A cup and a half milk
- One stick of butter

Instructions:

1. First and foremost, we'll gather our fruit and place it in our pot, along with one cup of sugar, and bring it to a boil. Let's say 10 minutes. And then you add half a cup of water to soften things up a little bit.

2. Once it's come to a boil, stir it occasionally to make sure it's still simmering for 10 minutes. I've combined one and a half cups of flour with one cup of sugar in a mixing bowl.
3. I'll add one and a half cups of milk to this, which will be plenty for our crust. I'll put this to the side once I've mixed it and it'll be finished.
4. One stick of butter is all I have (this is gonna go in the Chimp.) Once it's melted, I'll add my crust ingredients to the baking dish, followed by the fruit with a little spoon. The fruit is added last.
5. Simply pour it in a little at a time until it's all in, then place it in the chimp for 35-40 minutes.
6. Remove the butter from the grill and stir in our crust ingredients, taking care not to splatter it because the butter is still hot. Stirring is not allowed. Toss in your fruit.
7. One at a time, spoon it in; don't worry about the crust; it will fall over the fruit. Stirring is not allowed. Once all of the fruit is in, carefully pour the juice over it and return it to the grill to cook for 35 to 45 minutes at 400 degrees.

Nutrition:

Protein 23g

Fat 10g

Calories 180g

Carbs 0g

146. SMOKED BREAKFAST CASSEROLE

Preparation Time: 15 minutes

Cooking Time: 30 minutes

Servings: 2

Ingredients

- 2lbs ground pork sausage
- 1 cup Diced Onion
- 1 cup Diced Bell Pepper (red and green mixed)
- 1 cup Sliced Mushrooms
- 10 large Eggs
- 2 cups Shredded Cheese
- 1 cup Sour Cream
- 1 Tablespoon Hot Sauce
- 1 Tablespoon Butter
- 1 Tablespoon Olive Oil
- Salt and Black Pepper to taste
- 1 package Crescent Roll Sheet Pastry

Instructions:

1. Sausage should be browned over medium heat and drained on a paper towel-lined tray.
2. Sauté veggies in butter and olive oil until soft, about 3-4 minutes.
3. Combine the sausage and veggies in a mixing bowl and set aside.
4. Crack eggs into a large mixing dish and whisk them together. Combine the cheese, sour cream, spicy sauce, and a sprinkle of salt and black pepper in a mixing bowl. To mix the ingredients, whisk them together.
5. Spread crescent roll dough on the bottom of a 9X11 inch baking sheet sprayed with cooking spray.
6. Evenly distribute the sausage and veggies throughout the dough, then top with the egg mixture. Refrigerate the dish for at least 1 hour before serving.
7. Preheat the Traeger pellet grill or any smoker to 3500 degrees Fahrenheit for cooking.
8. Cook for 1 hour on a barbecue pit, flipping the pan every 30 minutes to ensure equal grilling.

9. The casserole is done when the top is golden and the sides break away from the pan slightly. Remove the fruit from the pit and chop into serving sizes. Serve with sour cream, crumbled bacon, pico de gallo, and other toppings.

Nutrition:

Protein 23g

Fat 10g

Calories 180g

Carbs 0g

147. SMOKING STUFFED PEPPERS

Preparation Time: 15 minutes

Cooking Time: 30 minutes

Servings: 2

Ingredient

- 6 Multi colored Bell Peppers
- 1 pound Ground Beef
- 1 pound Italian Sausage
- 1 Onion diced
- 1 pint of Mushrooms diced
- 1 cup of shredded Italian blend Cheese plus extra for topping
- 1 bunch of Flat Leaf Parsley
- 4 cloves of fresh Garlic minced
- 1 cup rice (cooked by package Instructions:s)

Instructions:

1. After washing and draining the bell peppers, trim the tops with a sharp knife. Remove the peppers' stems and any seeds on the interior. Save the top ring of the peppers for the filling and throw away the stems. Set aside the onions, pepper tops, and mushrooms in diced form. In a sauté pan over medium high heat, brown the ground beef and Italian sausage. As the meat cooks, season it with Cavendar's Greek spice. When the beef combination is brown, drain it on a paper towel and leave it aside. In a small amount of olive oil, sauté the onions, pepper tops, and mushrooms for 3-5 minutes.

2. Cook for 3 minutes more, until the vegetables have softened, before adding the garlic and parsley. Season with a pinch of Greek seasoning as well.

3. In a large mixing basin, combine the meat and veggies. It's ready to shove into the peppers once you've added the shredded cheese.

4. Stuff each Pepper cavity to the top with the stuffing. This may be done ahead of time, and the peppers may be stored in the refrigerator until ready to use. The smoking procedure is straightforward. You'll need an indirect-heating smoker or grill. Preheat your smoker to 300°F and add some wood for smoke flavor.

5. Place the peppers on a wire rack or directly on the grill grate after the smoker has reached the desired temperature. Make sure the peppers are balanced during the cooking process so they don't topple over.

6. Cooking time for the stuffed peppers is roughly one hour. They should start to brown and become soft, but the pepper itself should retain some firmness. You don't want your peppers to be soggy.

7. Top the peppers with grated cheese just before they're done, at the 50-minute mark. The stuffed peppers are ready to remove from the stove and serve as soon as the cheese has melted.

Nutrition:

Protein 37g

Fat 10g

Calories 180g

Carbs 0g

FISH AND SEAFOOD RECIPES

148. LOBSTER TAIL

Preparation Time: 25 minutes

Cooking Time: 30 minutes

Servings: 2

Ingredients

- 4 Lobster Tails 8oz each
- 3 Sticks Unsalted Butter
- 4 cloves Garlic minced
- ½ cup Fresh Parsley chopped
- Juice of 1 Lemon
- 2 tablespoons Fresh Lemon Zest
- 2 teaspoons Crushed Red Pepper
- ¼ cup Olive Oil
- 1 TBS Kosher Salt
- 1 TBS Cracked Black Pepper

Instructions:

1. For indirect cooking, prepare a charcoal grill or a smoker (2 zone fire on a grill) The temperature should be 3750 degrees Fahrenheit.
2. Split the lobster tails lengthwise in half and season with salt, pepper, and olive oil.
3. Melt butter in an aluminum pan on the hot side of the grill.
4. Simmer for 5 minutes with garlic, parsley, lemon zest, lemon juice, and red pepper in butter.
5. Place lobster tails on the indirect side of the grill, flesh side down, and cook for 5-6 minutes. Brush the butter mixture on the shell side.
6. Place each tail shell side down on the grill after dipping it in the butter mixture. Brush the meat with the butter mixture once more.
7. Cook for another 4-5 minutes, or until the lobster meat has turned opaque and the shells have become brilliant pink.
8. With the remaining butter mixture, fresh parsley, and lemon wedges on the side, serve.

Nutrition:

Protein 33g

Fat 30g

Calories 230g

Carbs 0g

149. FISH TACOS

Preparation Time: 15 minutes

Cooking Time: 30 minutes

Servings: 2

Ingredients

- 2 pound Snapper Filet (any white fish can substitute).
- 2 tbsp. Mexican Style Dry Rub
- 2 tablespoons melted butter
- 2 lemons.
- 2 jalapeo peppers
- 1 bunch Cilantro, fresh
- 12 cup Crema de Cilantro Lime

Mexican Style Rub:

- You will need 3 Tablespoons of Killer Hogs AP Rub.
- 2 teaspoons chili powder
- Paprika, 2 tbsp.
- Cumin, 2 teaspoons
- 1/2 tsp Onion Granules
- Cayenne pepper, 1/4 teaspoon

- 1/4 teaspoon ground chipotle chili pepper
- Oregano, 1/4 teaspoon
- a quarter teaspoon cinnamon
- Crema de Cilantro y Lime
- 1 cup Mexican Crema
- 1 tablespoon chopped cilantro
- 1 teaspoon fresh lime juice
- 2 tablespoons coarsely chopped jalapeo
- 1 tsp zest of lime
- a pinch of Mexican seasoning

Instructions:

1. Preheat the grill to 350-3750°F or medium high heat for indirect grilling.
2. Apply vegetable cooking spray on the skin side of the snapper. Apply a generous amount of Mexican Style Rub on the flesh side.
3. Limes should be cut into tiny rounds, while jalapenos should be cut lengthwise. On the cooking grate, arrange lime slices, jalapeño slices, and cilantro sprigs. To keep the snapper filet from adhering to the grate, place it on top.
4. Cook for 10-15 minutes, or until the flesh becomes white and readily flakes with a fork.
5. Allow to cool for a few minutes after removing from the grill.

6. Warm corn tortillas on the grill grate for 30 seconds on each side to serve. Place parts of the salmon on each of the doubled tortillas. Garnish with fresh shredded cabbage, cilantro-lime crema, pickled red onion, or any toppings of your choice.

Nutrition:

Protein 35g

Fat 30g

Calories 20g

150. SHRIMP AND GRITS

Preparation Time: 20 minutes

Cooking Time: 30 minutes

Servings: 2

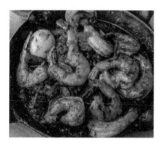

Ingredients

- 1lb Raw Gulf Shrimp Jumbo 13-15count peeled & deveined, tail on
- 1lb Andouille Smoked Sausage
- 6 slices Bacon crumbled (reserve drippings for sauce)
- 8oz Butter
- 1/3 cup Worcestershire Sauce
- ¼ cup Flat leaf Parsley chopped
- ¼ cup Green Onion (white parts) chopped
- 3–4 cloves Garlic
- 2 Lemons halved
- 2 Tablespoons Killer Hogs Hot Rub
- 16oz Chicken Broth
- 1 cup Stone Ground Yellow Corn Grits

- ¼ cup Parmesan Cheese grated fine
- ¼ cup Cream Cheese

Instructions:

1. Preheat the Big Green Egg or another grill to 3500 degrees Fahrenheit for grilling.
2. Place the Andouille Sausage on the grill and cook for about 30 minutes, rotating as required, until the internal temperature reaches 1650 degrees.
3. Bring the chicken stock to a boil over medium-high heat, then add the grits. Reduce the heat to low and cook the grits, stirring often, for 20-30 minutes or until thick. Keep heated until ready to serve by stirring in the Parmesan and cream cheese.
4. Season both sides of the shrimp with the Hot BBQ Rub.
5. Remove the sausage from the grill and cut it in half lengthwise before chopping it into tiny chunks.
6. Place the sausage and 1 tablespoon of bacon drippings in a cast iron pan on the grill. Brown sausage on all sides for 2-3 minutes.
7. Sauté for a few minutes with the garlic, parsley, and green onion. Stir in the Worcestershire sauce and the juice from 12 lemons, then slowly drizzle in the butter.

8. Grill the seasoned shrimp for 12 minutes on each side. Toss the shrimp in the iron skillet to coat them. Remove the shrimp from the grill after 1-2 minutes of cooking in the sauce.

9. To serve, spoon the grits onto a big dish or platter, then top with the shrimp and sauce. Finely sliced green onion and crumbled bacon serve as garnishes.

Nutrition:

Protein 45g

Fat 10g

Calories 210g

Carbs 10g

151. SMOKED CRAB LEGS

Preparation Time: 10 minutes

Cooking Time: 20minutes

Servings: 2

Ingredients

- 10lbs Snow Crab Legs
- 1lb Real Butter
- 2 Tablespoons Killer Hogs The BBQ Rub
- 1 Tablespoon Dried Parsley
- ½ teaspoon Crab/Shrimp Boil seasoning
- Juice from 1 lemon
- For Serving
- Drawn butter
- Lemon slices
- Cocktail sauce

Instructions:

1. Preheat the Charcoal Smoker to 2500 degrees Fahrenheit and prepare it for indirect cooking. For smoke, use 1 chunk of seasoned cherry wood.
2. In a small saucepan, melt the butter on low.
3. Stir together the BBQ Rub, the Crab/Shrimp boil seasoning, the parsley, and the lemon juice.
4. Dredge each crab leg cluster in the butter mixture using a half-size aluminum steam pan. The leftover butter mixture will be used to baste the chicken.
5. Place crab clusters on the grilling grate and smoke for 12 hours. Using the saved butter mixture as a basting agent every 10 minutes.
6. After 30 minutes of smoking, remove the crab legs from the grill. At this time, your legs should be sizzling.
7. Serve immediately with additional lemon wedges and drawn butter.

Nutrition:

Protein 36g

Fat 20g

Calories 80g

Carbs 0g

152. CHARGRILLED OYSTERS

Preparation Time: 15 minutes

Cooking Time: 30 minutes

Servings: 2

Ingredients

- 1 Dozen Raw Oysters
- 8oz Salted Butter softened
- ¼ cup Grated Pecorino Romano Cheese
- 2 Cloves Garlic minced
- 2–3 Lemon wedges
- 1 Tablespoons Italian Leaf Parsley
- 1 teaspoon Killer Hogs AP Rub

Instructions:

1. The temperature on a Big Green Egg or equivalent charcoal barbecue for direct cooking should be 475-5000 degrees Fahrenheit.
2. Allow the butter to come to room temperature before using it. Mix in the remaining ingredients after they've softened.
3. Cook for 3-4 minutes, or until the liquid in the oysters begins to bubble, directly on the barbecue grate.
4. 1 heaping spoonful of the butter mixture should be spooned onto each oyster.
5. Cook for a further 3-4 minutes, or until the tops of the oysters are lightly browned and the sides begin to curl.
6. Remove off the grill with care and serve with a squeeze of fresh lemon juice and Crystal hot sauce on top.
7. Serve with Saltine Crackers or directly from the shell.

Nutrition:

Protein 23g

Fat 10g

Calories 180g

Carbs 0g

153. SHRIMP

Preparation Time: 10minutes

Cooking Time: 50 minutes

Servings: 2

Ingredients

- 2lbs Fresh Gulf Shrimp (16-24ct)
- Killer Hogs The BBQ Rub.
- 1/2 lb Real Butter salted
- ¼ cup Worcestershire Sauce
- 1 Lemon quartered
- ¼ cup Flat Leaf Parsley chopped

Instructions:

1. 2 pieces' hickory wood for smoke flavor on a smoker or grill set for indirect cooking up to 2500 degrees.

2. Leave the tail on when peeling and deveining shrimp. (Most grocery stores and fish markets have already done this.)

3. In a microwave-safe container, melt butter, stirring often.

4. Combine butter, Worcestershire sauce, lemon juice, and parsley in a mixing bowl.
5. The BBQ Rub should be applied on both sides of the shrimp (or your favorite bbq seasoning blend)
6. Pour the butter mixture over the shrimp in an aluminum pan. On the shrimp, it should come up about a quarter of the way.
7. Close the cover on the smoker or grill and place the pan on it. Maintain a temperature of 2500 degrees Fahrenheit with mild hickory smoke.
8. After 10-15 minutes, gently stir the shrimp. Shrimp will still have a transparent appearance.
9. Shrimp are ready after a total cooking period of 25-30 minutes. Serve with crusty French bread for dipping, garnished with a squeeze of lemon juice and a dash of fresh parsley.

Nutrition:

Protein 23g

Fat 10g

Calories 180g

Carbs 0g

154. Bacon-Wrapped Shrimp

This tender Traeger bacon-wrapped shrimp are one of my favorite appetizers for the spring and summer months! Cookouts, potlucks, family gatherings, or just a regularly old day - your family will adore this flavor-packed shrimp appetizer!

Prep Time: 5 Minutes

Cook Time: 20min

Serving: 5

Ingredients

- 1 pound raw shrimp (16-20 per pound size)
- 1/2 teaspoon salt
- 1/4 teaspoon garlic powder
- 1/2 - 1 pound bacon, cut in half

Instructions

1. Make sure your Traeger is preheated to 350° before using.

2. Use paper towels to remove the shells and tails from the shrimp, and place them on a tray to dry. To get the finest results, you should be sure that the shrimp is completely dry before wrapping it with bacon.
3. Add salt and garlic powder to the shrimp and stir to distribute the seasoning.
4. To add an interesting texture, cover the skewers with pieces of bacon and then fasten them with a toothpick.
5. Spray a baking rack with cooking spray before placing it in the oven.
6. Start cooking your shrimp by cooking for 10 minutes. Then, flip the shrimp over and cook for another 10 minutes.
7. You will likely end up with overdone shrimp if you cook for more than 5 minutes with uncrisp bacon.
8. Allow to cool, then enjoy.

Nutrition:
Calories: 204
Fat: 14.07g
Carbs: 17.4g
Protein: 4.1g

155. Grilled Crab Legs

Prep Time 15 Minutes

Cook Time 30 Minutes

Ingredients

- 4-6 pounds snow crab leg clusters
- 1 cup melted butter
- 2 cloves garlic, minced
- 1/4 cup dry white wine
- 2-3 tablespoons Old Bay seasoning
- 3 tablespoons chopped fresh parsley

Instructions

1. Thaw the crab clusters in the fridge or in a basin of cold water thoroughly.
2. Preheat the grill to 375° according to the manufacturer's instructions.
3. Put the crab in a 9x13-inch cake pan or a foil grill pan.

4. Mix the ingredients for the sauce together and pour over the crab legs in the pan.
5. Close the cover and place the pan on the grill rack.
6. Cook for 10 minutes on the grill, then baste with the butter mixture and cook for another 10 minutes. Grill for a further 5-10 minutes after basting, then serve hot.

Nutrition:
Calories: 810
Fat: 38.07g
Carbs: 20.4g
Protein: 4.1g
Fiber: 9.1g

156. Dill Smoked Salmon

Fresh salmon is brined and then smoked on a wood-pellet grill with garlic dill seasoning!

Prep Time: 10 Minutes

Brine Time: 16 Hours

Cook Time: 4 Hours

Total Time: 20 Hours 10 Minutes

Ingredients

- 2 large salmon filets

Brine

- 4 cups water
- 1 cup brown sugar
- 1/3 cup kosher salt

Seasoning

- 3 tablespoons minced garlic
- 1 tablespoon chopped fresh dill

Instructions

1. Brining only works if the fish is thawed thoroughly. Use tweezers to remove the pin bones.

2. Once the sugar is dissolved, combine the brine ingredients until the bag is full. Seal the bag or cover the container, and set it in the refrigerator to marinate overnight. To brine your salmon, first clean and then thoroughly dry the salmon, and then place it in the brine and refrigerate for 16 hours.

3. Place the salmon in the liquid, let it sit for a minute, then remove and wipe dry with paper towels. Allow the solution to hang out for two to four hours, uncovered, for the pellicle to develop. IT IS VERY IMPORTANT THAT YOU FOLLOW THE INSTRUCTIONS.

4. Warm the salmon in a hot skillet with the garlic and dill.

5. After igniting the fire, you should turn your smoker to smoke so that the fire will maintain a steady heat, and lay the salmon on a cooking rack that has been coated with cooking spray.

6. Place the smoker rack on the cooking surface, and cover the cooker.

7. Allow the smoker to get over 180° F, but do not allow it to dip below 130° F.

8. Let it cool to room temperature and then wrap it well and store it in the fridge for up to a week.

Freezing and vacuum sealing are other options as well.

Nutrition:
Calories: 139
Fat: 5.07g
Carbs: 17.4g
Protein: 4.1g

157. Blackened Fish Tacos

These easy Traeger grilled blackened fish tacos are an easy and healthy way to add some more fish in your family's diet! Super flavorful and fresh.

Prep Time: 5 Minutes

Cook Time: 10 Minutes

Total Time: 15 Minutes

Ingredients

- 18 ounces fresh fish filets
- 4 tablespoons blackening seasoning
- Limes for garnish
- Shredded cabbage
- Corn tortillas

Instructions

1. Follow the proper procedure and preheat your grill to 400°F. While your cast iron pan is heating up, place it in the oven.
2. Liberally sprinkle a spice called blackening seasoning all over your fish, except on one side.
3. Gently take the pan from the grill using a pot holder, and spray well with cooking spray. To spray while it is on the grill, do not use an aerosol can. Spray cooking oil may catch fire easily
4. Return the pan to the grill and drop the fish in as soon as you do. Then, immediately place the cover on the grill and seal the lid.
5. Or until the bottom is browned and a crust has formed, cooking for 4-5 minutes on each side.
6. Using a broad spatula, carefully turn the fish only once. Cook for an additional 4-5 minutes with the lid closed.
7. Thickness is important when cooking fish fillets, therefore it's difficult to predict how long it will take. Thin filets cook more rapidly because they are thinner.
8. The inside of your fish is now opaque and flakes easily.
9. Makes a tasty meal when served with corn tortillas, limes, and a variety of taco toppings.
   Nutrition:

Calories: 104
Fat: 12.07g
Carbs: 17.4g

Protein: 18.1g

158. MOLASSES GLAZED SALMON

Preparation Time: 15 minutes

Cooking Time: 30 minutes

Servings: 2

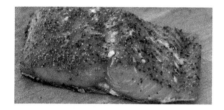

Ingredients

- 2 Sockeye Salmon filets cut into 4–6oz portions
- 8oz Molasses Glaze* recipe to follow
- ¼ cup Pastrami Rub* recipe to follow
- *Molasses Glaze*
- ¼ cup Molasses
- ¼ cup Dark Soy Sauce
- 2 Tablespoons White Cooking Wine
- red pepper flakes (pinch)
- In a small saucepan, mix together the ingredients for 2-3 minutes over medium heat, stirring occasionally. Allow to cool in a small container or basin before coating the fish.
- *Pastrami Rub*
- ¼ cup Coarse Ground Black Pepper

- 2 Tablespoons Kosher Salt
- 2 Tablespoons Turbinado Sugar (Raw Sugar)
- 1 Tablespoon Granulated Garlic
- 1 Tablespoon Coriander
- 1 teaspoon Ground Mustard
- 1 teaspoon Onion Powder
- Combine ingredients in a small bowl and store in an airtight container for up to 1 month.

Instructions:

1. Preheat the Traeger grill to 3250 degrees Fahrenheit for indirect grilling with pecan pellets for smoky taste.
2. Refrigerate each piece of salmon for at least 30 minutes after brushing it with Molasses Glaze (recipe below).
3. Season the salmon filets with pastrami seasoning and set them skin side down on the grilling grate.
4. Cook until the thickest section of each filet reaches 1350 degrees Fahrenheit.
5. Before serving, remove the salmon from the grill and let it rest for 5-10 minutes.

Nutrition:

Protein 23g

Fat 10g

Calories 180g

Carbs 0g

BAKING RECIPES

159. SMOKED MAPLE BACON CUPCAKES

Preparation Time: 15 minutes

Cooking Time: 30 minutes

Servings: 2

Ingredients

CUP CAKE MIX

- Yellow cup cake mix

BUTTERCREAM

- 4 cups powdered sugar, sifted
- 1 cup softened butter
- 1 TBSP maple flavoring
- 4 TBSP Heavy cream
- 1 pinch salt

BACON

- ½ cup Killer Hog's The BBQ Rub, or your favorite rub
- ½ cup brown sugar

Instructions:

1. Our cake and bacon were cooked on the Pitboss Grills Pitboss for this recipe. First and foremost, check sure your grill is in good working order. To avoid any "off" tastes being transmitted to your cake from leftover fat or unpleasant smoke, cook your cake first. Preheat the grill to 350 degrees.

2. We then proceeded to make our cupcakes. We made some delicious yellow cupcakes with a box cake mix. To truly enhance your box cake mix game, make some modifications instead of following the conventional recommendations on the box. Substitute water for milk, add one additional egg, and twice the amount of melted butter instead of oil. One cup milk, four eggs, and one cup melted butter were used in this recipe. You'll want to combine these ingredients until they're completely combined. Next, we spoon out even amounts of batter into our paper cupcake liners with a big ice cream scoop. They're ready to put on the grill after the cupcake tray is filled. In around 20 minutes, check them out. To prevent your cakes from sinking in the centre, try to keep the grill covered for as long as possible. Bring them inside to chill while you prepare the bacon. Reduce the temperature of your grill to 300 degrees.

3. For the bacon, follow these instructions: 12 cup Killer Hog's Barbecue Rub 12 cup sugar (brown) Apply to both sides of your bacon in an equal layer. You should avoid salty rubs because your bacon will provide all of the salt you'll need for this recipe. Our bacon was cooked on a cooling rack in a metal pan. This allows the fat to drain off the bacon, allowing the sugars to caramelize and making cleanup a breeze! Cook your bacon for 45 minutes on the smoker. You'll want to keep an eye on it and flip it around halfway through. Remove it from the oven and set it aside to cool fully.

4. To make the buttercream, combine the following ingredients. To begin, put your butter in the mixer. Then, sift in your powdered sugar. Mix until the butter and sugar are totally incorporated and the texture is creamy. After that, add your maple flavour and stir until completely combined. Add a pinch of salt after thatFinally, begin to pour in the heavy cream. Add a small amount at a time until you get the desired consistency. We find that using all 4 TBSP in this recipe results in a buttercream that is wonderfully smooth and spreadable. Make care to fully incorporate your cream and scrape down the edges! After everything has been combined, we prefer to "whip" the buttercream on high speed until it is light and fluffy.

5. It's now time to put the finishing touches on the room. Our cupcakes were iced using a 1M Wilton tip. Starting from the outside and working your way up and to the middle creates a wonderful cloud of icing, whilst starting from the center and working your way out creates a lovely "rosette" design. Finish it up with a couple slices of candied bacon.

Nutrition:

Protein 23g

Fat 10g

Calories 180g

Carbs 0g

160. SMOKED CHOCOLATE BACON PECAN PIE

Preparation Time: 15 minutes

Cooking Time: 30 minutes

Servings: 2

Ingredients

- 4 eggs
- 1 cup chopped pecans
- 1 tablespoon of vanilla
- ½ cup semi-sweet chocolate chips
- ½ cup dark corn syrup
- ½ cup light corn syrup
- ¾ cup bacon (crumbled)
- ¼ cup bourbon
- 4 tablespoons or ¼ cup of butter
- ½ cup brown sugar
- ½ cup white sugar
- 1 tablespoon cornstarch
- 1 package refrigerated pie dough

- 16 oz heavy cream
- ¾ cup white sugar
- ¼ cup bacon (finely chopped)
- 1 tablespoon vanilla

Instructions:

Pie:

1. Preheat the smoker to 350°F.

2. In a mixing dish, combine 4 tablespoons butter, 12 cup brown sugar, and 12 cup white sugar.

3. In a separate dish, whisk together 4 eggs and 1 tablespoon cornstarch; add to the mix.

4. In a large mixing bowl, combine 12 cup dark corn syrup, 12 cup light corn syrup, 14 cup bourbon, 1 cup chopped pecans, 1 cup bacon, and 1 tablespoon vanilla extract.

5. Roll out the pie dough and place it in a 9-inch pie pan.

6. Flour the dough lightly.

7. Evenly distribute 12 cup chocolate chips around the pie plate.

8. Transfer the mixture to a pie pan.

9. Smoke for 40 minutes at 350°F or until the middle is firm.

10. Allow to cool before serving with bacon whipped cream (see below).

Bacon whipped Cream:

16 oz heavy cream, 34 cup white sugar, 14 cup finely chopped bacon, and 1 tablespoon vanilla) in a high-powered blender until the liquid thickens. This recipe can be split into six tiny pie plates or custard dishes, or it can be served whole.

Nutrition:

Protein 23g

Fat 10g

Calories 180g

Carbs 0g

161. BREAKFAST CHEESEBURGER

Preparation Time: 10 minutes

Cooking Time: 1 hr

Servings: 2

Ingredients:

- 4 bacon, strip
- 6 ounce lean beef, ground
- 2 burger buns
- 2 cheese, sliced
- 2 egg
- Pepper
- Salt

Instructions:

1. Often it'll only be one of those busy days when you have to get things done. If that's the case today, pit boss grills is here to help. Start your day off right with this filling breakfast burger with bacon, egg, and cheese recipe.
2. Start the grill on "smoke," leaving the lid open, until a fire forms in the burn pot (3-7 minutes). Preheat the oven to 400°f.
3. Separate the ground beef into two small patties. Brush the grate with grease, then apply the patties and grill for 2-5 minutes per hand, or until finished, pressing down to get a decent sear.
4. Remove the burgers from the grill and assemble your sandwich. Start with the bottom bun or bread slice, followed by a slice of american cheese, bacon, hash browns, an egg over simple, and the top bun or bread slice. It's all time to eat!

Nutrition:

Protein 23g

Fat 10g

Calories 180g

Carbs 0g

162. BLUE CHEESE BISCUITS

Preparation Time: 10 minutes

Cooking Time: 1 hr

Servings: 2

Ingredients:

- 2 cups self rising flour
- 1 tablespoon baking powder
- 1 3/4 cup buttermilk
- 1 stick of unsalted butter grated
- 1 teaspoon sugar
- 4oz blue cheese crumbled
- Pinch of salt
- 3 tablespoons butter melted (optional)
- 2 teaspoon dried parsley (optional)

Instructions:

1. Preheat the grill to 425°f for indirect cooking.
2. In a mixing cup, combine the flour, baking powder, salt, and sugar.

3. Stir in the grated butter (which should be very cold). Gently fold in the blue cheese.
4. Pour in the buttermilk and stir gently until a dough emerges.
5. Roll the dough out onto a floured surface to a thickness of 1/2 inch. Cut the dough into biscuits.
6. 1 1/2 tablespoons canola oil in a cast iron skillet
7. Cook the biscuits in the skillet for 25-30 minutes, or until they are brown on top and around the sides.
8. (optional: brush the last 5 minutes of cooking with melted butter mixed with a little dry parsley.)

Nutrition:

Protein 23g

Fat 10g

Calories 180g

Carbs 0g

163. CHEESECAKE WITH SMOKED CHERRY COMPOTE

Preparation Time: 15 minutes

Cooking Time: 30 minutes

Servings: 2

Ingredient

SMOKED CHERRY COMPOTE

- 5 oz pitted cherries
- 2 tbsp sugar
- 1 tbsp lemon juice
- 3 tbsp water
- 1 tbsp cornstarch

CHEESECAKE CRUST

- 1 c graham cracker crumbs
- 1/4 c melted butter
- 3 tbsp white sugar
- Pinch of salt

CHEESECAKE FILLING

- 1 pkg cream cheese
- 2 tbsp sour cream
- 2 tsp vanilla
- 1 egg
- 1/2 c white sugar
- 2 tsp lemon juice

Instructions:

1. Cheesecake with Smoked Cherry Compote
2. In a small metal pan, combine the cherries, lemon juice, and water. For 40 minutes, smoke at 240°F using Pitboss Competition mix.
3. Remove the meat from the smoker and set it aside to cool.
4. Once cool, place in a small saucepan with the smoked cherry combination and put to a low simmer.
5. Cornstarch should be added. Allow 10-15 minutes for cooling.
6. Crust for Cheesecake
7. Combine all ingredients in a medium mixing basin.
8. In the bottom of a spring form pan, place the graham crumb mixture.
9. Filling for Cheesecake
10. Preheat the smoker to 300 degrees.
11. Combine all ingredients in a medium mixing dish with a hand-held blender. Blend until the mixture is completely smooth.
12. Fill a 5-inch graham crusted pan halfway with the cheesecake mixture.
13. Smoke for about 1 1/2 hours at 300 degrees.
14. The centre of the cheesecake should be slightly jiggly but not moist.
15. Remove from heat and chill for 30 minutes in the refrigerator.

16. Add the cherry compote once it has cooled.

Nutrition:

Protein 23g

Fat 10g

Calories 180g

Carbs 0g

164. PEANUT BUTTER COOKIES

Prep Time: 5 Minutes

Cook Time: 15min

Serving: 5

Ingredients

- 1 Egg
- 1 Cup Peanut Butter
- 1 Cup Sugar

Instructions:

1. Preheat your grill to medium-high heat and keep the lid open until the burn pot catches fire (3-7 minutes). Preheat oven to 400 degrees Fahrenheit. Whisk together all of the ingredients in a mixing basin. Bake for 15-20 minutes in your Grill with tablespoons of dough on a prepared baking sheet. Allow the cookies to cool for 5 minutes on the baking sheet before serving.

Nutrition:

Protein 23g

Fat 10g

Calories 185g

Carbs 0g

165. BLUEBERRY VANILLA CHEESECAKE

Preparation Time: 15 minutes

Cooking Time: 30 minutes

Servings: 2

Ingredient

CRUST

- 1 1/2 C. graham cracker
- 1/4 C. brown sugar
- Good pinch salt
- 1/4 C. strainer bacon fat

FILLING

- 2 tsp smoked vanilla
- 1 tbsp AP flour
- 1 pkg cream cheese
- 1/4 c sugar
- 1 egg
- 1 1/2 tbsp bourbon

BLUEBERRY TOPPING

- 3/4 c frozen blueberries
- 1/2 tsp cornstarch
- Splash of bourbon
- 1 tsp smoked vanilla
- 1 tbsp sugar
- 1 1/2 tbsp maple syrup

Instructions:

For the crust

1. In a mixing dish, combine all of the ingredients. Hand-mix until a crust or shell can be pushed into a pie pan. Fill shells with the mixture.

For the cheesecake

2. Smoke vanilla for 30 minutes at 235°F in your preferred Pitboss Grills. Combine all ingredients in a hand mixer and blend until smooth.
3. Fill tart shells halfway with the mixture.
4. Bake for 90 minutes at 235°F on your favorite Pitboss Grills smoker, or until you can touch the surface of the cheesecake without it sticking to your finger.

For the blueberry topping

1. Defrost the blueberries first, then filter off the liquid. That liquid should be saved for later. Except for the cornstarch, mix all ingredients in a saucepan.

2. On medium-low heat, cook for 5-10 minutes. Combine cornstarch and saved liquid after your mixture has begun to decrease.
3. Simmer for another 2-3 minutes with the blueberry liquid and cornstarch in the saucepan. Allow the compote to cool before applying it on the cheesecakes.

Nutrition:

Protein 23g

Fat 10g

Calories 180g

Carbs 0g

APPETIZERS AND SIDES RECIPES

166. TACOS WITH PINEAPPLE POMEGRANATE SALSA

Preparation Time: 20 minutes

Cooking Time: 30 minutes

Servings: 2

Ingredients

- an additional 1/2 cup of virgin olive oil
- Lime zest and juice.
- Half an ounce of tequila.
- An individual teaspoon of Louisiana spicy sauce.
- crushed red pepper (1 tbsp).
- Two tablespoons of kosher salt.
- 2 cloves of garlic, smashed.
- a tablespoon of minced ginger.

- Two pounds of fresh baby Gulf shrimp from Alabama's Yellow River.
- one unpeeled pineapple
- One-quarter cup of light brown sugar.
- one pomegranate
- a heaping 1/4 cup of pineapple juice
- coarsely cut cilantro leaves.
- 6 tortillas de maíz azul.
- 1 cup raw or 1 cup cooked Napa cabbage julienned

Instructions:

1. In a dish of room temperature water, soak 6 wooden skewers.

2. Heat the grill to medium.

3. In a large mixing basin, whisk together the first 8 ingredients until emulsified.

4. Peel the shrimp and remove the veins. Set aside after tossing in the marinade until well covered.

5. Cut the pineapple into 1/2 inch broad rings after removing the peel and core.

6. Brush both sides of each pineapple ring with brown sugar and cook until caramelized (2-3 minutes per side).

7. Halve the pomegranate and smash the uncut sides with a wooden spoon over a big mixing bowl until all the seeds fall out.

8. Toss the grilled pineapple with the pomegranate seeds in a large mixing dish.

9. Stir in the cilantro and pineapple juice until fully combined.

10. Arrange shrimp on skewers in an even layer and cook for 2 minutes on each side.

11. Pour the leftover marinade into a small saucepan and heat over high heat on the grill. Remove from heat once it has thickened and reduced by 1/3.

12. Heat tortillas for about 30 seconds on each side on the grill. Distribute Napa cabbage equally on tortillas to construct. Drizzle a spoonful of the reduced marinade over each chicken breast. 1 skewer of shrimp and 1 tablespoon pineapple pomegranate salsa on top of each.

Nutrition:

Protein 23g

Fat 10g

Calories 180g

Carbs 0g

167. EASY PEAR COBBLER

Preparation Time: 15 minutes

Cooking Time: 30 minutes

Servings: 2

Ingredients

- 2 Large Cans Pear Halves in Syrup
- 1 C Flour
- 1 C Whole Milk
- 1 C Sugar
- ½ Tsp. vanilla extract
- Non-Stick Spray
- 1 Stick butter
- Cranberries
- Brown Sugar

Instructions:

1. Preheat the oven to 400 degrees Fahrenheit. In a large mixing bowl, stir together flour, milk, sugar, and vanilla extract while it's cooking. Using nonstick spray or a buttery pan, oil your baking dish. In the bottom of a greased pan, melt one stick of butter, then add the Pitboss. The butter will melt after a few seconds. Remove the pan from the oven and coat the bottom with melted butter. Pour the batter into the baking pan. Place split pears in an ordered pattern on top of the batter, then top with a handful of cranberries. Brown sugar should be strewn throughout the whole pan.

2. Preheat oven to 400°F and bake for 40 minutes, or until golden brown on top. Allow 15-20 minutes to cool before serving.

Nutrition:

Protein 26g

Fat 10g

Calories 180g

Carbs 0g

168. PINEAPPLE WITH BROWN SUGAR GLAZE

Preparation Time: 15 minutes

Cooking Time: 30 minutes

Servings: 2

Ingredients

- 1 fresh pineapple
- ¾ stick butter
- ¾ C brown sugar

Instructions:

1. Slowly soften the butter in a bowl until it melts. Stir in the brown sugar immediately to mix. The sugar will take a minute or two to absorb. Preheat the Pitboss to 350 degrees Fahrenheit.

2. Peel your pineapple with a knife and cut it into 34-inch pieces. Place the slices on your Pitboss and cook for 5 to 7 minutes a side on each side. Before turning and repeating, you just want to acquire some decent color and grill marks on the first side.

3. Remove the pineapple slices from the oven and immediately coat each side with the butter mixture. Quickly serve the brown sugar pineapple.

Nutrition:

Protein 47g

Fat 10g

Calories 180g

Carbs 0g

169. BANANAS FOSTER BREAD PUDDING

Preparation Time: 20 minutes

Cooking Time: 30 minutes

Servings: 2

Ingredients

- Day-old bread
- 2 cups of milk
- 5 eggs
- 1 tsp vanilla
- butter extract
- 1/2 tsp cinnamon
- 1 oz rum
- 1/2 cup brown sugar
- 1/4 cup white sugar
- 1/2 stick butter
- 2 overripe bananas

Instructions:

1. Except for the bananas, combine all of the ingredients in a mixing bowl. We're going to beat up the eggs, combine them with the milk, add the rest of the ingredients, and then pour it over the bread and let it set till it's nice and sticky. We'll slice up the bananas into little cubes and mix them in after it's done. Then you'll place it in your butter casserole dish, or spray it with butter, or use cast iron. Then you'll preheat your grill to 350 degrees. Any pellet will do; I'm just going to use a competition mixture. Once you've poured the bread ingredients in here, all you have to do now is seal the top tightly and wait 30 minutes before checking it.

2. Check it after 30 minutes with a toothpick or a knife inserted straight in. If it comes out clean, it's done; remove it and set it aside for approximately five minutes before serving. If you're going to someone's house, this is a nice dish to bring. You can just heat it up for a second if it's precooked. I'm going to combine my eggs and milk in this bowl. I'm using five huge eggs once more. I'm going to throw a teaspoon of vanilla in there, along with a dash of butter essence and 1/2 teaspoon of cinnamon.

3. Mix everything together, then add the rum and sugar. Add 1/2 cup brown sugar, 1/4 cup white sugar, and spiced rum once everything has been beaten. Once that's all beaten up, we'll put it in a huge mixing basin and add the bread. We're going to cut up the bananas now.

4. Preheat your Pitboss Grill to 350 degrees. Half a stick of salted butter, diced, should be placed in the bottom of the pan. Even it out, then drizzle the remaining butter all over the top. After 30-40 minutes at 350 degrees, it will be ready.

5. You may create a sauce while the Bananas Foster bread puddings are cooking. Combine half a cup brown sugar, one ounce spiced rum, 1/2 a stick butter, and roughly one ounce half-and-half in a mixing bowl. Bring to a simmer, then reduce to a thicker consistency. Serve over the Bananas Foster bread pudding with ice cream.

6. Bananas Foster and bread pudding are combined in this classic Louisiana dish. I served it with a rum butter sauce and ice cream. Please, give me my spoon!

Nutrition:

Protein 48g

Fat 10g

Calories 180g

Carbs 0g

170. SAUSAGE AND POTATO SKILLET

Preparation Time: 15 minutes

Cooking Time: 30 minutes

Servings: 2

Ingredients

- Sausage links
- Small potatoes (whole)
- Celery
- Onion
- 1/2 cup broth
- Dash of Worchestershire
- 1 tbsp stone ground mustard
- Garlic salt to taste

Instructions:

7. In a cast-iron pan, add the sausage.

8. In a cast iron skillet, place the potatoes.

9. Celery and onion should be added at this point.

10. Toss in 1/2 cup stock and a pinch of Worchestershire sauce into the skillet.

11. Mix in 1 tablespoon stone ground mustard and season with garlic salt to taste.

12. Cook for 2.5 to 3 hours at 250°F.

Nutrition:

Protein 45g

Fat 18g

Calories 180g

Carbs 0g

171. ORANGE VANILLA GRILLED FRENCH TOAST

Preparation Time: 25 minutes

Cooking Time: 30 minutes

Servings: 2

Ingredients

- 8 slices day-old sourdough bread
- 4 eggs
- ¼ C milk
- ½ tsp vanilla extract
- 1 tsp ground cinnamon
- ¼ tsp ground nutmeg
- 2 TB sugar
- ¼ tsp orange zest

Instructions:

1. Whisk together all of the ingredients (excluding the bread) in a large mixing bowl until well combined.
2. Fill a small basin halfway with the egg mixture. Preheat the oven to 350 degrees Fahrenheit. Bring the bowl with you to your Pitboss. Place the first slice of bread on the pellet grill after soaking it for about 5 seconds on each side. Continue to layer pieces of bread until all of them are in place.
3. After 3 minutes, flip the first piece. You may sprinkle the done side with extra fresh cinnamon and orange zest as you flip it over.
4. The slice should be golden brown after another 2 to 3 minutes.
5. Remove the grilled bread from the Pitboss and top with melted butter and warm maple syrup to serve.

Nutrition:

Protein 23g

Fat 10g

Calories 180g

Carbs 0g

172. CITRUS HERB SALT

Preparation Time: 25 minutes

Cooking Time: 30 minutes

Servings: 2

Ingredients

- 1 C high-quality, coarse kosher salt
- 2 tsp rosemary
- 2 tsp thyme
- 2 tsp granulated garlic
- 2 Limes – zested
- 1 Lemon – zested

Instructions:

1. To begin, use a high-quality salt. Don't skimp on the salt and use iodized—you'll need a coarse salt for this.

2. Combine all herbs in a bowl (use fresh herbs for enhanced flavor). Zest the lemon and two limes in a separate dish (zesting the citrus over the salt mixture could add too much liquid to the equation).

3. Combine the zest with the salt and herbs in a zip-top bag and store.
4. Shake the bag once a day for the first several days to ensure that all of the components have a chance to be dried out by the salt.
5. This will allow the salt to absorb all of the herbs' and zest's tastes. Use as required.

Nutrition:

Protein 40g

Fat 20g

Calories 200g

Carbs 0g

173. HOMEMADE JALEPENO POPPERS

FILLING

- 12 oz Cream Cheese
- Pitboss All Purpose Rub
- Shredded Pepper Jack Cheese

POPPERS

- 16 Jalepeno
- 1 lb. Bacon

Instructions:

1. Set your Pitboss Grill to 180°F. Mix the cream cheese, pepper jack cheese, and dry rub together in a mixing bowl. Fill sliced jalapenos halfway with cheese mixture.

2. Wrap the bacon around the cheese-filled Jalapeos and fasten with a toothpick. Place the stuffed/bacon-wrapped peppers on a sheet pan or our Jalepeno Popper Rack and cook for 30 minutes on the Pitboss Grill. Cook for another 30 minutes after raising the temperature to 375 degrees.
3. Remove From The Grill And Save For Later!

Nutrition:

Protein 23g

Fat 10g

Calories 180g

Carbs 0g

174. CHOCOLATE BREAD PUDDING

Preparation Time: 10 minutes

Cooking Time: 1 hr

Servings: 2

Ingredients:

Instructions:

1. Preheat a pellet smoker or other grill/smoker to 350°f for indirect smoking.

2. Tear the french bread into small pieces and put them in a big mixing bowl. Soak the bread in 4 cups of heavy cream for 30 minutes.

3. In a medium mixing cup, combine the eggs, sugar, melted butter, and vanilla extract. Gently swirl in the box with white chocolate morsels. Season with nutmeg and salt to taste.

4. Pour the egg mixture over the soaked french bread and blend well.

5. Place the mixture on the smoker in a well-buttered 9 x 13 inch casserole bowl.

6. Cook for 1 hour, or until the bread pudding is set and the surface is brown.

7. Melt the butter in a sauce pot over medium heat. Continue to cook for 3-4 minutes, or until the alcohol has evaporated and the butter has begun to brown.

8. Heat the heavy cream until it reaches a gentle boil. Remove from heat and gradually incorporate white chocolate morsels, stirring constantly, until the whole pack has melted. Serve with a touch of salt over bread pudding.

Nutrition:
Calories: 164
Fat: 3.07g
Carbs: 17.4g
Protein: 14.1g
Fiber: 5.1g

175. FRENCH DIP SLIDERS WITH SMOKED PROVOLONE CHEESE

Preparation Time: 10 minutes

Cooking Time: 2 hr 30 minute

Servings: 2

Ingredients:

- 1 ¾ cup beef stock
- 3 lbs. Beef top round roast, boneless
- 1 tbsp olive oil
- 2 tbsp pit boss chop house steak rub
- 1 8 oz. Block of provolone cheese
- 1 red onion, sliced thinly
- ¼ cup sherry
- 1 dozen slider rolls, sliced

Instructions:

1. Make these french dip sliders with smoked provolone cheese for a crowd-pleasing party appetizer or casual dinner.

2. Set your pit boss grill to smoke mode and turn it on. Set up a gas or charcoal grill for low indirect fire.

3. Place an ice tray on the lower shelf of the smoke chamber and cover the upper shelf with cheesecloth. Place an 8-ounce block of provolone on the smoke chamber's top shelf.

4. Smoke the provolone for 2 hours, turning halfway. Check the ice tray on a regular basis to avoid raising the temperature of the chamber above 90°f.

5. Remove the cheese from the smoker and let it sit at room temperature for 20 minutes before wrapping it in cheesecloth and placing it in a sealed plastic bag. Refrigerate for at least two days before using to soften the smoke flavor.

6. Preheat your pit boss lockhart grill to 400 degrees fahrenheit. Set the barbecue to medium-high heat whether you're using a gas or charcoal grill.

7. Season the roast with pit boss chop house steak rub after rubbing it with olive oil.

8. In the bottom of a cast iron pan, place the roast on top of the red onion. Cook for 15 minutes on the grill with the pan. Reduce the heat to 325°F on the grill, then add the beef stock and sherry and continue to roast for another 30 minutes, or until the internal temperature reaches 125 to 130°F.

9. Remove the roast from the grill and set aside for 10 minutes before slicing thinly.

10. On a sheet tray, assemble sliders by putting sliced beef on the bottom half of each pan. Place the top half of the roll on top of the onion and provolone cheese. Reserve the jus in a metal gravy boat or porcelain ramekin for serving.

11. Return the rolls to the cast iron skillet and grill for 5 minutes, or before the cheese melts. Serve immediately with jus for dipping.

Nutrition:

Calories: 164.1

Saturated Fat: 0.5 g

Dietary Fiber: 6.4 g

Total Fat: 3.9 g

176. HOT DOGS

Preparation Time: 10 minutes

Cooking Time: 1 hr

Servings: 2

Ingredients:

- 1/3 lbs binder flour
- 1 tbsp black pepper
- 2 tsp coriander
- 1 3/4 cup distilled ice water, divided
- 1 tbsp garlic powder
- 7 1/2 lbs ground beef
- 5 lbs ground pork
- 2 tsp mace
- 3 1/2 oz maple cure
- 1/4 cup mustard powder
- 3 tbsp paprika
- 1/4 cup salt
- 24 - 26 mm sheep casings, pre-flushed

Instructions:

1. Nothing beats the sizzle and snap of a freshly grilled hot dog. Homemade hot dogs are simple to make with the right equipment and will fill your fridge with tasty franks to last you the whole summer.
2. Cover sheep casings in warm water in a glass bowl or measuring cup and soak for 1 hour.
3. Whisk together paprika, mustard powder, black pepper, garlic powder, coriander, mace, and salt in a shallow cup. Place aside.
4. Combine ground beef and ground pork in a big mixing bowl. By side, combine the ingredients, then apply the maple cure and 3/4 cup plus 2 tablespoons of chilled ice water. In a medium mixing dish, combine seasoning and binder flour, then add 34 cup plus 2 tablespoons water. Combine for the beef combination.
5. Hand-mix the meat mixture for 5 minutes, or until the meat is tacky. Divide the mixture into two wide mixing cups. One bowl should be refrigerated while the other bowl's mixture is stuffed.
6. Prepare the sausage stuffer and wrap a 12 inch horn in sheep casing. Place a sheet tray with a little water on it underneath the stuffer's nozzle and begin filling the casings.

7. If the casings are complete, twist them off to the desired length. Refrigerate for at least 24 hours.

8. Preheat your pit boss platinum series lockhart to 250°f. Set up a gas or charcoal grill for low, indirect fire. Pull both side handles open to raise the amount of smoke and temperature in the smoking cabinet.

9. Remove hot dogs from the smoking cabinet and serve hot with your choice toppings, or put in an ice water bath for 15 minutes, then dry at room temperature before refrigerating or freezing for later use.

Nutrition

Calories: 164.1

Saturated Fat: 0.5 g

Dietary Fiber: 6.4 g

Total Fat: 3.9 g

177. BROWN BREAD WITH MOLASSES & ROLLED OATS

Preparation Time: 10 minutes

Cooking Time: 2 hr

Servings: 2

Ingredients:

- ½ c quick oats
- 2 tbsp butter
- 1 tsp kosher salt flakes
- 1 c boiling water
- 1/3 c molasses
- 1 packet rapid rising yeast
- 1 c whole wheat flour
- 1 ½ c unbleached white flour

Instructions:

1. Combine the butter, salt, and rolled oats in a big mixing bowl.

2. Pour 1 cup of hot water over the rolled oats mixture. Combine molasses and whole wheat flour in a mixing bowl. The resulting mixture would be very moist and sticky. Allow to cool until lukewarm.

3. Stir in the contents of the quick-acting yeast packet. It should be mixed into the sticky rolled oat/flour dough.

4. Gradually stir in 1 cup of white flour. As you knead the dough, turn it out onto the counter and incorporate the remaining 1/2 cup. Knead the dough until it is smooth, elastic, and no longer sticks to the counter. This should take no more than ten minutes.

5. Shape into a big loaf or two smaller loaves and put in greased loaf pans.

6. Cover with a clean dish towel and set aside for an hour to rise (until the bulk as doubled). This can be determined by how hot your kitchen is. I left my loaves to grow in the oven when the interior oven light was switched on. The light's heat provides the ideal temperature for a one-hour growing cycle.

7. Preheat the pit boss pellet grill to 350 degrees fahrenheit.

8. Bake for 40 - 50 minutes on the lower rack of a preheated pit boss with the lid down, or until the loaf sounds hollow when pressed. Let cool on a wire rack.

Nutrition:

Protein 23g

Fat 10g

Calories 180g

Carbs 0g

VEGETARIAN RECIPES

178. SMOKED GUACAMOLE

Preparation Time: 10 minutes

Cooking Time: 1 hour

Servings: 2

Ingredients:

- 7 whole avocados, seeded and peeled
- 1 whole poblano pepper
- 4 whole ears corn, husked
- 1/4 cup chopped cilantro
- 1/4 cup chopped tomato
- 1/4 cup chopped red onion
- 2 tablespoon lime juice
- 1 teaspoon cumin
- Chile powder
- 1 tablespoon minced garlic
- Salt and pepper

Instructions:

1. When you're about to roast, preheat the pitboss to 180°f with the lid closed for 15 minutes. If available, use super smoke for the best taste.
2. Place the avocados cut-side up on the grill grate and smoke for 10 minutes.
3. Remove the avocados from the pitboss and raise the heat to 450°f.
4. Place the entire poblano pepper and corn directly on the grill grate until the pitboss has reached temperature. Cook for 15 to 20 minutes, or until a pleasant char has formed.
5. Remove the burnt corn cobs from the cobs and set aside.
6. Cover the poblano pepper with plastic wrap and set aside for 10 minutes before removing the skin. Add the pepper, diced, to the corn kernels.
7. Coarsely mash smoking avocados in a big mixing tub, leaving some chunks. Combine the peppers, corn, and remaining ingredients in a mixing bowl. To merge, mix it together.
8. It's best to get guacamole as close to serve time as possible. Seal in an airtight bag with a sheet of plastic wrap against the top of the guacamole for short-term storage. Have fun!

Nutrition:

Protein 53g

Fat 10g

Calories 180g

Carbs 0g

179. VEGETABLES WITH LEMON HERB VINAIGRETTE

Preparation Time: 10 minutes

Cooking Time: 35 minutes

Servings: 2

Ingredients:

- a quarter cup of red wine vinegar
- a two-tablespoon portion of Dijon mustard.
- 1 garlic clove, minced.
- A quarter teaspoon of kosher salt.
- The ground black pepper added was just 1/4 teaspoon.
- Lemon juice in 2 tbsp.
- a single spoonful of honey
- Use one-tablespoon (6g) of fresh dill.
- Chopped 1 teaspoon chives.
- one-half cup of olive oil
- 1 large bag of half-diced baby bells with three different colors.

- 2 carrot bunches, each containing two full bunches of carrots.
- half-filled baby squash packets
- 100-percent peeled baby white onions, around a pound.
- ½ gallon of peeled baby red onions
- 1 pound fresh snow peas.
- One entire carton of cherry tomatoes in red, white, and green.
- half of a full baby eggplant
- kosher salt.
- Black pepper

Instructions:

1. Set the temperature to high and preheat for 15 minutes before cooking. Preheat your pitboss barbecue basket on the grill.
2. For the lemon herb vinaigrette, combine the following ingredients: in a shallow mixing cup, combine red wine vinegar, dijon mustard, garlic, salt, black pepper, lemon juice, sugar, dill, and chives.
3. When whisking, slowly drizzle in the olive oil. Shake the dressing in a container with a lid until it is emulsified. Place aside.

4. Toss all vegetables in olive oil and season with salt and black pepper to taste. Cover the lid and barbecue for 5 minutes with all of the vegetables in the pitboss grill basket.

5. Open the grill and toss the vegetables. Close the cover and continue to barbecue for 5-10 minutes. Take off the grill and toss with the lemon herb vinaigrette.

6. Enable to cool to room temperature before serving hot, or refrigerate and serve cold. *cook times can differ based on the temperature set and the air temperature.

Nutrition:

Protein 23g

Fat 10g

Calories 180g

Carbs 0g

180. WINTER SUCCOTASH

Preparation Time: 10 minutes

Cooking Time: 1hour

Servings: 2

Ingredients:

- 1 small shallot, minced
- 3 tablespoon lime juice
- 1 tablespoon sherry vinegar
- 1 tablespoon dijon mustard
- 1 tablespoon honey
- 1/4 cup extra-virgin olive oil, plus more as needed
- 3 tablespoons finely chopped herbs, such as basil, mint and/or chives
- Kosher salt and freshly ground black pepper
- Succotash
- 2 cup diced butternut squash
- 1 pound mixed mushrooms, such as shiitake or king trumpet, stems trimmed

- 12 stalk asparagus, ends trimmed and sliced into 2 inch pieces
- 3 head bok choy, halved through the stem
- 2 tablespoons extra-virgin olive oil
- 2 teaspoons kosher salt

Instructions:

1. When you're about to serve, preheat the pitboss to 450°f with the lid closed for 15 minutes.
2. In a shallow mixing cup, combine the shallot, lime juice, vinegar, mustard, and honey. To make a vinaigrette, slowly whisk in 1/4 cup extra-virgin olive oil. Stir in the herbs gently, then season with salt and pepper to taste. Place aside.
3. In a big mixing bowl, combine the mushrooms and butternut squash, and in a separate mixing bowl, combine the asparagus and bok choy. 2 tbsp olive oil drizzled over the vegetables toss with a teaspoon of salt to cover, adding up to 2 teaspoons more oil if necessary.
4. Spread the butternut squash and mushrooms on one baking sheet and the asparagus and bok choy on another, using additional sheets if possible to keep the vegetables from crowding.

5. Place the tray with the butternut squash and mushrooms on the grill for 25 to 35 minutes, or until the butternut squash is partially caramelized and a fork can be inserted.
6. Cook for another 10 to 15 minutes after adding the asparagus and bok choy to the grill.
7. Place the grilled vegetables in a big mixing dish. Drizzle a few teaspoons of the vinaigrette over the vegetables and toss to cover, seasoning and vinaigrette to taste.
8. At room temperature, serve

Nutrition:

Protein 23g

Fat 10g

Calories 180g

Carbs 0g

181. ASPARAGUS & HONEY-GLAZED CARROTS

Preparation Time: 10 minutes

Cooking Time: 1 hour

Servings: 2

Ingredients:

- 1 bunch asparagus, woody ends removed
- 1-pound carrot, peeled
- 2 tablespoons olive oil
- Sea salt
- 2 tablespoon honey
- Lemon zest

Instructions:

1. Both vegetables should be washed in cold water. Drizzle olive oil over asparagus and season generously with sea salt. Drizzle honey over carrots and gently brush with sea salt.

2. When you're about to roast, preheat the pitboss to 350°f for 15 minutes with the lid closed.

3. Cook the carrots for 10-15 minutes, then add the asparagus and cook for another 15 to 20 minutes, or until they're cooked to your liking.
4. Garnish the asparagus with fresh lemon zest. Have fun!

Nutrition:

Protein 65g

Fat 10g

Calories 180g

Carbs 0g

182. SWEET POTATO KOFTAS

Preparation Time: 10 minutes

Cooking Time: 35 minutes

Servings: 2

Ingredients:

- 1 large sweet potato (or a few smaller ones), peeled and chopped
- ½ tsp onion powder
- ½ tsp coriander powder
- ½ tsp cumin powder
- ½ tsp pepper
- 1 tsp salt
- 110g (1 cup) breadcrumbs, preferably from stale bread
- A few tablespoons of vegetable oil

Instructions:

1. Begin by bringing the sweet potatoes to a boil in a medium saucepan. Boil for 20 minutes, or until the sweet potato is tender and squishy.
2. Light your grill and heat it to approximately 180°c (356°f), or until the charcoal is clean. Enable your plancha to heat up on top of the barbecue.
3. Shake off as much extra water as you can from the sweet potatoes. Mash them in a big mixing tub. At this point, combine all of the remaining ingredients and mash it together with a spoon.
4. Once all is fully combined, form a handful of sweet potato mash into a short, chunky sausage shape. Repeat with the remaining mixture, then place the sweet potato koftas on your barbecue's plancha grill – i like to use the flat side of the plancha with these koftas because it makes it easier to transform them and brown them equally all over. Cook the koftas for 5-10 minutes on either hand, or until golden brown. Keep turning them to prevent them from burning!
5. When the koftas are finished, remove them from the grill and serve them in a pita bread with lots of lettuce and vegan garlic mayonnaise.

Nutrition:

Protein 23g

Fat 10g

Calories 180g

Carbs 0g

183. ASPARAGUS WITH HOLLANDAISE SAUCE

Preparation Time: 10 minutes

Cooking Time: 25 minutes

Servings: 2

Ingredients:

- 1 bunch of fresh asparagus
- 50ml or 3 tablespoons extra virgin olive oil
- 1 clove peeled crushed garlic
- Salt and freshly ground black pepper
- For the hollandaise sauce
- 2 eggs
- 2 teaspoons white wine vinegar
- 2 teaspoons lemon juice
- 4oz or 110g unsalted butter
- Salt and pepper

Instructions:

1. Toss the asparagus in a marinade bowl with the olive oil, garlic, salt, and pepper. The marinade would not necessarily tenderize the meat; it is just a simple way to incorporate spices without having to leave it for an extended period of time.

2. Place the asparagus spears on a medium to low heat grill or hotplate and cook until the stalks are flaccid and slightly wrinkled, taking care not to burn. This usually takes 5 to 8 minutes.

3. Pour the vinegar and lemon juice into a saucepan and bring to a boil over medium heat.

4. As the saucepan heats, crack the eggs into a food processor, season with salt and pepper, and blitz for a minute. While the processor is still running, slowly drizzle in the lemon juice/vinegar mixture.

5. Return the saucepan to the heat and apply the unsalted butter after the food processor has been turned off. Switch the food processor back on and drizzle in the butter until the butter has melted and begun to bubble (but not burn).

6. You should now have a lovely thick yellow sauce that complements this grilled asparagus recipe perfectly. Serve the sauce directly to reduce the chance of it splitting (you don't want to reheat or simmer it).

Nutrition:

Protein 23g

Fat 10g

Calories 180g

Carbs 0g

184. SALSA VERDE

Preparation Time: 10 minutes

Cooking Time: 30 minutes

Servings: 2

Ingredients:

- 1 ½ lbs. Tomatillos, peeled
- 2 jalapeños, halved
- 1 white onion, quartered
- 2 garlic cloves, peeled & smashed
- 1 tbsp olive oil
- ½ tsp kosher salt
- ½ tsp black pepper, ground
- 1 lime, juiced
- 1 tbsp apple cider vinegar
- ½ cup cilantro, chopped
- 1 tsp cumin, ground

Instructions:

1. Preheat the pit boss to 225 degrees fahrenheit. Set up a gas or charcoal grill for low, indirect fire.

2. Wrap a sheet tray in foil. On the plate, arrange the tomatillos, jalapeos, onion, and garlic. Season with salt and pepper and drizzle with olive oil. When the meat is resting on the grill, move it to the smoking cabinet and smoke it.

3. Cook the tri tip over indirect fire on the barbecue. For medium rare, cook for 18 to 20 minutes, or until the temperature reaches 125°f. Remove the tri tip from the grill and set aside for 10 minutes to rest.

4. Increase the temperature to 450°f by opening the sear slide. Over open fire, sear the steak for 2 minutes per hand. Remove from the grill, rest for 10 minutes on a cutting board, and slice against the grain into bite-size bits for nachos.

5. Meanwhile, take the vegetables out of the smoking cabinet and place them in a blender or food processor. Combine the lime juice, vinegar, cilantro, and cumin in a mixing bowl. Blend thoroughly, then season with salt and pepper to taste.

6. Set up a nacho assembly station and layer the following ingredients in a big cast iron skillet: tortilla chips, cheese, tri tip, bell pepper, tomato, jalapeo, cheese, then repeat. Cook for 10 to 15 minutes, or until the cheese has melted and the sides begin to bubble. Remove from the grill and top with avocado, onion, cilantro, and sour cream. Serve immediately.

Nutrition:

Protein 33g

Fat 10g

Calories 280g

Carbs 6g

185. MEDITERRANEAN VEGETABLES WITH PESTO DRESSING

Preparation Time: 10 minutes

Cooking Time: 1hour

Servings: 2

Ingredients:

- For the grilled Mediterranean vegetables
- 2 aubergines
- 2 courgettes
- 4 red bell peppers
- Light olive oil for brushing
- A couple of handfuls of fine salt
- A few basil leaves, to garnish

Ingredients:

- For the pesto dressing
- 35g (¼ cup) toasted hazelnuts, whole
- 50ml (¼ cup) good quality olive oil
- A large handful of fresh basil leaves

- ½ tsp rock salt
- 1 small clove garlic, peeled
- 1 tsp fresh lemon juice
- nuts (hazelnuts)

Instructions:

1. The aubergine should be cut into 1cm slices, and the courgette should be cut into 12cm slices. Place all of the slices in a colander (or two if one is too small!). And scatter a pinch or two of salt over the cuts, ensuring equal coverage – this brings out a lot of the bitter juices contained in courgette and aubergine. Allow them to sit for 30 minutes before properly rinsing off the salt.

2. Light the grill and hold it before the flames jump out at the grill. Grill the entire red peppers over fire until the skin is charred and blistered all over – there should be no red parts on the outside; it should all be dark! Once this has occurred, remove them from the grill and place them in a plastic bag to sweat for about 10 minutes.

3. Enable the flames to die down after you've removed the peppers and place your plancha on the grill to heat up before cooking your vegetables. Heat your grill to 100-150°c (212-302°f) – grilled Mediterranean vegetables need only a low temperature.

4. Remove the red peppers from the bag and peel off the blackened flesh, which should come off quickly. Prepare the peppers for plancha grilling by cutting them in half and seeding them.
5. Brush the vegetable slices with olive oil before placing them on the plancha. Allow the aubergines to cook for 5-10 minutes per hand. Cook for 3-5 minutes on each side for the courgettes and red peppers.
6. Serve the grilled Mediterranean vegetables with a drizzle of pesto seasoning and a few basil leaves on the side.

Instructions:

For the pesto dressing

1. Blend together all of the pesto ingredients in a blender, and blitz! Taste and adjust with additional salt, lemon, basil, nuts, or garlic as required.
2. I've found it almost impossible to develop a fail-safe pesto recipe because basil leaves vary in strength, so there isn't a correct ratio in my opinion. Simply keep tasting and modifying until the pesto is just right! Have fun!

Nutrition:

protein 23g

fat 10g

calories   180g

carbs 0g

186. TRI TIP NACHOS

Preparation Time: 10 minutes

Cooking Time: 1hour

Servings: 2

Ingredients

- 2 jalapeños, halved
- 1 tbsp. apple cider vinegar
- 1 avocado, diced
- 1 tsp black peppercorns, ground
- 8 oz. cheddar jack cheese, shredded
- 3/4 cup cilantro, chopped
- 1 tsp cumin
- 2 garlic cloves, peeled and smashed
- 1 jalapeno pepper, minced
- 1 tsp kosher salt
- 1 lime, juiced
- 1 tbsp olive oil
- 1/2 tbsp pit boss smoked infused classic sea salt
- 4 oz queso fresco, crumbled

- 1/2 red bell pepper, chopped
- 1/2 minced red onion
- 1 roma tomatoes, diced
- 1/4 cup sour cream
- 1 1/2 lbs tomatillos, husked and washed
- 8 oz tortilla chips
- 1 lb tri tip roast
- 1 white onion, quartered

Instructions:

1. Level up your appetizer game with these epic smoked tri tip nachos.

Nutrition:

Protein 23g

Fat 10g

Calories 180g

187. PINEAPPLE SALSA

Preparation Time: 10 minutes

Cooking Time: 1hr 30 min

Servings: 2

Ingredients:

- Cilantro
- 1 large onion, diced
- 1 pineapple, chopped
- 1 tbsp. pit boss mandarin habanero spice
- 1 red bell peppers
- 5 tomatoes, roma
- 1 bag tortilla chip

Instructions:

1. Preheat your grill to 250°f and roast the vegetables for 30 minutes, whole. To give your wood pellet grill a 100% hardwood smoke, use hickory pellets.
2. When the vegetables roast on the grill, cut a whole pineapple in half and make a cup out of one hand. Remove the core and combine the remaining diced pineapple with some freshly diced cilantro in a cup.
3. Peel the tomatoes until the vegetables have finished roasting. Roasted carrots, red peppers, and tomatoes, diced place in a mixing dish.
4. Add a tablespoon of mandarin habanero and blend with a hand blender until the mixture is chunky.
5. With the remaining roasted tomatoes and onions, make a guacamole.

Nutrition:

Nutrition:
Calories: 112
Fat: 3.07g

Carbs: 17.4g
Protein: 4.1g

188. ROOT VEGGIES

Preparation Time: 10 minutes

Cooking Time: 1 Hour

Servings: 2

Ingredients:

- 6 carrots, peeled
- 3 parsnips, peeled
- 1 sweet potato, peeled
- 1 ½ t oil
- 1 ½ tsp thyme
- Sprinkle of kosher salt flakes
- Grinding of pepper

Instructions:

1. Heat the pit boss pellet grill to 350°f.
2. Halve the parsnip lengthwise.
3. Cut the sweet potato in half lengthwise and then into 1/3-inch thick slices.

4. Depending on the size of the carrots, cut them in half lengthwise or make them whole. Make all of the vegetable slices at the same size… That way they'll all be finished at the same time.
5. In a mixing cup, combine the cut parsnips, sweet potato, and entire young carrots. Drizzle the olive oil over the vegetables and toss them about until they are finely covered with the oil.
6. Toss the vegetables once more with the thyme.
7. Put the vegetables on a grill rack if you have one. If not, line a baking sheet with foil and arrange the vegetables equally on the plate.
8. Roast on the pit boss grill with the lid down until smooth and well browned (about 40 minutes).

Nutrition:

Calories: 164.1

Saturated Fat: 0.5 g

Dietary Fiber: 6.4 g

Total Fat: 3.9 g

189. VEGETABLE SALAD

Preparation Time: 10 minutes

Cooking Time: 40 minutes

Servings: 2

Ingredients:

- 1/2 lb. asparagus, trimmed
- 2 small zucchini
- 1 large red onion, ½" thick slices
- 1 orange bell pepper, quartered and seeded
- 1 red bell pepper, quartered and seeded
- 2 romaine lettuce hearts, cut lengthwise in half
- ¼ c fresh basil leaves, cut into thin strips
- 1 tbsp. Dijon mustard
- 2 cloves garlic, minced
- 1 tbsp. fresh oregano, minced
- ¼ c balsamic vinegar
- Salt & pepper to taste

Instructions:

1. Heat the pit boss pellet grill to 600°f. Switch to open flame cooking mode until the temperature has been hit. Open flame 1 by pressing the arrow (of-1).

Carefully remove the grill grates and ez-access hatch, and replace with the direct flame insert. On the bottom level of the heated grill, arrange asparagus, zucchini, red onion, corn, and bell peppers. Cook until the veggies are cooked and slightly browned, stirring occasionally. While cooking for 10 to 15 minutes, turn the veggies every 10 to 15 minutes. Remove the veggies off the grill after they've finished cooking.

2. Grill the romaine lettuce pieces, flat side out. Remove as finely burnt.

3. Chop the grilled vegetables into bite-sized bits. Place the burnt romaine hearts in a flat bowl and shred them. Place the grilled vegetable chunks on top of the lettuce. Remove the burnt corn from the cob and spread it over the other vegetables.

4. To make the dressing, whisk together the balsamic vinegar, dijon mustard, garlic, salt, and black pepper in a mixing cup. Slowly pour in the olive oil while stirring. Drizzle the dressing over the broccoli and burned romaine. This salad can be served warm or chilled.

Nutrition:
Calories: 338.9
Fat: 23.7g
Carbs: 17.4g
Protein: 4.1g
Fiber: 5.1g

190. SIMPLE ARUGULA SALAD

Prep Time: 15 minutes

Cook Time: 20 minutes

Total Time: 35

Ingredients

- 4 lbs boneless skinless chicken breast
- 1 container arugula
- Olive oil, balsamic glaze, – or your favorite salad dressing for salad for night #1
- Your favorite BBQ Rub, you can make your own with my all-purpose BBQ rub recipe

Instructions:

1. Prepare your grill for direct heat by filling it with Kingsford Charcoal Briquettes (charcoal spread out evenly on the bottom versus only on one side). If you want to learn how to start a charcoal grill or construct direct and indirect zones on your grill, check out my GRILL SCHOOL series, which will teach you the basics of grilling!

2. To prevent your chicken from sticking to your barbecue grates, brush them with avocado oil or similar high-heat oil.
3. Grill the chicken thighs on direct heat until an instant read thermometer, such as the Thermapen or the Thermopop, registers 170 degrees internal temperature.
4. Before cutting into the chicken, remove it from the grill and let it rest.
5. On the first night, serve with arugula salad and thinly sliced heirloom tomatoes drizzled with balsamic glaze and olive oil.
6. If you want carbs, a grilled Texas Toast or bread may easily be added to the dinner to complete it.
7. On evenings 2 and 3, save the leftover chicken for supper.

Nutrition:

Protein 23g

Fat 10g

Calories 180g

Carbs 0g

191. CHICKEN TINGA FOR CINCO DE MAYO

Preparation Time: 15 minutes

Cooking Time: 30 minutes

Servings: 2

Ingredients

- 3 pound chicken (I use half bone-in, split chicken breasts and half skinless boneless thighs).
- 1 big white onion, thinly slivered
- 1 big Vidalia onion, peeled and halved
- Avocado or grape seed oil, for example, is a high-heat oil.

- 4 cups chicken stock
- 4 cloves garlic, peeled
- 2 tsp. kosher salt
- ¼ tsp. dried Mexican oregano
- ¼ tsp. ground thyme
- ¼ tsp. cumin
- ¼ tsp. ground marjoram
- 1 dried bay leaf

- 7 oz. can of chipotle peppers in adobo sauce
- Roma tomatoes (28 ounces) (I prefer fresh that are charred in a cast iron skillet and skins removed, but fire-roasted canned tomatoes also work when in a pinch)
- Chicken seasonings (garlic salt, cumin, smoked paprika)

Instructions:

1. Season chicken thighs with garlic salt, cumin, and smoky paprika to taste. To produce a crust on each side, brown in the oil in a Dutch oven.
2. Add the halved onions, garlic, spices, and bay leaf to the chicken stock plus 1 cup of water. Bring to a low boil, then reduce to a low heat and cook for 30 minutes, covered.
3. Season chicken breasts with salt and pepper, then cook in your preferred smoker until the internal temperature reaches 165 degrees. This is going to be a game changer!
4. When the smoked chicken is done, peel it apart, let it cool, and shred it.
5. Remove the cooked chicken and onion halves from the broth and pour it into a separate dish. Once the chicken thighs have cooled, shred them.

6. In the same Dutch oven that the chicken was cooked in, heat the oil and sauté the slivered white onions until translucent, about 4 minutes.

7. Reduce the strained broth with the onions for 15 to 20 minutes, or until it has been reduced by half.

8. Combine the boiling onion and garlic halves, one chipotle can, and the tomatoes in a blender. Blend for 1 to 2 minutes, or until smooth.

9. Cook for another 15 to 20 minutes after adding the blended chipotle/tomato mixture to the reduced stock.

10. In a large mixing bowl, toss the shredded chicken with the sauce until it is well combined and coated. Allow 15 minutes for the stew to simmer on low heat.

Nutrition:

Protein 34g

Fat 16g

Calories 210g

Carbs 80g

192. CHICKEN SAUSAGE AND APPLE SALAD

Prep Time: 10 min

Cook Time: 30 min

Total Time: 40 hour

Ingredients

- 3 chicken sausage links
- 1 large fennel bulb, sliced into quarters
- 1 large crisp red apple
- 2 cups arugula
- olive oil, to taste
- red wine, to taste
- sea salt (I used citrus finishing salt, which you can create yourself using this recipe!)
- fresh ground pepper

Instructions:

1. On a medium high grill, around 350-400 degrees, cook the sausage and fennel quarters. When checking the temperature of the chicken sausage using an internal read thermometer like the Thermapen, it should register 170 degrees (note, Aidells and Al Fresco are precooked but for non-precooked Sausage you need to make sure you hit this internal temp). After a few minutes, the fennel should soften and develop wonderful char marks. Remove the fennel and chicken sausage from the pan and put aside to cool. After that, finely slice the apple and place it on top of an arugula bed.

2. Fennel and sausage should be sliced and layered on top of each salad. Drizzle with olive oil and red wine vinegar (recipe for citrus infused olive oil is below). Season with sea salt and freshly ground pepper (I used a citrus finishing salt).

Nutrition:

Protein 37g

Fat   10g

Calories 180g

Carbs 0g

193. EGGPLANT PARMESAN

Prep Time: 15 min

Cook Time: 30 min

Total Time: 45 hour

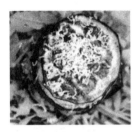

Ingredients

- 1 large eggplant, thinly sliced into rounds
- 1 lb sausage, removed from casing
- 1 large tomato (you may use tomato sauce instead of tomato slices; the sauce will make layering simpler, but nothing beats a fresh heirloom tomato!)
- 1 fresh basil and oregano sprig
- Parmesan cheese, grated over each piece of eggplant
- Extra virgin olive oil to drizzle over the tomatoes, eggplant, and arugula
- Sea salt, to taste
- Fresh ground pepper
- Balsamic

- Arugula

Instructions:

1. Grill eggplant slices until tender and excellent charmarks have developed on a medium high grill (350-400 degrees). Remove the grill pan from the heat and set it aside to cool. In a skillet, sauté the sausage until it is fully cooked and the juices run clear.

2. Begin assembling your "eggplant stack" by arranging your vegetables. Begin with an eggplant round, then top with a tomato slice, a drizzle of olive oil, salt, and pepper. Finally, grate roughly 1 tablespoon of parmesan on top. Add the sausage crumbles now. Rep with more eggplant, tomato, herbs, olive oil, parmesan, and so on. Cover with grated cheese and the last (3rd) eggplant round. Bake for 10 minutes at 350°F, or until the parmesan cheese has melted.

3. Place the remaining sausage on top of arugula salad drizzled with olive oil and balsamic vinegar, and toss with the arugula salad. With a glass of decent red wine, you've got yourself an Italian-inspired lunch that you can feel good about eating! *There are no carbohydrates and just a little amount of dairy in aged cheeses. What's your favorite way to eat eggplant?

Nutrition:

Protein 37g

Fat 10g

Calories 195g

Carbs 0g

194. CINNAMON AND SUGAR ROASTED PUMPKIN SEEDS

Preparation Time: 10 minutes
Cooking Time: 40 minutes
Servings: 2
Ingredients:
- 2 tablespoon melted butter
- 1 teaspoon cinnamon
- 1 pumpkin seeds ground
- Sugar, 2 tablespoons

Instructions:
1. Set your grill to smoke mode, wait for the fire to catch, and then preheat to 350 degrees' f (177 degrees c).
2. Rinse the seeds under cold water after cutting them from the pumpkin to remove any remaining pulp.
3. To coat the pumpkin seeds, throw them in a bowl of melted butter, then season with cinnamon and sugar. On a baking sheet, spread the seeds in a single layer. Cook for 25 minutes, or until softly golden.

Nutrition:
Calories: 120.8kcal
Carbohydrates: 4.9g
Protein: 3.7g

Fat: 9.7g

195. BLISTERED CURRY CAULIFLOWER

Preparation Time: 10 minutes
Cooking Time: 20 minutes
Servings: 2
Ingredients:
- 1 whole head cauliflower
- 2 tablespoons extra-virgin olive oil
- 1 clove garlic, grated
- 1 teaspoon curry powder
- 1/2 teaspoon ground turmeric
- 1/2 teaspoon kosher salt, plus more as needed
- 1/2 teaspoon freshly ground black pepper, plus more as needed
- 1/3 cup chopped roasted, salted almonds
- 1/4 cup currants, rehydrated and drained
- 1/4 cup fresh chopped mint
- 2 teaspoon lime zest

HAAS SAUCE
- 3 tablespoon Sherry vinegar
- 1 tablespoon Dijon mustard
- 3 clove garlic, peeled
- 2 cup parsley leaves, loosely packed
- 2 cup mint or basil leaves, loosely packed
- 3/4 cup extra-virgin olive oil
- Black pepper
- Kosher salt

Instruction:

1. When you're about to roast, preheat the pit boss to 450°f with the lid closed for 15 minutes.
2. Remove the core from the cauliflower head and cut the florets into 1/2 inch sections.
3. In a big mixing cup, combine the cauliflower, oil, garlic, curry powder, turmeric, cinnamon, and pepper. Toss the cauliflower until it is uniformly coated. Spread the cauliflower out on a big baking sheet, being careful not to clutter everything.
4. Place the sheet pan on the grill and cook for 15 to 20 minutes, rotating halfway through, until the cauliflower is tender and golden brown.
5. Meanwhile, prepare the Haas sauce, also known as chimichurri. In a food processor, combine the vinegar, mustard, and garlic cloves. To mix and split up the garlic, pulse a few times.
6. Add the herbs and wait until evenly diced, stopping only to scrape down the sides of the processor. Add the olive oil and pump until the herbs are coarsely chopped and a thick sauce emerges. If required, season with up to 1 teaspoon of salt and a pinch of pepper. Add more olive oil or 1 tablespoon of water to make the sauce thinner.
7. Toss the cauliflower with the almonds, currants, mint, and lime zest after it has been grilled. Season with salt and pepper to taste. With a drizzle of Haas sauce, serve warm or at room temperature.

Nutrition:
Protein: 4.7g
Fat: 9.7g
Calories: 150.6kcal
Carbohydrates: 4.9g

196. BAKED GRANOLA

Preparation Time: 20 minutes
Cooking Time: 1hour 30 minutes
Servings: 2
Ingredients:
- 1/2 cup honey
- 1/2 cup brown sugar
- 1/2 cup butter
- 1 pinch salt
- 2 teaspoon vanilla extract
- 2 teaspoon ground cinnamon
- 1/2 teaspoon almond extract
- 5 cup oats, steel-cut
- 1 cup raw unsalted sunflower seeds
- 1/2 cup toasted wheat germ
- 1 cup salted mixed nuts
- 2 cup dried fruit (such as cherries, raisins, cranberries, blueberries, pineapple, etc.)

Instruction:
1. In a shallow saucepan, combine the honey, brown sugar, butter, and salt. Get the mixture to a low boil over medium-low heat. Cook, stirring regularly, for 5 to 8 minutes.
2. Take the pan off the heat and add the vanilla, cinnamon, and almond extract. Allow to cool slightly.

3. Butter the bottom and sides of a rimmed baking sheet lightly.
4. In a big mixing cup, combine the peas, sunflower seeds, wheat germ, and coarsely chopped nuts.
5. Hot syrup can be poured over the oat mixture. Mix thoroughly with melted butter in your hands. Press the mixture onto the baking sheet that has been prepared.
6. When you're about to roast, preheat the grill to 300°f with the lid closed for 15 minutes.
7. Bake the granola for 1 hour, or until lightly browned. Allow to cool before breaking into chunks in a big mixing cup.
8. Combine the coconut and dried fruit in a mixing bowl. Keep it in an airtight bag. Have fun!

Nutrition:
Protein 58g

Fat 14g

Calories 21.9g

Carbs 3.0g

197. GRILLED BABY CARROTS AND FENNEL WITH ROMESCO

Preparation Time: 10 minutes
Cooking Time: 45 minutes
Servings: 2
Ingredients:
- 1-pound slender rainbow carrots or regular carrots with tops on
- 2 fennel bulbs, stalks and cores removed and halved
- 1-pound fingerling potatoes, washed and halved lengthwise
- 1/4 cup olive oil
- Kosher salt
- 1 tablespoon thyme or rosemary leaves

Instructions:
1. When you're about to roast, preheat the pit boss to 500°f with the lid closed for 15 minutes.
2. Trim the carrot tops to 1 inch in length. Peel the carrots and cut the bigger ones in half so that they are just about 1/2 inch thick. Cut the fennel bulbs into 1/2 inch thick slices lengthwise. In a big mixing cup, combine the onions, fennel, and potato slices. Drizzle with olive oil and season with salt to taste. Toss the vegetables in the oil to coat uniformly.

3. Place the vegetables on a baking sheet. Insert a few herb sprigs into the vegetables as well.
4. Place the pan directly on the grill grate and cook, stirring regularly, for 35 to 45 minutes, or until the vegetables are browned and softened. Allow time for cooling.

Nutrition:

Protein 52g

Fat 17g

Calories 225g

Carbs 7.0g

198. ROASTED CAULIFLOWER

Preparation Time: 10 minutes
Cooking Time: 40 minutes
Servings: 2
Ingredients:
- 1 head cauliflower, fresh
- 2 tablespoon extra-virgin olive oil
- 2 clove garlic clove
- 1 1/4 teaspoon smoked paprika
- 1/2 teaspoon salt
- 1/2 teaspoon black pepper
- 1 cup parmesan cheese

Instructions:
1. When you're about to cook, •preheat to 180°f with the lid closed for 15 minutes. If available, use super smoke for the best taste.
2. Place the cauliflower on a sheet tray and cut it into medium florets. Place the sheet tray on the grill for 20 minutes to burn.
3. When the cauliflower is burning, combine all of the ingredients except the parmesan cheese in a mixing bowl.
4. Cut the cauliflower after 20 minutes. Double the grill temperature to 450°f and preheat for 15 minutes with the lid closed.

5. When the grill is heating up, toss the cauliflower with the spice mixture and return it to the sheet tray.
6. Return to the pit boss and roast for 10 minutes, or until it has a nice golden brown hue.
7. Sprinkle the parmesan over each slice in the last few minutes of Instructions, and close the lid until the cheese is melted. Have fun!

Nutrition:
Calories: 80.8
Protein: 3.1 g
Dietary Fiber: 4.0 g
Potassium: 468.8 mg

199. SMOKED HUMMUS WITH ROASTED VEGETABLES

Preparation Time: 10 minutes
Cooking Time: 45 minutes
Servings: 2
Ingredients:
- 1 1/2 cup chickpeas
- 1/3 cup tahini
- 1 tablespoon garlic, minced
- 6 tablespoons extra-virgin olive oil
- 1 teaspoon salt
- 4 tablespoon lemon juice
- 1 red onion, sliced
- 2 cup butternut squash
- 2 cup cauliflower, cut into florets
- 2 cup fresh Brussels sprouts
- 2 whole Portobello mushroom
- Salt
- Black pepper

Instructions:
1. When you're about to roast, preheat the grill to 180°f with the lid closed for 15 minutes.
2. Drain and rinse the chickpeas and lay them out on a sheet tray for the hummus. Place the tray on the grill grate and smoke for 15-20 minutes, or until the optimum amount of smoke is reached.

3. Combine smoked chickpeas, tahini, garlic, olive oil, salt, and lemon juice in a food processor and process until fully combined but not fully smooth. Transfer to a bowl and set aside.
4. Preheat the grill and raise the temperature to high.
5. Drizzle the vegetables with olive oil and lay them out on a sheet plate. Place a sheet tray under the grill for 15-20 minutes, or until the vegetables are lightly browned and cooked through.
6. Place the hummus in a serving bowl or platter and top with the roasted vegetables to eat.
7. Serve with pita bread and drizzled with olive oil. Have fun!

Nutrition:
Calories 433.
Fat 20.3 g (31.3%)
Saturated 3.1 g (15.3%)
Carbs 51.9 g (17.3%)

200. GRILLED VEGETABLE SALAD

Preparation Time: 10 minutes
Cooking Time: 40 minutes
Servings: 2
Ingredients:
- 1/2 lb. asparagus, trimmed
- 2 small zucchini
- 1 large red onion, ½" thick slices
- 1 orange bell pepper, seeded & cut into quarters
- 1 red bell pepper, seeded & cut into quarters
- 2 romaine lettuce hearts, cut in half lengthwise
- ¼ c fresh basil leaves, cut into thin strips
- 1 tbsp. Dijon mustard
- 2 cloves garlic, minced
- 1 tbsp. fresh oregano, minced
- ¼ c balsamic vinegar
- Salt & pepper to taste

Instructions:

1. Heat the pit boss pellet grill to 600°f. Switch to open flame cooking mode until the temperature has been hit. Open flame 1 by pressing the arrow (of-1). Remove the grill grates and the ez-access hatch with care and substitute with the direct flame insert. Arrange asparagus, zucchini, red onion, corn, and bell peppers on the hot grill's lower shelf. Cook, stirring sometimes, until the vegetables are tender and slightly charred. Turn vegetables every 10 to 15 minutes while grilling for 10 to 15 minutes. When the vegetables are cooked, remove them from the barbecue.

2. Grill the romaine lettuce pieces, flat side out. Remove as finely burnt.

3. Chop the grilled vegetables into bite-sized bits. Place the burnt romaine hearts in a flat bowl and shred them. Place the grilled vegetable chunks on top of the lettuce. Remove the burnt corn from the cob and spread it over the other vegetables.

4. In a mixing cup, combine the balsamic vinegar, dijon mustard, garlic, salt, and black pepper to create the dressing. When whisking, slowly drizzle in the olive oil. Cover the broccoli and burnt romaine with the dressing. This salad can be eaten either warm or cold.

Nutrition:

Protein 43g

Fat 17g

Calories 201g

Carbs 4.0g

CONCLUSION

Pellet grills may be used in a variety of ways. In a pellet grill, you can barbeque, smoke, roast, grill, and even bake or braise. We've used them to make anything from crispy chicken wings to braised short ribs to smoked pork chile verde and crème brulee at BBQ University.

It is a fact that pit boss pellet grills have become the latest trend. For sure, they do offer lots of convenience and ease that almost every BBQ lover dreams of owning one. Despite being a big investment due to their high cost, the will for sure give you a run for your money and purchasing the right pellet grill will last for a pretty long time.

Only two firms made pellet grills as late as 2008. (Traeger and its rival, MAK, also based in Oregon). The expiry of Traeger's initial patents, however, allowed competitors to enter the market. Pellet grills have been popular in recent years, with more than 20 different types available in North America. Even competitive barbecuers have begun to adopt this innovative smoker and are winning, which has enraged some old school pit masters. Why? Because it's "too damned simple" to smoke on a pellet grill, they say. (Does this sound familiar?)

So, do you think a pellet grill is suitable for you?

We hope you found the information to be quite useful and that you are now able to determine which pit boss pellet grill is ideal for you. We done our best to lay down all of the aspects you should think about while purchasing one.

Do Not Go Yet; One Last Thing To Do

If you liked this book or found it useful, I'd appreciate it if you could leave a quick review on Amazon. Your support is greatly appreciated, and I personally read all of the reviews in order to obtain your feedback and improve the book.

Thanks for your help and support!

CPSIA information can be obtained
at www.ICGtesting.com
Printed in the USA
LVHW081915220721
693399LV00003B/25